TITLE PAGE

The Way

Dedication

I dedicate this book to you, the reader, and to everyone who wished they had more time. I hope *The Way* helps you achieve True Success!

Acknowledgments

I want to say a special thank you to my mother and father for all the love, belief, discipline, time, inspiration, patience, and all the other support they have given to me throughout my life. Additionally, I want to acknowledge and express the deepest gratitude to my mom for her thoughtful help and intelligent hard work on editing *The Way*.

I also want to thank my brother and sister who helped, coached, and pushed me. To my nephew for all his belief and hope. To all my friends and other people who helped me along this path. To all my teachers who inspired me to find the truth and not give up. To all who came before, sought the truth, found answers, and shared in a manner so we could all benefit. And to God for everything.

MAIN TITLE PAGE

The Way

7 REVOLUTIONARY STEPS TO LIVING A MEANINGFUL LIFE & MAKING A REAL DIFFERENCE IN THE WORLD

Your Ultimate Guide to

Positive Relationships

Optimal Health

True Success &

Lasting Happiness!

Volume I

ANDREW CALDERELLA

Copyright Page

The Way: 7 Revolutionary Steps to Living a Meaningful Life & Making a Real Difference in the World. Your Ultimate Guide to Positive Relationships, Optimal Health, True Success & Lasting Happiness!

Volume I | First Edition

Copyright © 2020 by Andrew Calderella
The 7th Foundation
PeaceAce@7Way.Me | www.7Way.Me | www.PeaceAce.com

Published by: Speaker House Publishing
City of Publication: Boise, Idaho
Printed in the United States of America

ISBN Electronic: 978-1-7331249-3-5
ISBN Softcover: 978-1-7331249-2-8
ISBN Hardback: 978-1-7331249-4-2

USA Library of Congress Control Number: 2019908859

Publisher's Cataloging-In-Publication Data
(Prepared by The Donohue Group, Inc.)
Names: Calderella, Andrew, author.
Title: The way : 7 revolutionary steps to living a meaningful life & making a real difference in the world : your ultimate guide to positive relationships, optimal health, true success & lasting happiness! / Andrew Calderella.
Description: First edition. | Boise, Idaho : Speaker House Publishing, [2020-]
Identifiers: ISBN 9781733124928 (v.1 : softcover) | ISBN 9781733124942 (v.1 : hardback) | ISBN 9781733124935 (v.1 : ebook)
Subjects: LCSH: Conduct of life. | Quality of life. | Interpersonal relations. | Health. | Success. | Happiness.
Classification: LCC BF637.C5 C35 2020 (print) | LCC BF637.C5 (ebook) | DDC 158.1--dc23

Copyrighted material. All rights reserved. No part of this book may be reproduced, stored in a retrieval system, or transmitted in any form or by any means without written permission from the author or *The 7th Foundation*.

DISCLAIMER

This book is not intended as a substitute for the medical advice of physicians or the counsel of licensed mental health professionals. The reader should regularly consult a physician in matters relating to their health and particularly concerning any symptoms that may require diagnosis or medical attention. The author and publisher hereby disclaim any liability to any party for any injury, loss, damage, or disruption caused by this information, errors or omissions, whether such errors or omissions result from negligence, accident, or any other cause.

TABLE OF CONTENTS

About the Author vii
Preface Dear Reader xi
Chapter 1 What is the True Goal of Life? 1
Chapter 2 How to Achieve the True Goal of Life ... 18
Chapter 3 Get On Your True Path Right Now 31
    Step 1: Know 31
    Step 2: Want 32
    Step 3: Choose 33
    Step 4: Center 35
Chapter 4 Understanding Life 57
Chapter 5 Understanding People 93
Chapter 6 Understanding God 114
Chapter 7 Understanding Your Place 137
Chapter 8 Living a Meaningful Life 160
    Step 5: Be 160
Chapter 9 Finding Unity 196
    Step 6: Unite 196
Chapter 10 Connect & Make a Real Difference .. 234
Chapter 11 Mending the Broken 266

TOC

Chapter 12 True Power & Being the Solution..... 283

Chapter 13 The Keys to Leadership & Wealth.... 307

Chapter 14 Achieving Global Harmony 347

Chapter 15 Creating Lasting Peace & Happiness 371

Chapter 16 Living Perfection............................... 405

    Step 7: Perfect 405

Chapter 17 Your Next Steps 426

My Notes 449

ABOUT THE AUTHOR

Andrew was born in Detroit, Michigan, USA, on March 18, 1966. He is not someone that you would have expected to write a book. He was born with a lazy eye, which made him legally blind in one eye. As a result, he wore a patch over his good eye to improve his vision. He has dyslexia and other "learning disabilities," so he struggled with reading, writing, and arithmetic. Little was known about "learning disabilities" at the time, so learning and adapting to life's challenges at an early age was difficult.

Along with these issues, he was also bullied by his peers and adults, with one elementary school teacher even going as far as to ridicule him in front of the class, telling him to drop out of school and get a job because he was too stupid ever to graduate.

He learned to compensate. He even became an avid reader and listener to books with a lot of extra effort on his part, the support of his mother, sister, a special teacher, and aid from services for the blind and handicapped. It's important to note that along with these "learning challenges" came some great gifts that allowed him to do and see things others could not. He has also always been a very spiritual person with a special connection to nature.

He went on to not only graduate from high school as the Vice President of the student body but went on to earn a BA in Speech and Communications as well as minors in Religious Studies and Eastern Philosophy. After graduation, he then spent a few years teaching English in Japan and traveling the world, which enhanced his knowledge before returning to the USA.

Throughout his life, Andrew has always worked hard. He was forced into it because of his learning disabilities, but he also likes doing a good job even if no one will see or know about it. Andrew has won many accolades throughout his career and is known as an innovator, out of the box thinker, and someone who gets the job done. He started working when he was very young by doing odd jobs and selling things for money or trade.

For example, in elementary school, he created a little business selling collectibles he got from the ice cream man that got so popular the principal called his parents to shut it down because it was taking all the other children's lunch money.

At various times he was a paperboy, lifeguard, swimming teacher, gas station attendant, construction worker, stock boy, cashier, appliance repairman, handyman, gardener, janitor, dishwasher, landscaper, food server, personal trainer, security guard/bouncer, martial arts and self-defense teacher, cook, furniture mover, teleprompter operator, teacher, salesman, sales manager, IT manager, recruiter, recruiter manager, marketer, trainer, public speaker, business partner, business owner, startup developer, website programmer, internet marketing and SEO expert, founder, owner and CEO of Consulting Ace Inc. since 1999, and now the author of *The Way* and the creator of *The 7th Foundation*.

Andrew has additionally always been very healthy and fit and is what many would call a health and fitness fanatic. He stopped eating all forms of junk food, by choice, at 13 years old after learning about the benefits of real food compared to the harmful effects of junk food. Since then, he has studied all facets of food, health, the human body, mind, longevity, and ways to train and repair ourselves.

About The Author

He participated in sports while in school, including track, cross-country, basketball, and crew (rowing team). He has competed in triathlons, is an expert swimmer, mountain biker, and yoga practitioner, as well as earned degrees in many forms of martial arts. Andrew was also forced to learn even more profound lessons of the body and mind as he was injured seriously many times in life. While some of these injuries left him with permanent issues, today, few people could recognize any physical limitations aside from the inability to sit in one place for too long.

There is so much more to Andrew as he has lived quite the adventurous life and has had many nail-biting and mind-blowing experiences. It would take a whole book even to begin to tell his story correctly. You will learn a little more about him in the first chapter of this book. Hopefully, the little taste we have given you here is enough to see that most people would not have picked Andrew as someone who should write a book. However, knowing his life and knowledge base, Andrew is definitely someone we want doing so.

"Learning Disabilities" Note: What society has negatively labeled as "Learning Disabilities" are really just "Learning Differences" and alternative ways of thinking that often come with great gifts. This simply means, in most cases, the cookie-cutter teaching methods that work for most everyone, just need to be altered to reach these people. If we can master educating this group, it will help our society, for many, if not most, of our greatest achievers and thinkers, have one or more of these issues.

A <u>few</u> of whom include: Leonardo da Vinci, George Washington, Alexander Graham Bell, Thomas Edison, Albert Einstein, George Patton, Winston Churchill, Henry Ford, Walt Disney, Pablo Picasso, Ludwig van Beethoven,

The Way

John F. Kennedy, Temple Grandin, Daymond John, Gavin Newsom, Cher, Stevie Wonder, Agatha Christie, Woopie Goldberg, Steve Jobs, Erin Brockovich, Solange Knowles, Keira Knightley, Henry Winkler, W.B. Yeats, Keanu Reeves, Richard Engel, Michael Jordan, Earvin 'Magic' Johnson, Anderson Cooper, Harry Belafonte, Jay Leno, F. Scott Fitzgerald, Justin Timberlake, Tom Cruise, Tim Tebow, John Lennon, Muhammad Ali, Charles Schwab, Will Smith, Vince Vaughn, William Hewlett, Octavia Spencer, Tommy Hilfiger, Michael Phelps, Robin Williams, Steven Spielberg, Richard Branson, Elon Musk, and Greta Thunberg. To learn more about "learning difficulties" and gifts, see www.7Way.Me/LD.

THE 7TH FOUNDATION

The mission of *The 7th Foundation* is to be a catalyst that spurs meaningful positive change within people's lives and our society in order to create a world of lasting peace and happiness that everyone can enjoy.

Our motto is "All for one, one for all, united we stand, divided we fall!" which we have borrowed from The Musketeers.

We are dedicated to spreading the message found within *The Way* and helping the founder with his great mission. We are a consulting group and think tank dedicated to solving the problems facing people and our world. We offer and are developing a lot of products and services, as well as planning events that may be of interest to you. You can learn more about Andrew, The Mission, and *The 7th Foundation* by visiting www.7Way.Me.

PREFACE
DEAR READER

Welcome and peace. Thank you for reading. This book is not about me. It was written because I discovered something truly important that can help a lot of people, our society and world.

Since this discovery, I have been compelled to get this message out in as many ways as possible. The ultimate goal of *The Way*, *The 7th Foundation*, *The One Movement*, and everything else that will follow, is to be a catalyst that spurs meaningful positive change within people's lives and our society in order to create a world of lasting peace and happiness that everyone can enjoy.

WHAT WILL YOU LEARN?

By reading this book, you will gain critical knowledge in many key facets of life. This knowledge will help you to be your best physically, mentally, emotionally, spiritually, financially, in relationships, as a family, and in society. This critical information will not only help you meet your goals; it will take you to the next level and beyond.

Within this book, you will find out what "The Goal of Life" really is, what "True Success" really means, "Why You are Here," and the "Meaning and Purpose of Life." You will learn of *"The Way"* and its "7 Steps," where you will discover your "True Path" that will lead you to your "True Self," "True Life," and a better world for all.

You will learn the "10 Laws" that make up a core belief system that will keep you on your "True Path" throughout your life as well as how to maintain all that is good and how to continually improve. You will also be given the keys to power, wealth, business, government, and other vital systems of society so you can make a real difference. You will likewise discover how to put your best foot forward, build positive relationships, and unite with other people to create meaningful, lasting, positive change within people's lives, and within our society.

Within these volumes, you will find out how to do everything more efficiently and effectively. You will learn how to train and maintain your mind, body, emotions, and spirit. This information includes things like how to get the best healing sleep throughout your life, how to be mindful, and how to utilize five different ways to meditate effectively. You will learn how to fuel your body correctly with air, light, water, food, and information, as well as how to properly care for your body and optimize your health so you can live a longer, healthier life.

Along with all that knowledge, you will also learn how to create a nurturing, loving family and how to raise positive, productive, and happy children. Add all of this together and combine it with everything else within *The Way*, and you get something much greater than the sum of its parts.

ONE BOOK IN THREE VOLUMES

Basically, the main questions and problems of life, as well as their answers and solutions, have been placed into one book that is divided into three volumes: *The Way*, its *Life Manual*, and the *Child & Family Guide*.

The Way covers the main philosophy and all "7 Steps." The *Life Manual* is designed to work with "Step 5: Be" of *The Way* yet can be used anytime by jumping to the section of interest. The *Child & Family Guide* can also be used anytime yet will become of even greater value after an understanding of *The Way* and *Life Manual* has been gained.

Preface: Dear Reader

Know that this is not the work of one person, a few, or even a team. *The Way* is the collective work of humanity and took thousands of years to create. The solution, I have named *The Way*, was only made possible because I was able to join the knowledge and wisdom from our most celebrated minds throughout the ages. To be clear, this is not about me; it's about the message.

For this reason, before we start on our journey into *The Way*, it's essential to understand a couple of key points.

First – What is it?

The Way is a philosophy and a set of best practices on how to live a meaningful life and make a real difference in the world. I have taken this philosophy as if written on scrolls and have adapted the wisdom to fit within this modern-day book chapter format (with every chapter mainly about one thing and most chapters are about the same length).

To put it another way, I did not write a book called *The Way*. Instead, I have adapted the philosophy called *The Way* and put it into book format. Doing it this way means I did not artificially stuff information into *The Way* to make parts longer, nor did I cut out critical information just because it was a little long for one chapter. For instance, some chapters may contain a few steps, while other steps span a few chapters.

The Way, as a collective work, is larger than most books because it's a Complete Solution and will help you meet your current goals faster and take you to the next level and beyond. It's a "Transformative Guide" and "Life Reference" that includes details and lists that you will need at different times throughout your life.

It's the handbook for humanity, showing us how to win at this great game of life.

The Way as a Transformative Guide means *The Way* is designed to change you in positive ways through merely understanding the message. Here you simply read the book and then follow the instructions going as far as you desire at the speed of your choosing.

The Way as a Life Reference: *The Way, Life Manual, and Child & Family Guide* are designed as a quick reference book that you can use anytime. Within this book, you find the details and lists that you will need at different times of life. In this way, once you understand the steps and the layout of the manual and guide, you can jump to crucial sections when you and yours are in need.

The Way and its accompanying *Life Manual* and *Child & Family Guide* are short once you understand how they are divided and how much knowledge and wisdom they contain. On a basic level, if you compare how many books and how much time it would take you to find all the bits of knowledge within *The Way*, it's a real bargain for collecting this information took me the majority of my life. *The Way* is designed to get you to where you need to be fast, saving you time and money along the way.

SECOND – FOR WHOM IS THIS BOOK WRITTEN?

"The whole of life, from the moment you are born to the moment you die, is a process of learning." - Jiddu Krishnamurti

It's important to note that *The Way* is for everyone. Every person needs clarity of purpose and action. Yet we are all starting from different places, some of us with little knowledge in some areas, others with deep expertise. The problem is that as a writer, I can't know what you know or don't. Nor can I write a custom book for everyone.

Preface: Dear Reader

The problem is compounded by the fact that any part of *The Way* and its *Life Manual* or *Child & Family Guide* can make all the difference to those who do NOT have this information.

To say it another way, any missing piece or misunderstanding can mean the difference between success and failure. It's like building a superstructure that is to last the ages. We need to make sure that we are all on the same page, that all the bases are covered, and that the foundation is firm if we are to build something truly grand.

Therefore, *The Way* will confirm key universal truths as it reveals nuances and missing information. The sharing of this common fact base in the context of *The Way* is what gets us all "on the same page." Being on the same page allows us all to take the precise actions that are needed to reach the ultimate goal of life and make a real difference in the world.

Example: One of my publishers, who has read hundreds of self-help, self-development, and success books as well as publishes them, found great wisdom within *The Way* that they had not found anywhere else. This knowledge helped them through a very challenging life event.

You don't have to understand or accept all the information within *The Way* as you go. Just take what you need and leave the rest for now. By the time you get to the end, the wholeness of the message can resonate and bring clarity to earlier parts. You can always reread *The Way* and use our other helpful resources to enhance your understanding and capabilities.

While the fragments of knowledge found within *The Way* may have deep meaning and provide immediate help, it's understanding them all as a whole in the context of

The Way that brings greater enlightenment, positive change, lasting peace, and happiness. So regardless of where you start, know that in the end, it's all the parts working together that *The Way* becomes a catalyst for positive change within your life and our world. It's through using *The Way* as a guide to transform yourself as well as a reference throughout your life that it becomes a catalyst transforming you into a continuously improving person and our world into a nicer place to live for everyone.

A Note on Quotes

I have used many quotes within this book, and in some cases, the word "he" is used. To be clear, I interpret "he" and "him" in these quotes to include everyone, not just men or a select group of men.

Notes on Analogies

For some readers, I have included the definitions of two types of analogies to help in understanding their use and why they can be helpful yet also be detrimental to our collective understanding. An analogy is a comparison between two things that are quite different. I sometimes use an analogy in the form of simile and metaphor to help gain perspective about the concept being discussed.

- **Simile:** A phrase that describes something by comparing it to something else using the word "like" or "as."

  Examples:
    - He went white as a sheet.
    - He moves like a cat.
    - Her attitude towards me was cold as ice.

- **Metaphor:** Includes all language that involves figures of speech or symbolism and does <u>not</u> <u>literally</u>

represent real things. It's used to describe somebody or something that is not meant literally but instead is used as a comparison. One thing used or considered to represent another.

Examples:
- Her voice was like silk.
- His gaze is like steal.

Example: The ship moved to the light.
- The Ship represents the self.
- Light represents good.
- Movement indicating a desire, choice, and action.

The Problem: It's important to note that sometimes analogies can be detrimental to our real understanding as it may put a false perspective in your mind when you think about that "thing."

For Example, the idea of a business or government as a hierarchical pyramid structure with one person at the top running everything does not represent the true nature of these complex systems. A motor or engine with many different components working together would be a more accurate and fairer analogy of these types of systems. Another *example* is representing God as an old white man with a beard limits our understanding of God.

Therefore, it's essential to keep in mind that an analogy is not an accurate comparison and is used only to highlight a partial perspective and therefore limits an understanding of the whole.

Ok, now that we have the preliminaries out of the way, let's start our journey into *The Way* by finding out what the true goal of life really is.

Chapter 1
What is the True Goal of Life?

*"The true nature of anything is
the highest it can become."* – Aristotle

Whom do you want to be? What do you want out of life? For most of humanity, the answer is simply to be "successful." However, what does "success" truly mean, and how do you get there from where you are right now, exactly?

The truth is you are a special, unique, and precious individual with amazing positive gifts to offer. With the right nurturing, knowledge, and a conducive environment, you can become this greater, truly successful person or "True Self."

Being human means that we are all different yet similar. Throughout time, humanity has sought answers to every question we can conceive of and overthrow those who would oppress us. At our core, we, the human race, are seekers of truth, freedom, and the right way of doing things.

Humanity has assigned labels and created disciplines to study everything. Everything we create is based on the collective knowledge that has been passed down and improved upon, generation by generation. In the past few thousand years, our understanding of everything has come a long way.

During all this time, some questions have stood out like: Is there a purpose or meaning to life? Why am I here? What should I be doing? Is there a point to all this?

The Way

How do I become my best? How can I be happy every day? Is there something greater or God? How can I be significant, influential, and really make a positive difference? What happens after I die?

The reason these questions stand out is that as a people, the majority of us throughout time have been seeking a direction and a purpose in life. We seek our special people and a way to fill that void within us. We look for that missing piece that will make us complete. To use a metaphor, we all innately want a clear path out of the darkness into the light.

We all innately want what is good and positive for us, our loved ones, and our world. Being human also means all of us have been on a mission since our birth. The instinctual mission is to find a way to not just survive but to thrive and be happy. My mission has led me to never stop asking "why" and "how" as the answers given to the most important questions of life did not seem complete or correct. This incompleteness and wrongness left me very unsatisfied, and I could not just let it go.

One of the greatest gifts we were all given as a species is that we can learn from others, build on their work, and go further in life. All of us need to seek to learn from the right people because this practice will save us from making mistakes, saving us time, helping us go further, faster, and with less effort.

My quest to find the answers to the most fundamental questions of life led me through a lot of trials and into deep research. I read and listened to thousands of books and other media in all the critical areas of life. I attained college degrees and studied our religions, spiritual paths, philosophies, and the most spiritually enlightened, resourceful, successful, and wisest among us.

During my quest, I discovered answers to many of life's most important questions and problems.

IS TRUE SUCCESS FOUND IN POWER, WEALTH, FAME, OR HOLINESS?

"Nearly all men can stand adversity, but if you want to test a man's character, give him power." - Abraham Lincoln

To understand these greater truths, we first need to understand the difference between "success" and "true success." Throughout human history and into this current age, as a society, we see "success" generally tied to a position of power, fame, or having a lot of wealth. With the most "successful" of us having the most power, fame, and/or wealth.

Our society's focus in these areas guided me to study the lives of the most "successful" people throughout all human history, i.e., our greatest leaders and rulers, as well as the most wealthy, famous, and powerful. Also, through my work and travels, I made friends and worked with a lot of very "successful" people. What I found shocked me because there is a recurring problem that shows up in many, if not most, of these "successful" people's lives.

Over and over throughout our long history, we find that those of us at the highest levels of "success," with great power, fame, wealth, beauty, and intelligence, are also often corrupt. We can plainly see how petty, mean, self-righteous, unhealthy, arrogant, spiteful, lazy, greedy, lustful, dishonest, and disruptive, so many of them are. They often work hard to stoke the negative feelings of hate, division, jealousy, anger, and envy whenever possible.

These "successful" people often do not treat everyone as equals, nor do they treat others as they would want to be treated if the situation was reversed.

Just like so many, they cheat, lie, and exaggerate everything to make them seem right no matter what the truth or cost. If ever questioned or when errors are pointed out, they cast themselves as the victim of unfair attacks.

For verification of this fact, we need only look to the media in our current age and our collective history. For here we can plainly see the tragedies of these "successful" lives spread out before us with all the acts of abuse, lack of self-control and direction, waste of money and time, bad relationships, lies as well as the other corruptions of character and needless trauma and drama.

We can clearly see how the most "successful" rulers and leaders throughout all human history often treat us, "the masses," and our precious world as their personal disposable resource, game, or toy. We "the masses" are most often thought of as pieces on a board or numbers in a calculation rather than as people.

Sure, there are exceptions to this general rule, but that is the problem, they are only exceptions. Throughout all our history, we see that few "successful" people and organizations use their power and excess wealth for something truly good. Few go beyond giving the minimum to charities and only do that so they can get some positive press

For example, few pay <u>everyone</u> who works for them in <u>every</u> job enough to live a happy life. Few do things that really help fix something broken in our society like:

- Building or improving a school, community center, gym, or health clinic.
- Helping a family get back on its feet after losing everything in a disaster.

What is the True Goal of Life?

- Funding a new business which has a solution to fix a real problem.
- Sending kids to college or to trade schools who can't afford it.
- Sending city kids to summer camp in the country.
- Planting a forest or funding a park.
- Sponsoring a cleanup project.
- Improving an orphanage.
- Adopting a child.

The options for good works are endless, yet what is so desperately and obviously needed is not being done by the majority of the "successful" who have the means to do so. This is because if they had been doing what needs to be done, our society and world would be in a much better state. Consequently, those we call "successful" are clearly as flawed as the rest of us.

Throughout human history, we also see those of us who have achieved high levels of understanding, status, or ranking within a spiritual path or religion as being "successful." My travels, my conversations with people, my degrees and studies in religion, spirituality, history, and philosophy helped me understand our world's faiths, religions, and spiritual paths. This understanding allowed me to find more pieces to the puzzle on how to live a meaningful life and be our best.

However, I also found some very disturbing things that shook me to my core. So many "holy" people, like the very "successful," were often the most self-righteous, judgmental, arrogant, troubled, corrupt, depressed, unhealthy, close-minded, confused, and out of touch. Some of these holy people have confessed sins and shared with me how deeply their organizations are corrupt, along with how they have been this way for a very long time.

Here too, we need only look at history and the media of our current age to see these crimes being committed and the systemic corruption within these "holy" organizations. It also became apparent that often these "holy" men and woman at the pinnacle of their faith, live lives that are so far removed from what we "normal" everyday people live. This has left them without the knowledge of how to help us and has made many afraid of the real world.

Again, as with other "successful" people, there are exceptions here too, for many wonderful holy people help us realize virtue in life and a path to the divine. The problem is that these are again exceptions and not a consequence of being holy.

THE CHALLENGE OF "SUCCESS"

"Try not to become a man of success but a person of value." - Albert Einstein

Clearly, the many good deeds that are desperately needed are not done on a large scale by the so-called "successful" people and organizations who have the resources or else our world would not be as it is. The same is true of our faiths. If we manifested the true virtue found within them, our holy organizations would not be as corrupted and harmful as many have become. Instead, the so-called "successful" and "holy" would have created an exceptional world over the past couple of thousand years.

This pervading corruption does not mean that it's wrong to be wealthy, famous, powerful, intelligent, beautiful, or spiritual/holy. These aspects just need to be managed correctly if we are to reach our full potential individually and collectively as a species.

What is the True Goal of Life?

In fact, being wealthy, famous, powerful, intelligent, beautiful, and/or spiritual/holy are key aspects of society and can be helpful if handled correctly.

The solution is found within context and merit, as well as how and when it is used. Things have been wrong for a very long time. To fix our society's issues, we all need to join together, not be divided, and point fingers. To truly win, we must turn our enemies into friends.

The fact is what society calls "successful" as measured by power, fame, wealth, beauty, intelligence, and holiness is not "True Success." If this were so, these conditions would naturally create better people and a better society. After thousands of years of being led by these so-called "successful" people, the world would be much healthier and more peaceful than it is now.

What humanity has generally called "success" is really a human challenge filled with temptations and tests that, if not overcome, will corrupt us. As has been said, "power corrupts, and absolute power corrupts absolutely." Knowing this is key, for often, understanding what is not true, helps us find what is. Our collective focus on this false ideal of "success" has hurt humanity as this becomes an emotional topic that makes and breaks lives and relationships. However, the great news here is that finding our flaws is what allows us to fix them.

The truth is that <u>all of us</u>, even those we currently call "successful," feel the same emptiness, and have the same questions. To be clear, this void is when you feel that missing piece deep within. It's that ache of desperation, the fear of failure, the fear of getting lost, and being alone. It's the fear of never really being loved or appreciated or understood. It's the fear that you may fall into a shadow life of smothering darkness from which you can never escape.

This desperation you feel is an instinctual need we all share, as basic as being lost in the wilderness and wanting to go home. This feeling is designed as a perpetual energy source, forcing us to focus and take actions that fill this void. We all want to fill this void within us. We all need to find the real answers and to make some sense of everything. We are all looking for a way to live so we can be happy, thrive, and not be corrupt. We are all seeking our special people, so we are not alone, so we can be at peace and live a meaningful, hopeful, happy life.

Seeking "True Success" in Tragedy & Hardship

"There are uses to adversity, and they don't reveal themselves until tested…the difficulty can tap unexpected strengths."
- Sonia Sotomayor

So, if having power, wealth, fame, beauty, intelligence, or holiness is not "True Success," what is? "They" say the most profound answers to life are found within the hardships and heartache of life. I am not sure who "they" are, but for me, this proved to be accurate, for I found the most important answers to the meaning of life within the hardships and heartache of life.

For me, these hard lessons started when I was young. I was born with a lazy eye, which made me legally blind in one eye. As a result, I wore a patch over my good eye to improve my vision. I have dyslexia and other "learning disabilities," so I struggled with reading, writing, and arithmetic. (see the "About the Author" to learn more.).

Little was known about "learning disabilities" at the time, so learning and adapting to life's challenges at an early age was difficult. Along with these issues, I was also bullied by my peers and some adults. One elementary school teacher even going as far as to ridicule me in front of the class, telling me to drop out of school and get a job because I was too stupid ever to graduate.

While these circumstances added trials to my life, they also came with gifts. Along with "disabilities," I gained some abilities that allow me to see and do things most other people cannot. All of these circumstances have taught me to persevere, be empathetic, to seek real answers, and so much more.

Other foundation pieces to what "True Success" really means were shown to me by all the parents and child patients in those hospitals and testing centers I visited because of my or my sister's issues. When I was very young, during one of those difficult hospital trips when my sister had almost died, I had a very important conversation with a little girl who had a disease and was dying.

This conversation took place in a hospital section just for kids. She was here with my sister and other children who were either very ill, dying, or working hard to recover from great trauma. My sister had just had another operation to save her life and was there recovering. This little girl was maybe 9 or 10 years old, and at one point, as we were talking about many things, we started discussing how difficult this was for her.

It was during this part of the conversation that I was given the greatest key to "True Success," even if I did not know it at the time. She said that what was important above all else was love and that, without love, nothing else mattered. After she was done, I thought about it and said that I thought a lot of other stuff mattered and started listing things. She stopped me and pointed to the horrible machines that had tubes connected to her.

She talked about how ugly and scary this whole place was and how there is no park to play in. She talked about how she can't even see her friends or go anywhere.

Then she said, with a little tear running down her cheek and a crack in her voice, "without my parents and others here…loving me…I would not want to wake up any more…but it's ok…because I have them…and they love me…so I can still be happy sometimes when I am awake…I still have hope I might get better…and be free to play like you do with your friends."

After she was done, I had a vision of her life here, being in this horrible place for months and months and maybe never leaving. I thought of my sister in this same place with the doctors cutting her and all the tubes in her and how she was in so much pain. I thought about what it would be like if I were completely blind or sick and stuck here. It scared me!

I think at that moment something broke and was awakened within me as I saw her, the other children, and my sister all in this same place of horror, yet love making it ok or at least bearable somehow. It was clear how my parent's love for their children gave them the strength to go that extra mile and far beyond for my brother, sister and me, and how that made all the difference in the world to us.

As with many of these moments of moving conversations with random people throughout my life, I would not forget this moment, for it was one of those moments that change who you are on a deep level. I think a part of me never really left that hospital room with my new little dying friend. I always hoped she made it out and was free to play in the sun with her friends again.

What is the True Goal of Life?

My journey into the hardships of life also meant having to heal my body and mind many times after being hurt. Along with all the broken bones, cuts, scrapes, bruises, concussions, sprains, and other traumas many of us go through, some very serious things happened to me, a few of which I have included here.

For example, I have been attacked many times by dogs; after one attack, I almost lost my leg due to an infection from a dog bite. I have been in several car accidents. One of them left me unable to walk or stand normally for many years, and I still suffer from some related issues.

My hardships also meant that throughout my life, I have been in many fights. At a young age, I started being attacked, for as I said, I was a target of bullies because of my patch and "learning disabilities." As I grew, I studied martial arts and learned to defend myself and protect others. So, while in college, I got a job as a bouncer at a nightclub. As you can imagine, I had many altercations while in this job.

One of the most traumatic occurred late one night when a knife fight broke out. I stepped in, disarmed one of the fighters who had been stabbed, and confronted the other with the captured blade. I then gave him a choice of either fighting me or running now. I convinced him to leave. I then was able to save the life of the other fighter who had been stabbed in the chest.

Another time when I was a teen, I confronted a friend for sexually assaulting my girlfriend at a party when I was not there. I sat down with him for a while, listening to him lie, rationalize, and try justifying his actions as no big deal. Then, as he was trying to get me to leave and be cool with everything he said and did, I called him on his dishonor. As he was shaking my hand, I crushed his in my grip.

After a short time and some harsh words, I let him go, and he put his hands up to fight. The fight lasted for only a few seconds, but I unintentionally gave him a concussion, shattered his jaw and other injuries. He luckily woke up from a coma a few days later and eventually recovered.

I have lost dear friends and loved ones to horrible vehicle accidents and disease. I have been cheated and cheated on, lied to, manipulated, and betrayed many times. I have overcome an addiction to chewing tobacco, which I started while in high school playing sports, as well as depression and suicidal thoughts.

"The greatest glory in living lies not in never falling, but in rising every time, we fall." - Ralph Waldo Emerson

I have watched my sister endure severe illnesses and painful operations throughout her life with such strength while also attaining many college degrees and helping so many teens. I almost lost my brother, who was hit by a car, yet saw him fight his way back so fast so he could support his family. My whole life, I saw my father work so hard providing for us, yet he died young with such grace even as cancer destroyed his body. I am reminded of what is truly important every day as I care for my mother, who has health issues and endured so much yet is always a never-ending source of positive faith, belief, and strength.

All of these hardships have taught me many valuable lessons. They have shown me what is truly important and led me to discover what "True Success" really means.

TRUE SUCCESS & THE TRUE GOAL OF LIFE

It took me a long time to discover the full answer because I am male and because our society's idea of who is "successful" is not correct. It's also because while *The Way* is simple at its core, it's complicated in the details spanning many disciplines. So, it took me a while to discover the fullness of *The Way* because it was jumbled together within a lot of other knowledge.

In the end, the core truth of what it is to be "Truly Successful" was found back where I started with my little dying friend. For this answer, we need only look at what a loving mother wants for her child.

She wants her child to be healthy, happy, safe, loved, and to have long-lasting positive relationships. She wants them to grow to be a good and kind person who works hard and feels passionate about something worthwhile, ideally doing that as a means of support where they not only survive but thrive. A "True Life" where her child grows with the ability to overcome obstacles, challenges, and finds all they need to live a happy and meaningful life. In the end, this is what we all want. This is the "True Goal of Life!"

Your Problem

"Every problem has in it the seeds of its own solution. If you don't have any problems, you don't get any seeds."
- Norman Vincent Peale

The problem is that if you are to be "Truly Successful" and become your "True Self," live a meaningful life and make a real difference in the world; you need to integrate a wide variety of vital information into your life as quickly as possible.

As humans, our problem is compounded because we are all born ignorant and dependent on other people, and it's often what we don't know that will hurt us the most. The problem is made even more complex because the answers we seek are multifaceted and span many disciplines, and we are all starting from different points of understanding.

At the time of this writing and throughout human history, many live unhealthy, unfulfilling lives without any or only a few positive close relationships. Most of us live a life that is full of confusion and a lot of trauma and drama. Most of us live a life where we are left feeling lost, lonely, isolated, confused, frustrated, worried, dissatisfied, and desperate part, or even most of the time.

We all feel that void and are looking to fill it with the right pieces. The fact is most of us want positive change that creates a positive, permanent future. However, knowing and wanting to fix the wrongness within ourselves and our society is not enough to become "Truly Successful." To be "Truly Successful," you must know what actions to take and then act.

Doing all the research and reading the thousands of books and other materials in all the different genres to find the knowledge on how to be your best physically, mentally, emotionally, spiritually, financially, in relationships, as a family, and in society is certainly not easy or even possible for everyone. It may even seem impossible to you. This is why *The Way* was created.

THE SOLUTION

"It always seems impossible until it's done."
- Nelson Mandela

Collecting the questions and answers that will allow us all to thrive has been and is my mission. As I grew up in America, traveling the world, living in other countries, talking with people from everywhere, and learning, I gathered more and more pieces to this puzzle in the form of books, notes, recordings, sayings, inspirational pictures, and writings of mine.

What is the True Goal of Life?

Some of the pieces to this grand puzzle came to me at the oddest times, where I was compelled to save them somehow. Often, I awoke in the middle of the night to write the pieces down or had to pull over in my car to make a note. On many occasions, I stopped everything in life to research and/or write nonstop for days on end. All this time, I could feel that all these threads I was collecting were part of a much grander truth, and they just needed to be woven together in the right order somehow.

It was such an amazing day when I finally saw the key pattern within this weave of the information. I discovered *The Way* on April 3, 2015, while sorting the beginning and the ending of "The Book" I have been working on for over 30 years covering how to be our best physically, mentally, emotionally, spiritually, financially, in relationships, as a family, and in society. Within "The Book" and its "4 Pillars" of "Self," "Society," "Universe," and "God," I kept finding my references noting different concepts as "Key" to "True Success."

When I collected them all and put the "7 Keys" together in the right order, it was like a secret code got unlocked. At that moment, I saw these "Keys" were "Steps," and I discovered *The Way*. After this discovery, I wrote for three days straight without much sleep or doing anything else. I truly learned what obsession and compulsion meant that day. I then worked over five years to finish the book at the exclusion of most other things. *The Way* is the book I wish I found when I started my quest.

"True Success" is a journey where you find your "True Path" and then go from "working to become" to "being" your "True Self." As you join with others who are doing the same, the whole process becomes easier. It's this unbeatable combination of being on your "True Path" following *The Way;* while you join with others doing the same, that becomes the immovable and unstoppable positive force. This positive force is the power that will transform you into your "True Self" and our world into a wonderful place for everyone to live.

To say it another way, it's through clarity, focus, action, and unity that you will transform yourself into your "True Self" and create a world everyone can be proud to call home.

YOUR CHALLENGE

"The ultimate measure of a man is not where he stands in moments of comfort and convenience, but where he stands at times of challenge and controversy." - Martin Luther King, Jr.

Right now, at this moment, you are at a major crossroads on your life's mission. You found this message at this time for a reason. The fact is that if you really want to be "Truly Successful," a person who is influential, significant, and makes a real difference in the world, you need to integrate a wide variety of vital information into your life as quickly as possible.

This life's journey of mine has allowed me to collect these key bits of knowledge we all need. I have spent my life preparing *The Way* for you, so now you need only take a few moments of your life to benefit from these insights. You found *The Way* at this time because it's the foundation you need. This vital information will help you meet your current goals and take you to the next level and beyond.

WHAT IS THE TRUE GOAL OF LIFE?

You, your happiness, and our world are truly important. What you do with your life really matters. It matters to you, your loved ones, our society, to God, and to me. There is not and will never be another you. You are unique and special. You can be happy, healthy, at peace, have great relationships, and help this world in so many ways.

So, the question is, will you take this opportunity to look a little deeper? Will you take the opportunity to become your "True Self" that is in front of you right now?

If *The Way* is the answer or even contains part of the solution you have been missing, you don't want to let this opportunity slip by and always regret and wonder who you could have been. So, investing a little time to learn *The Way* is the right thing to do. You have nothing to lose and yet possibly everything to gain. The choice is yours.

"The will to win, the desire to succeed, the urge to reach your full potential… these are the keys that will unlock the door to personal excellence." - Confucius

Chapter 2
How to Achieve
the True Goal of Life

"Great goals make great people." - Roy Bennett

As we have learned, the primary goal of life is to become "Truly Successful." Knowing this leads us to ask the question, "how <u>exactly</u> do you become "Truly Successful?"

The answer to this question is to follow *The Way*.

What is *The Way*?

The Way is "Living Rational Positive Action"

Why "Living Rational Positive Action?"

Living

Because following *The Way* is something that we do all the time. We can only act within the flow of the now. Therefore, if we are to become our best, it must be a part of our life as we flow in time from moment to moment. The goal here is to live it and not just read about it or honor the ideas once in a while.

Rational

Because *The Way* is logical, reasonable, and includes implementing a plan that is customizable to fit your life. Being rational means that you can understand new things and change your mind when new facts arise. It means you are mentally healthy and, therefore, able to make "rational" decisions based on reality and truth. In this sense, *The Way* is a rational path leading to the ultimate goal of life.

POSITIVE

Because *The Way* is good as it naturally leads us to what we really want for ourselves, our loved ones, and our world. The positive is about producing "good" results. Good is something we naturally prefer. This fundamental knowledge of the positive is instinctive. The idea of "positive," "good," and "better" within a human life is expressed by virtues.

Virtues are traits or qualities that humanity has deemed positive, good, admirable, and at times, <u>morally</u> good and righteous. While there may be "top virtues" like being positive, good, hopeful, resilient, persevering, and rational, we do not rank or order them. This is because it takes many virtues to cover all parts of life, and some are more relevant to a moment than another. Virtues are more like a bouquet of flowers, where many can be equally beautiful and important. They are peers where none are better, and all are equal.

Some key virtues include being: positive, happy, hopeful, optimistic, peaceful, good, free, grateful, humble, reasonable, rational, resilient, brave, persevering, independent, curious, flexible, intelligent, wise, knowledgeable, honorable, creative, open-minded, polite, respectful, considerate, helpful, kind, caring, empathetic, sympathetic, tolerant, a great listener and communicator, a healthy skeptic seeking to understand before being understood, successful, disciplined, determined, dedicated, confident, enthusiastic, motivated, faithful, courageous, punctual, productive, responsible, a hard worker, doing a great job, going the extra mile, efficient, mindful, effective, diligent, frugal, prepared, handy, organized, clean, fair, just, honest, trustworthy, forgiving, affectionate, loving, charitable, compassionate, alert, sharp, focused, relaxed, cool, calm, collected, controlled, centered, patient, rightfully loyal, fit, healthy, strong, graceful and coordinated.

These positive human qualities are at the core of what we hold in the highest regard as a species. Virtues are at the heart of all our faiths, organizational codes, and all success, self-help and development books. They are the foundation of what a loving mother wants for her child. Virtues are the positive ideals we all aspire to. Knowing that we all seek virtue is a critical insight and one that can save you a lot of time. Therefore, you can focus on learning all the virtues and integrating them into your life.

Note that the opposite of virtue is called a failing, vice, or sin, with the most virulent named the 7 deadly sins. These 7 include pride, envy, gluttony, lust, anger, greed, and sloth. Some others include: lying, cheating, stealing, bearing false witness, mispresenting, callousness, deceiving, disparaging, & being hateful, unfair, unequal, impolite, mean, obnoxious, petty, rude, selfish, self-righteous, spiteful, uncaring, malicious, wasteful, prejudice, and xenophobic. All human failings are overcome by virtue.

For example, living rational, positive action, being mindful, and developing good self-discipline and control gives you key abilities that will help you overcome all vice. The key to ending a vice is to work on ingraining needed virtues in your life instead of focusing on the negative that you want to stop or give up. To say it another way, you focus on filling your life with the positive, not the loss of a negative.

ACTION

Because it's only through action in the now that you can make anything real. For virtue to mean anything, you must realize them in your life.

You express virtues within your words and actions. Therefore, for you to be your best, you must have unity of purpose, belief, and intention.

We call an action plan that is doing something the best way a "best practice." A "best practice" is often something that we continuously work to improve upon to ensure that we don't miss something. Also, there may be more than one "best practice" or variation that works better for some people than others or, in some circumstances, better than others. Therefore, knowing all the top variations of a "best practice" can be more valuable as you can find the one, or the few that work best for you in all situations.

"We are what we repeatedly do.
Excellence, then, is not an act, but a habit."
- Will Durant

Putting Virtue into Best Practice Examples:

- Living the "virtue" of "being healthy" includes the "best practices" of proper sleep, workouts, fuels, and more.
- Living the "virtue" of "being punctual" includes the "best practice" of leaving in plenty of time, time tracking, alarms, and reminders.

What good are "best practices" without a rational and real way to integrate them into our lives? As you go through *The Way*, you will learn how to integrate them. In the end, our goal is to have positive habits based on the "best practices" covering key areas of life we ultimately live without having to try.

The Way is not about being "without" or "stopping." *The Way* is about abundance and doing, where you crowd out the bad and negative and replace it with the good and positive naturally. It's through integrating key virtues through best practices into your life in 90-day cycles that allows you to build foundational habits, find your "True Path," and become a better and better person. If you create good solid habits during the good times, then during the bad times, it will be easy for you to maintain a positive lifestyle because you have built the habits.

In this light, we can see *The Way* as a practical guide on how to integrate the best practices for living a meaningful life and making a real difference in the world.

THE WAY & THE 7 STEPS SHORT EXPLANATION

As we have learned, *The Way* to achieve the ultimate goal of life is to "Live Rational Positive Action," and this is accomplished by following the "7 Steps." Below I have briefly outlined each of the "7 Steps" and their associated chapters for easy reference. *Note* some steps span multiple chapters while others are contained within one. This volume of *The Way* covers the main philosophy and all "7 Steps."

> **The Way** - Chapter 2
> **Step 1: Know** - Chapter 3
> **Step 2: Want** - Chapter 3
> **Step 3: Choose** - Chapter 3
> **Step 4: Center** - Chapter 3 to 7
> **Step 5: Be** - Chapter 8
> **Step 6: Unite** - Chapter 9 to 15
> **Step 7: Perfect** - Chapter 16
> **Your Next Steps:** - Chapter 17

Steps 1, 2 & 3: The first three steps allow you to get on your "True Path" from any point in life very quickly.

Steps 4 & 5: These two steps give you the keys to daily life and show you how to live them.

Steps 6 & 7: The last two steps show how to create positive relationships, make a real difference in the world, and refine everything as you go forward.

Volume II: Life Manual: This manual provides more details on the "Foundations of Life" covered within "Step 5: Be." The keys found within this manual help you to optimize your health and life and can be used anytime by jumping to the "Life Foundation" of interest.

Volume III: Child & Family Guide: This guide provides vital information and shows us how to raise positive, motivated children and build a happy, productive family. This guide can also be used anytime yet will become of even greater value after an understanding of *The Way* and *Life Manual* has been gained.

Ok, now that we have a basic understanding, let's discover how and why *The Way* can work for everyone. After that, we will go into each of the "7 Steps" in detail.

How The Way Works for Everyone

"When I let go of what I am, I become what I might be."
- Lao Tzu

Even though we might not all look the same, speak the same language, have the same physical or mental abilities, be the same age or gender, on a fundamental level, we all need, want, and feel the same things at some point.

The fact that we all share this "Human Condition" means we are all forced to do, and deal with, many of the same issues every day if we are to survive and thrive.

The underlying factors of being human remains the same for all of us, no matter our circumstances.

What is the Human Condition?

The "Human Condition" is a combination of all the characteristics and circumstances under which we all live. These factors generally fall into two categories, called "Universal and Life Conditions." Universal covers things related to our earth, solar system, and the universe. Life conditions are tied to our human body and society.

Universal Condition Examples:
- Spacetime
- Gravity
- Hot and cold
- Magnetics
- Cause and effect
- Entropy
- Day and night
- Seasons
- Earthquakes
- Storms

Life Condition Examples:
- Birth and extensive effort needed to raise children
- Old age and death
- Body care
- Need for sleep, light, food, air, and water
- Ignorant at birth
- Fight or flight responses
- Need other people for us to be happy
- Many people working together needed to thrive
- We can pass on knowledge and build systems which can help future generations

The Way

Why Do We Live Under These Human Conditions?

The "Human Condition" is what structures our life and society. It's an ever-present catalyst and energy source that we are driven by regardless of our desire.

For example, as time passes, we act and move in space and time (spacetime). As we move, these conditions affect us. We have no choice but to be affected.

These conditions focus our attention on essential aspects of what it is to be a sentient life form. It does all of this and much more in a repetitive manner. We can see this repetitive structure in the similarities between "a day" and "a life." In both cases, we awaken, learn, get tired, and surrender our consciousness.

Life	Day
Born	Awaken
Young	Morning
Adult	Day
Old	Evening
Die	Sleep

This repetition is designed to force us to think, choose, and act in specific ways individually and collectively every day. These conditions allow for an opportunity to learn and improve by implementing a better way of doing something the next time.

Over time this primary repetitive cycle provides a significant opportunity for us to gain a deeper understanding, to refine and perfect many critical aspects of ourselves and our world. This is especially true as we pass on knowledge and infrastructure from generation to generation. The key here is to use these conditions to spur us on in positive ways individually and as a society.

This is because if we do not understand how they focus us and then plan and choose wisely, many negative outcomes will occur. In the end, the human conditions under which we live are here to focus us so that key ways of being are ingrained within us.

How Do the Human Conditions Focus Us?

Looking at all the human conditions and their effects on our lives, we find that they focus us on the preservation of our life, those we care for, and on changing our environment and society. We can break down these developmental aspects of the "Human Condition" into three main categories: "Self-Creation," "Self-Control," and "Societal Development."

SELF-CREATION

Self-Creation is the ability to create oneself into who we want to be. We are all born ignorant, and, by our very nature, as we grow, we use free will and choice to create ourselves.

- **Free Will** is the power of independent action and the ability to act or make choices as a free and autonomous being and not solely as a compulsion or predestination. However, freedom of choice and action are confined, defined, influenced, and limited by our shared "Human Condition." Free will means we can choose anything within limits.

    For example, you can't choose not to eat or sleep and continue to live. You can't cool a nuclear reactor with your mind. Humans cannot fly around in space without protection, or we would die.

This idea of "constraint" applies to everything, including things like randomness and chaos, because they are constrained by the universal conditions and, therefore, not truly random or chaotic.

- **Choice** is to be able to decide which we feel is best or most appropriate. Our decisions are exercised in action. As we get older and more capable of understanding ourselves and our world, the more choices we make. It's through the accumulation of the right knowledge that we gain the wisdom to make the right choices and create ourselves into who we want to be.

SELF-CONTROL

Self-Control is the ability to control our behavior, especially in terms of actions, reactions, and impulses.

Examples of Self-Control Issues: Your power of free will and choice allows you to control your behavior physically (how you are doing it), mentally (what you are thinking), and emotionally (what you are feeling). Here are some *examples* of self-control issues within each state:

Physical
  o Sleep and Awakening: Do you adhere to a good pattern?
  o Body: Do you care and maintain your body correctly?
  o Fuel: Do you eat and hydrate correctly?
  o Violence: Do you hit and lash out?

Mental
- Self-Image: Do you think, treat, and talk about yourself in a positive way?
- Constant Mental Focus (CMF): What do you think about most often, is it positive?

- Moral Code: What are your core beliefs that influence your attitude toward everything?
- Attitude: Are you generally positive or negative?

Emotional
- What are you feeling, and why?
- How extreme are your feelings? Are they in proportion to the situation?
- How much significance are you giving your feelings? Do they rule your life?
- How well do you balance logic and emotion?
- Can you control your emotions?

SOCIETAL DEVELOPMENT

The human condition forces humanity to compete, as well as work together, cooperate, and share to survive. If we cooperate well with each other, we can thrive. Our society centers on individuals cooperating and competing in many forms. Our ability to cooperate and compete, as well as our ability to improve our skills and systems, is one of our greatest powers.

Basic Societal Competitive/Cooperative Systems Include:

- Family
- Relationships
- Tribes & Clans
- Countries
- Cities
- Businesses
- Governments
- Entertainment & Sports
- Basic Systems of Life: Food, water, clothing, housing, education, energy, health, sanitation, etc.

THE POWER OF COOPERATION & COMPETITION

Our shared human condition forces us to work together to compensate for and to overcome these conditions. Cooperating as we compete is key if we are to not only survive but thrive. This state creates an ever-present life challenge for us individually, and as a society, for here, we find opportunities to achieve higher states of being as well as temptations leading to corruption.

For example, think about a race at a sporting event that a lot of people would watch. We find cooperation in following the rules, the selection of locations, and all the details that allow for an event to happen. The competition comes in when we let the athletes run the race. However, even here, there are rules to follow as they all start at the same place. They will get disqualified if they trip or hit each other, take drugs, etc. People can even be tempted to bet everything on the race. The competitive spirit taken too far without cooperation becomes corruption.

HUMAN CONDITION SUMMARY

The fact is our shared human conditions force us all into situations where we can achieve greatness or be corrupted. These are purposefully designed life challenges and tests. The reason bad and negative things happen is generally for two reasons. One is that we have a societal problem that needs fixing. Or two, it's about character building and self-development.

Corruption is the acceptance of the unacceptable. In this light, the purpose of our human condition becomes clear. These conditions force us as individuals and as a society to make choices. These situations and our choices test our ability to live up to our conscience and positive moral code and stand against corruption. Therefore, it's key to realize that cooperatively competing correctly at a high level is one of our greatest gifts and is how we improve our culture and ultimately create our "True Society." It is also one of our greatest challenges that, if not handled correctly, can lead to our destruction.

> **THE REASON YOU ARE HERE**
>
> You are alive on this world right now because this whole repetitive setup under which you live is a training ground that is designed to teach and ingrain within you key foundational ways of being. The goal to ultimately prepare you for a greater reality. Because of the human conditions and especially spacetime, freewill, choice, and cooperation, we can all join together and create changes within our own lives and world. The goal is to manage these conditions in the most positive and productive way possible individually and collectively. This is how everything gets better and better. The Way is designed to help us all achieve this goal.

Chapter 3
Get On Your True Path Right Now

"A moment's insight is sometimes worth a life's experience."
- Oliver Wendell Holmes

Now that you have an overall idea of *The Way* and know why it can work for all of us, we will next go through each of the "7 Steps" in detail.

The first "3 Steps" of *The Way* are relatively short and logical. They are also very deep and essential to understanding yourself and all of humanity. This basic understanding is important because this is how, no matter where you or any of us start, *The Way* gets us all on our "True Path" right now.

Step 1: Know

"Ignorance, the root and stem of all evil." - Plato

First, we, as individual people, must perceive something and then learn about it to "know" it. Humanity innately "knows" good from bad and the positive from the negative without much thought.

For Example, you know being happy is better than being sad, being free is better than being a slave, drinking clean water is better than drinking poisoned water, and being loved is better than being hated.

Knowing this basic truth should seem simple and obvious. Simply acknowledging the fact that you know the "good" and "positive" is how you take the first step on your "True Path" to your "True Self."

STEP 2: WANT

"Desire is the starting point of all achievement, not a hope, not a wish, but a keen pulsating desire which transcends everything." - Napoleon Hill

Now that you know the good and positive, it should be obvious that you would naturally want it for yourself, your loved ones, and our world. Just as you would naturally want happiness, clean water, freedom, and love. This desire for the positive can manifest in many ways.

FOR EXAMPLE, THIS DESIRE CAN MANIFEST AS A DESIRE & HOPE:
- For a better life
- To fix a wrong
- For the best for our loved ones
- To understand life
- To do more with your life
- To be saved
- To be at peace
- To do something meaningful
- To run away from everything
- For the bad, wrong, and evil to stop and end
- To have good things happen in the world

The need, want, desire, hope, and aspiration for the good and positive has been hardwired into us and is spurred on by the human conditions under which we all live. Our innate desire for "the better" is a catalyst and an ever-present source of energy that can help fuel our journey.

So, the second step down the path to your "True Self" is simply finding and acknowledging the part of you that wants, desires, hopes wishes, and prays for the positive. No matter how weak or strong this sensation is at this point, just locating and observing it is enough. You don't have to know how or even believe good things will happen. You only need to realize you <u>want</u> the good and positive in your life.

STEP 3: CHOOSE

"Life presents many choices, the choices we make determine our future." - Catherine Pulsifer

Now that you know and want the positive, you must formally choose this as your path, just as you would naturally choose happiness, freedom, clean water, and love over sadness, slavery, poisoned water, and hatred. This is a general choice based on your desire, and as with the last step, it does not require you to know what actions to take or even believe it will happen.

No matter how tentative this choice is, it will be made firm and realized more deeply through understanding and living *The Way*. Your choice can be made anytime and reaffirmed throughout your life. It's in your formally "choosing" that you make the intangible into something real. Your decision can be made with your full heart in a formal verbal ceremony, or it may start as the faintest wish, hope, desire, dream, aim, goal, or aspiration using your inner voice.

When ready, say something like, "I choose a positive path" or "I choose *The Way*" or "I choose the positive" or "I follow *The Way*" or "I live *The Way*" or "I Live Rational Positive Action." You may also add or create your own positive wording for this declaration if desired. You can take this oath now and/or after you learn the whole of *The Way*.

Let Go of the Past

It does not matter who you were, only who you want to be and who you choose to become. Let go of the past. Choose to make yourself into the best version of yourself. It's ok if you did not have a happy or easy start. It does not matter what you have done, only where you end up. Direct all your experiences and energy into the ultimate goal of becoming the best version of yourself, and you will achieve it.

How to Make A True Choice

A true choice is linked to your true intention. True intention means that deep down at the foundation of who you are, you <u>WANT</u> this. If your intentions are true and you're willing to examine "who and what" you are so you may change, develop, and become better, then you can achieve this goal.

Your "want and desire" for good and for you to be your best must be greater than most other desires as it will then become an ever-present guiding positive force in your life that will help you change in the positive ways you choose.

For example, your desire to improve must be stronger than the desire to hold onto a belief or way of doing something just because of your role models, ancestors, parents, organization, society, or you are doing it that way. You must be willing to examine all of who you are and change where needed, for this is the only way to really improve.

Note: At this point, we are almost halfway through the "7 Steps," and I would like to think that we, as in most of humanity, would agree with the first "3 Steps" in this logic chain. It should be clear that you know and want the good within your life and that you must choose it if you are to attain your desire. The remaining four steps cover what is needed to manifest your knowledge, desire, and choice of the positive within your life as quickly as possible.

STEP 4: CENTER

"Educating the mind without educating the heart is no education at all." - Aristotle

Within Step 4, you continue down your "True Path" and put your choice for the positive and the good into rational action by confirming a complete "Core Belief System" or "Moral Code" that covers all areas of life. *Note* that "Step 4: Center" starts here in chapter 4 and runs through chapter 7.

WHY DO YOU NEED TO CONFIRM A CODE?

We all have a core value system. Core values are also known as a moral code and paradigms. They are fundamental to your success because they affect and determine your attitude, intentions, thoughts, judgments, choices, words, actions, reactions, emotions, feelings, and other beliefs. Add all of this together, and this is basically who you are.

This means that a small set of values affects and determines your view and how you feel about yourself, parents, foreigners, God, religion, education, government, our environment, the rich, the poor, politics, money, sex, drugs, violence, and everything else.

This critical insight is of paramount importance as it determines your fate/destiny and the fate/destiny of humanity. Our core values are the deciding factors that determine our success as individuals and as a species. Therefore, having a complete set of core beliefs that cover all aspects of life is imperative for becoming your best because they affect everything in your life.

You can see "Our Code" as firmware or as an operating system that determines all you do and say. Our core code is the lens that helps us interpret the world around us. So, by centering ourselves through choosing and adhering to a positive moral code that covers all aspects of life, we solve most of the problems of life and society.

How Does Your Core Value System Change?

A Paradigm Shift is a core belief that changes drastically. For us to develop as humans, our paradigms naturally change drastically as we go from a baby to a toddler to a teen and an adult.

Our core beliefs can also change for other reasons, all of which require a catalyst of some kind. A catalyst is something that is introduced and creates change. The catalyst and its effect can be positive or negative. The key to note here is that you determine the effect of the catalyst. Your control means that you can take a negative catalyst and turn it into positive energy. See the "Life Manual: Our Practice: The Power: Transmutation" for more on how to change the negative into positive.

The paradigm shift can create a change that takes place instantly, or it may take time to manifest. The key to any paradigm shift is not to fight it, but instead to take the time to understand what is happening or has happened. Through this deep understanding, you gain control and often can find even more positive change.

Paradigm Shift *Examples*:

- As a child, our perspective on cars was how cool it looked. As we got older and had kids, we then found safety as our primary concern. Here the paradigm shifts from cool to safety.
- We hate all people who have dark or light skin because we were taught this was right since we were a child. Then we serve in the military and work with people of many different shades of skin tone.

    We make friends with people that have different skin tones, cultures, and ethnic groups and then realize we are all just people. Here the paradigm shifts from hate to friendship and from falsely believing in separate races to understanding that we are one human race.

Traumatic events are catalysts that can cause a paradigm shift that drastically changes our lives. Again, this change can be positive or negative, depending on how you handle it. These close calls or near-death experiences can radically change the way you see those close to you and the world around you.

These events can literally make everything seem more vibrant and glow with the energy of life. You can feel the most profound appreciation for the simplest everyday things, and this experience can wash away all the little problems you have with people. Here the paradigm changes from commonplace to wonder and gratitude. This crucial insight holds great power for positive change in our everyday life and society, for we don't have to wait for such events to get the benefits.

THE 10 LAWS DEFINED

"Ethics is knowing the difference between what you have a right to do and what is right to do." - Potter Stewart

The "10 Laws" or "10 Commandments" below are a complete set of positive core beliefs that cover all aspects of life. These "10 Commandments" are at the center of *The Way*. We refer to these as "Laws" or "Commandments" or "Core Values" because they are self-mandated directives that make up the center of a value system that covers all of life. (*Note: I have used "Laws" most often in this book because it's a shorter word*).

It's my understanding that the "10 Laws" are at the core of all religions, spiritual paths, and our developed human conscience and sense of morality. All is written with the utmost respect and appreciation for all. You can follow *The Way*, honor God, your religion, spiritual path, and yourself without conflict.

The information contained within the "10 Laws" can help bridge the gap between believers and non-believers, science and religion, as well as east and west. These laws can help everyone gain an understanding of our world and our societal systems. It's this mass understanding that will naturally change our lives and systems for the positive.

As a set of personal absolute moral guidelines, the "10 Laws" guide you in every situation, which helps you stay on your "True Path." These "rules to live by" are a construct that you use to check yourself against throughout our day to ensure that you are on track. They are the yardstick to judge the rightness and wrongness of yourself, our society as well as other people.

Really knowing the meaning and intent behind each law and how the "10 Laws" work together as a whole is key to successfully implementing them in life. Any belief that is worth having must not be forced upon you, and it should be able to stand up to others, reason, morality, and your conscience. Therefore, first, we will provide the list of all the laws, and then we define each of these core values in detail.

The laws are grouped into "The Laws of Purpose," "The Universal Laws," and "The God Laws." For some people, at a glance, a few of the Laws may appear to be in conflict with your beliefs. If so, please read further for clarification, for you may find, as others have, that they are not what you assume.

Laws of Purpose
1. The Primary Purpose of Life is to Be Your True Self, Live a True Life, and Go to Heaven.
2. The Primary Purpose of Society is to Create Our True Society.

Universal Laws
3. Respect Life.
4. All People are Equal.
5. Treat People as You Want to be Treated.

God Laws
6. There is No God Other than God.
7. We are All Directly Connected with God, and this Connection Cannot Be Broken.
8. God is Our Sole and Final Judge, and We are Judged by Our True Beliefs, Intentions, Words, and Actions.
9. Respect God.
10. Worship Only God; God Does Not Require Worship; God Can Only be Freely Worshiped.

THE LAWS OF PURPOSE

"The first principle of ethical power is Purpose. By purpose, I don't mean your objective or intention-something toward which you are always striving. Purpose is something bigger. It is the picture you have of yourself-the kind of person you want to be or the kind of life you want to lead." - Ken Blanchard

It's through the unity of purpose within self and society that we create the circumstances for higher states of being to be realized in our life and world. Our lives, all callings, and our society are made better through the first "2 Laws of Purpose."

LAW 1
THE PRIMARY PURPOSE OF LIFE IS TO BE YOUR TRUE SELF, LIVE A TRUE LIFE, & GO TO HEAVEN.

"The whole point of being alive is to evolve into the complete person you were intended to be." - Oprah Winfrey

A primary purpose means we have an overall life goal, mission, and reason for existing. The primary purpose for each of us to become the best person we can, live a meaningful life, and to go to "heaven."

Here you are only competing with yourself, and comparisons with other lives are meaningless for your journey is "truly" unique and incomparable.

DEFINITIONS OF KEY TERMS:
- "True Path." The way to the ultimate self, life, and heaven.
- "True Self." The ultimate self.
- "True Life." Living the ultimate life.
- Heaven. The ultimate place to exist, live, and be.

WHY IS HEAVEN INCLUDED?

Heaven is included within the "First Law" for all of us who believe and because it's possible. For those who do not believe in heaven as the ultimate goal, the other concepts of becoming your best and living a great life are still valid primary purposes of life. You can change it to "The Primary Purpose of Life is to Be Your True Self and Live a True Life," omitting heaven from the law. For those wanting more, note that we will cover more about God and Heaven within the "God Laws" later within this step.

THE OTHER MAJOR PURPOSES OF LIFE

There are other definite major purposes or missions for your life beyond this primary. However, all other purposes in life are enhanced and supported by this "1st Commandment" because if you are at your best, everything else you do is better. In fact, following *The Way* helps you be prepared for your great callings when they arrive. Other great callings may include: being a parent and role model, doing meaningful work, a political calling, being an artist, helping people, solving world issues, and more.

THE VOID & YOUR TRUE SELF

As stated, there is no comparison with others for each of us is truly unique and only competing with ourselves. The key is to realize that it's more important to find the truth than to be right. Often, humans learn more through error, trials, and tribulations of life than an easy success.

In the end, your "True Path" to your "True Self" is one you must be willing to follow no matter where it takes you.

One of the keys to being truly successful is knowing that the fear of being lost, failure, and self-destruction is balanced with the hope of becoming your "True Self" and living a wonderful life. This positive image of your ultimate self, having great relationships, living a "True Life" is critical. To be "Truly Successful," you must realize this greater being, is you.

To say it another way, you are not channeling this greater self from anywhere else or trying to become something you are not. Instead, you are growing into, releasing, and manifesting your "True Self" within the body you inhabit within this world. Your "True Self" is who you really are; it just takes conscious effort to manifest.

So, take a moment right now and imagine the moment has finally arrived when you find that missing piece to fill that void within. Envision, there is a positive, powerful, beautifully glowing ball of energy in front of you right now. This glowing ball of positive energy is the answer to your deepest desires and is here for the taking right now. You naturally feel the rush of good feelings, like hope, and excitement, just knowing the moment is here, and the answer is right in front of you.

Now, you see yourself taking the wonderful ball of light, and as you do, it merges with you. You instantly become one with this positive energy. You understand and find peace. The world makes sense. You know why you are here and what to do. You have clarity of purpose. You know how to find your people and make the relationships you have better. You clearly see your unique path to get you to where you want to go. No matter how difficult or challenging, it all seems doable, and you know you can pass the test. You can clearly see being your "True Self" and living a "True Life" that is more wonderful than you ever dreamed.

For some of us, we may not know what we have been missing until it appears, and for others, the void within is keenly apparent. In either case, when a missing piece finally appears, we have no real choice as it's instinctual, we most often just go for it. Many of us even risk everything for an opportunity to fill this void when it arrives.

We take this missing piece when it shows up because we know if we let this, what may be a once in a lifetime opportunity go, it might never come again, and we might miss out on something we desperately need. We know this type of missed opportunity can create regrets leaving us always to wonder what could have been. This feeling of loss and missing out added to the hope of getting what we really need is why most of us just go for it when that missing piece seems to appear.

The problem with our human need to fill the void means we may try to fill it with wrong or incomplete pieces that can leave us worse off than we were before. In the end, we all would like to find the correct missing pieces so that we can become our "True Self" and live a "True Life," but we just don't know-how.

How Do You Find Your True Path, Become Your True Self, Live a True Life & Go to Heaven?

"Clarify your purpose. What is the why behind everything you do? When we know this in life or design, it is very empowering, and the path is clear." - Jack Canfield

To fulfill the primary purpose of life and other major callings, you simply follow *The Way* as it puts you on your "True Path" which leads to your "True Self" and "True

Life." To say it another way, *The Way* is the guidebook on how to master life's ultimate mission. Once you understand the fullness of *The Way,* this path will become clear.

For now, let's go a little deeper into the levels of self. We are doing this because knowing the different levels of human development is key to understanding ourselves, humanity, and our goal as individuals and as a society. We often refer to people acting at a low level or in very negative ways as being a savage or a barbarian, while those who have positive qualities as being civilized, enlightened, or their "True Self." This is important, so let's go into each level a little more deeply.

- **Savage:** Being a savage means we live close to an animal state. In this state, we are ignorant, simple, wild, naïve, uneducated, unsophisticated, and underdeveloped people. It's a state of unrestrained brutality, violence, and cruelty. While savages are mainly concerned with themselves, they will also protect those they care about at the expense of everyone else. If we are not part of the inner circle of the savage, we are its prey. Desperate circumstances can drive almost anyone into a state of a savage for a time.

    For example, having to care for a starving or sick child during a collapse of civilization. In these situations, we can find ourselves doing the otherwise unthinkable and acting like a savage. Being human means that when we are truly desperate, we will most often steal, lie, cheat, and even kill to survive and save ourselves and/or our loved ones.

- **Barbarian:** While a step above a savage, a barbarian distains civilization and other refinements such as caring for more than oneself and one's immediate inner circle. In this state, we are a little less ignorant, simple, wild, naïve, uneducated, unsophisticated, and underdeveloped. Yet, we still possess other negative qualities.

A barbarian may pay allegiance to a clan or tribe but still distains society and culture. "Might Makes Right," cruelty and uncivilized behavior is the norm. Barbarians believe that if one can take power and make others do what they want, no matter what that entails, it's right. Other than the basics to survive, barbarians do not pass down knowledge well. They are not interested in education or any real refinements.

Note on Savages and Barbarians: Savages and barbarians have an underdeveloped sense of morality, empathy, and sympathy. They can also be mentally and emotionally twisted, feeling pleasure from doing terrible things. This twisted viewpoint leads those of us who are savages and barbarians to see feelings like love, the desire to help and understand others, the admission of mistakes, open-mindedness, cooperation, caring, and consideration as weaknesses. Savage and barbarian mindsets are often the bottleneck preventing real solutions from being implemented because they see everything as us vs. them, zero-sum, and win-lose.

- **Civilized:** Civilized people are humane, moral, educated, ethical, polite, and reasonable. They work to create a wide range of societal systems to benefit all. The civilized have an appreciation for art, exhibit a refined level of manners, and are generally polite. Rules of behavior are centered on equality and fair treatment. For the most part, the civilized obey the law because they feel it's right or because they are afraid of the punishment if caught.

- **Enlightened:** Here, we possess all the traits of being civilized. However, higher moral virtues and other wholistic refinements are reflected within this person's life. They do what is right because it's right and not out of fear. They truly work to better themselves and the world around them.
- **True Self:** Here, we carry the traits of the civilized and enlightened yet also fully realize who we are as an individual. Our true talents have become manifest, and we are developing and working on using these abilities to the fullest degree.

Note: These human levels are not associated with the society around us.

For example, someone living in the Amazon forest in a primitive state can still be civilized, enlightened, and even their "True Self." Conversely, someone in a highly developed society can behave like a savage or barbarian.

It's important to remember that no matter how high our level of development is, most of us are a disaster away from becoming a savage or their prey. It's also important to remember that we are all born ignorant. Therefore, any society, even one that has very highly enlightened members, can revert to savagery and barbarism within a few generations if the institutions, knowledge, and ways of being are not maintained and passed down correctly.

Therefore, to ward against savagery and barbarianism, we must care for our societal systems, ensuring that they are running well for everyone. No matter how advanced our physical society becomes, we as a species must continuously be educated, over and over, generation by generation.

We must strive to improve how we raise all human beings, for this is how we prevent raising groups of savages and barbarians who will steal instead of work, hate instead of love, and destroy instead of build.

We need to prepare for disasters, actively work to prevent them, and help people out of disasters if we are to stop people from becoming desperate and falling into a barbarian or savage level mindset. Preparedness means each of us needs our emergency plans, supplies, and go bags As a society; we need to conduct major disaster, fire, and other safety-oriented drills in our homes, schools, workplaces, cities, and regions to help prevent problems and be prepared for when they happen.

See "Life Manual: Self-Care: Health Fundamentals: Disaster Preparedness." and our site www.7Way.Me/wd for information on how to create your own plans and bags.

We also need to ensure that those caught by a personal disaster have a way back. Support means having humane systems in place that help people through desperate transitions of life that get them to a good place. These systems include things like food banks, shelters, etc. as well as plans to help people become self-supportive like education, relocation, temporary housing, and training programs. In this way, our society can help the desperate, positively channel the negative energy, so that they can develop themselves and attain a conducive lifestyle that adds positively to society.

THE FUTURE IS OURS

"If you can tune into your purpose and really align with it, setting goals so that your vision is an expression of that purpose, then life flows much more easily." - Jack Canfield

When working to become your best, remember that what has come before does not have to come again or continue. Today is the first day of the rest of your life. Those of us who do not reach our full potential are a significant loss. This is because, for our society to achieve its full potential, it must be filled with good people all working to be their best.

In the end, as we all go about our primary mission, we naturally spread positivity, happiness, and peace in the world. It's through the process of you making your own life better that you help improve everyone else's — other people doing the same helps you. Each of us is a critical link in the chain of what it takes to truly make a positive difference in our world. Our effort directed at becoming better individually added together with everyone else means we will be building a more conducive environment for us all to thrive. This is one way, generation by generation, that we create a better and better world.

Law 2
The Primary Purpose of Society is to Create Our True Society

"No society can surely be flourishing and happy, of which the far greater part of the members are poor and miserable." - Adam Smith

You are not alone. You share this world and universe with other life, including other people. We all experience life from within human society. We all need a conducive environment in which to grow and live if we are to truly be our best and thrive. Therefore, our society must be its best if we are to truly thrive.

Now that we have covered the absolute need to create the best society possible or our "True Society," we need to get on the same page as to what that really means. Our human society is a combination of all our knowledge, customs, traditions, cultures, creations, systems, and ways of doing things. It's comprised of all our institutions, individual contributions as well as our cooperation throughout the ages.

The primary societal systems include government, economics/business, communications, health, justice, religion, media, and entertainment as well as the basics such as education, water, food, housing, clothing, sanitation, transportation, emergency services (fire, paramedics, shelters, etc.) and energy. Our quality of life and level of society depends on how well the systems are developed, our ease of access to these critical systems, and the quality of the products and services offered.

Another key facet of our human society worthy of note here is found in the different cultures within society that reflect different groupings. Because of our human condition, those in an area, or of a group, cooperating over time develop shared traits. These unique ways of doing things and rituals are woven together into what we call "Culture." These groupings are most clearly seen as cultures that span areas of the world and are related to continents, countries as well as segments of their populations and other groups.

For Example: American, Chinese, Russian, Indian, culture is one level. Another is when we go to a more regional and local view, such as in comparing the cultures of New York City - New York, New Orleans - Louisiana, and Outlook - Montana. These regions and localities have very different cultures. Within each of these, there are even more subcultures based on wealth, age, ethnicity, faith, and other demographics.

THE LEVELS OF SOCIETY

Our societal systems and cultures make up our society. The primary factor in determining the level of society is found in the societal system development and balance. These levels sound similar to the human developmental levels covered in "Law 1" and include primitive, civilized, enlightened, and "True Society." Let's go into them all now to ensure we are all on the same page.

- **Primitive:** At this level, most societal systems do not exist, or the ones that do are at a very low level. Frequently at this level, what is done is not being done in the best or most efficient way, often causing other problems.

For example, a primitive civilization may have a kitchen that consists of a wood-burning pit that they cook over. The problem is that the smoke causes health problems for all those in the home. Also, the land is being deforested, which is killing life and causing other issues like mudslides. Since there is no long-term energy solution, it leads to strife and famine.

- **Civilized:** At this level, societies have most, if not all, of the societal systems in place. The problem is that the systems at this level are often corrupted and out of balance. Thus, creating other issues in our society.

    For example, while a company may be making a lot of money and employing a lot of people, they are still underpaying them, creating a bad working environment, and destroying the world.

- **Enlightened:** At this level, all systems are developed to the point that creates a general feeling of happiness and peace within the people of the society. It's a world that is working with care and consideration respecting life and all people. Here we are working to truly balance and optimize all systems to make them the best they can be for everyone.

- **True Society:** At this level, we have mastered our natural world and societal systems. We have a world where people generally live in harmony with each other and our universe. We have created a conducive environment for everyone to grow into their "True Self." A "True Society works to preserve all that is good as it strives to refine everything it can.

A LITTLE MORE ABOUT OUR TRUE SOCIETY

"Really, the only thing that makes sense is to strive for greater collective enlightenment." - Elon Musk

Just as our fear of self-destruction is balanced by the hope of being our "True Self," so too is the apocalyptic destruction of our world balanced by the hope of our "True Society." Imagine a world in balance, thriving, and at peace, where all people have a real clear path to become the best they can be. A world of wonder, fun, challenge, and plenty, where everything is done in an artful way that adds happiness to everyday life. A garden world and healthy society where we can meet good people and explore wonderous cultures and thriving environments all over the world.

A place that is clean where we have truly mastered the human conditional forces of the universe and use this knowledge to live in harmony with nature even as we turn these forces to our advantage. A society where our systems are not corrupted but instead are led by those of real merit, with checks and balances in place and solid institutions to back it all up. Here is a world where all children receive what they need to thrive and learn the best habits as their primary way of doing everything.

Here you grow being challenged and provided with all you need to become your best. You would naturally develop long-lasting positive relationships and find your other life callings. You grow, live, and work in an artful garden world with different wonderous cultures to visit and explore. You grow up naturally living a meaningful life and making a difference in the world.

Now imagine our current human society taking up this challenge and working on perfecting and refining the societal systems and best practices generation after generation. Imagine that we are successful and what it would be like to be born into this "True Society." How would you like to be born into that world? Would you like this for your children or their children? Of course, you do, as do we all. This is the whole point.

How Do We Get There From Here?

It's this simple universal truth of what we all really want ("True Success" & our "True Society") understood by the many that allows positive change to happen. This is because there is tremendous energy in mass realization and focus. It's this power that creates a global paradigm shift. It's this shift that opens a path for meaningful positive change to happen within people's lives and our society. Over time, it's our positive actions that create a world of lasting peace and happiness that everyone can enjoy.

For those of us in the current age, it may seem a bit daunting or even impossible to get to this ideal world and society from here. That is because there is little unity, and we have not started the real work. All societies are products of the past. Our future society is a product of what we do in the present, which means that we can act in the present to create the society of our choosing for our future.

To get there, we must start now, for time is short and if we don't unite very soon, all will be lost. *The Way* provides vital information and the exact steps on how we can unite and create peaceful, lasting positive change. So, by knowing the fullness of *The Way,* you will be able to take positive actions that will lead to our "True Society."

To save our world, we need to stay focused on the true goal and find all the "wrongness" in society. We look for the wrongness, for it shows us what needs fixing. To say it another way, it's when we look at what "should be" and compare it to "what is" that we can see the "difference." This "difference," or this "wrongness," is what needs to be fixed and healed.

Collectively we are the "Superhero" we all need. Together we can discover what is wrong, then find and implement solutions. There is NO other way; we must unite to accomplish this goal. Throughout history, we have united in common cause during times of great need. Right now, humanity is connected like no time in all of human history. There are enough people, resources, and will power to create meaningful, positive change globally very quickly - we only need to focus and unite to succeed.

We, the human race, must share a foundation of knowledge and unity of purpose in key areas if we are to create our "True Society." While it may take several generations to realize our "True Society," working to achieve this goal as a species is the more significant point. Our collective work will have many benefits. This includes things like creating more: hope, peace, happiness, health, safety, security, productivity, long-lasting positive relationships, and so much more.

The whole process will also create less stress, desperation, and worry, thereby improving everyone's lives. In the end, we must realize that no matter how troubled our society is, it's ours, and the only one we have. There is no other choice. We must work together to <u>make</u> things better if they are to get better.

We can only truly change our society as "the masses" for our society reflects who we are, and it will take the vast majority of us joined together to fix and maintain everything. This is because our institutions, cultures, governments, organizations, environments, and everything else to be their best, they must be filled with good people, all looking to make everything the best it can be.

The fact is that through your daily interactions and choices, you can affect positive change within your life and our society naturally. Your actions matter because, as we have said, humanity can only build our "True Society" if the vast majority of people are working to be their best. This is the reason the first commandment within this value system is about becoming your best, and the second is about building a better world because it takes "all of us" added together that make up the big "we" that is needed to create and maintain the positive.

If we are all working together to achieve this goal, everything will get easier for everyone; things will get better and better, year by year, decade by decade, so that those down the road will always start even farther ahead. All of us working toward this end can take pride, knowing we have created hope and a better world for ourselves and future generations. Note that within "Step 6: Unite," we will outline how to peacefully force positive change within society in detail.

THE 2 LAWS OF PURPOSE SUMMARY

Bees aren't trying to pollinate flowers to help us all.
Their mission is self-serving, to make honey.
But pollen sticks to their legs and then gets spread to other
flowers, thus giving the world much beauty and food.
But to the bees, they are just on a personal mission.
– The Processional Effect - Buckminster Fuller

Law 1: The Primary Purpose of Life is to Be Your True Self, Live a True Life, and Go to Heaven.

Law 2: The Primary Purpose of Society is to Create Our True Society.

It should seem obvious that being the ultimate you, living the ultimate life, creating the ultimate society, and ending up in the ultimate place would be the primary foundational purpose or mission or goal of life and our society. After all, it's natural to want to live a fulfilling, meaningful, productive, and joyful life.

Our ability to find consensus and real solutions is why competition within cooperation works so well. The proper use of this skill is how we end up with something much greater than we intended. Cooperating and working hard to build a world that is consciously and rationally designed to facilitate all of us becoming our best is the eternal goal we have been striving for as a species since our creation.

As we have learned and must never forget, the way to our "True Society" starts with each of us doing our part. The better we are as individuals, and the more of us who join together, the better our chances of success. Using the two "Laws of Purpose" and working together, we can't lose.

The Meaning of Life

The two laws of purpose give us our direction, and it's this direction added to the human conditions that we find the meaning of life. The meaning of life is to "find meaning in your life" or to put it another way, the meaning of your life is to "make your life meaningful." *The Way* is living rational, positive action and is designed to help you develop, find, and create a meaningful life.

Chapter 4
Understanding Life

"A good person is the friend of all living things."
- Mahatma Gandhi

Within this chapter, we continue with "Step 4: Center" by starting to explore the laws that cover our relationship with our universe. These "Universal Laws" are a basic framework on how to deal with all that is not God or us.

The fact is, life holds great challenges, tests, dangers, rewards, and mysteries. "The Universal Laws" guide us on how to find meaning, greater happiness, and become better people while we help create a more harmonious society for all. As with "The 2 Laws of Purpose," these "3 Universal Laws" are needed because no one is an island, but instead, we are all part of a vast web filled with other people and life all wrapped within a complex society.

Law 3
Respect Life

Within our universe, energy is bound into many temporary forms, with life being the most unique, special, and precious. In fact, most of our universe is antithetical to our type of life. For life to exist on our world, a multitude of variables and coincidences had to line up just right.

Respecting life means that we give it careful consideration, thoughtfulness, and deference regarding how we act and react. The desire and need to use our natural world mindfully, to protect it, to refrain from violating it springs naturally through a sense of love, appreciation, admiration, wonder, and through the need for self-preservation and survival. For this is our home, our nest, our womb, and we are dependent on all other life and our planet. The life surrounding us allows us to live and greatly determines our quality of life. Caring for all life and our world is an ever-present societal level human condition task which we must master as a species if we are to survive and thrive.

To truly understand what was just written, let's go a little deeper into what life is and how you can help it thrive. However, before we get started, it's important to note, especially for first-time readers, that this chapter, while not long, does go into detail on exactly how to care for aspects of our world. Therefore, for some, it might feel a little out of place at times. Rest assured that this information is absolutely crucial if we are to survive and thrive. This knowledge will help you to improve the life around you and will help you see what we should be doing on a larger scale. It is also here to be used as a reference later.

What is Life?

The primary forms of life are sentient, animal, insect, plant, and microbial. Life on our world can take in food, adapt to the environment, grow, and reproduce. All life lives within ecosystems. *Note:* the exception to these rules are some extremophiles that live outside the need for supporting life or even hospitable environments and can survive in the most hostile environments all alone.

Sentient Life

Sentient life is the highest form of life. Sentient life is self-aware and has a choice-making consciousness with the ability to feel and perceive. Sentient life can think and act beyond mere reaction to immediate circumstances. Sentient life can plan and modify plans.

High-level sentient life can understand complexity in different ways and can learn, understand, gain knowledge, and show wisdom. As a group, they can manipulate the forces of nature, comprehend high-level math, use logic, reason, and understand other complex information. A "True Sentient" being is a combination of all the above plus a conscience (knowing right from wrong). The human race is a "True Sentient" life form.

Animal Life

Animal life includes amphibians, fish, mammals, reptiles, and birds. Animals are mainly limited to a reactionary and instinct-driven existence. However, all animals can suffer and do share some of the same higher cognitive abilities as humans. Mammals can display eight emotions. These emotions are seeking, rage, fear, lust, caring, pain, grief, and play. In fact, we have seen other emotions like play exhibited by other life forms such as birds, sea life, reptiles, and even spiders.

There are some creatures on our world that are called animals but are either sentient or very close. Some of these include elephants, dolphins, whales, apes, and possibly some birds. They all show higher cognitive abilities, and have passed basic sentient tests such as they grieve for their dead, have a sense of self, can see and admire themselves and others in a mirror. Also, they have language, use tools, and more.

Insect Life

Insect life includes flies, mosquitos, ants, roaches, etc. and are at the bottom of the food chain. Insects greatly outnumber all animal life and come in a wide variety. They are needed for our eco-systems to thrive as they are usually the primary food source for higher forms of life. They also work hard and improve our air, soil, and water.

Insects are also quite fascinating creatures in their variation and diversity.

PLANTLIFE

Plantlife includes photosynthetic organisms that use the energy of the sun, along with internal chemical reactions to grow and reproduce. Photosynthesis is where plants use the energy in sunlight to convert CO_2 and water to sugar and oxygen. We see them as trees and plants. They provide food, building materials, clean water, and air as well as help us spiritually and mentally.

While we consider plants primitive, they are still quite impressive as they do communicate with each other and other life through the air and underground using biochemicals. Plants will help other plants that they see as family or those they like by growing in ways that allow the other to also thrive. They can be trained like a dog to respond to stimulus as in the ringing of a bell to indicate food for a dog. For a plant, instead of a bell, a fan blowing air is used to signal sunlight. Some plants can learn to change their behavior in a very short time too. *For example, some can learn to protect themselves when dropped.*

MICROBIAL LIFE/MICROORGANISMS

Micro-life are forms of life that can divide themselves to reproduce or mutate into other forms of life. They are so tiny that we can't see them without a microscope. Microbial life is the lowest form of life on this planet and is the most abundant. They do not think or feel or have complex systems like brains or spinal cords. They are a simple form of life when compared to a human or animal, yet they are mighty in that they can help us live as well as hurt or kill us.

Microorganisms perform a vital part in the process of life. There are beneficial microbes and harmful ones.

We can see the micro life in and on our bodies as part of an ecosystem called a human microbiome. In fact, humans are a symbiotic life form comprised of trillions of microorganisms working together to maintain the vehicle we are using in this universe that we call a body. They are critical to our survival, protecting us from the harmful microbes, helping us digest food, and more. We could not live without them. See the "Life Manual: Fuel: Food Groups in More Detail: Supplements: Probiotics & Prebiotics" for more on protecting and strengthening your microbiome.

A balanced and symbiotic relationship with the micro life is needed. When we try killing them, we either make those who survive stronger and/or we kill off all of them, including the good. This killing of the good microorganisms within us, on us, and in our environment has adverse effects such as collapsing ecosystems and the breaking down of our bodies. This bad practice leaves us vulnerable to sickness and diseases from harmful microbes.

For Example: Taking antibiotics kills <u>all</u> micro life within our digestive tract and other areas within your body. This can make our digestive and other processes not to work correctly. The best approach is to keep our micro life in balance by crowding out the bad with the good.

"Phage Therapy" is a rising form of treatment against harmful microorganisms. A phage is the natural predator of microorganisms. The great thing about this type of therapy is that we can identify a phage to fight a specific harmful microorganism, often ending with a complete cure and no side effects. This therapy is used in many countries around the world for certain types of infections. This field of study is still developing and is more relevant than ever as the usefulness of antibiotics may be coming to an end.

How Does Life Survive?

In the end, all life (except some extremophiles) is dependent on other life to exist, and because of this dependency, life exists within ecosystems, and all ecosystems are dependent on each other.

A habitat or ecosystem is a symbiotic relationship between all life that includes microorganisms, plants, insects, animals, humans, and non-life such as minerals, water, air, gravity, and solar rays. All life and non-life are needed for an ecosystem to work.

Life needs many things to exist within a specific range (hot/cold, dry/wet, acid/alkaline, etc.). Tamper with one and the whole system can collapse. We can see ecosystems at the macro level such as a universe, galaxy, solar system, and planets and on the micro-level as continents, regions, deserts, forests, swamps, or even a small area like a yard or even a human body.

A basic *example* of mutual support within our global ecosystem is found between plants and mammals. Plants create oxygen, which mammals need to breathe-in. Mammals then breathe-out carbon dioxide, which the plants use. This circular support cycle allows both to live and must be maintained to the right level for continued survival.

We can see the whole universe as part of our ecosystem as it took the effect of gravity to form stars, and stars to create all the naturally occurring elements heavier than hydrogen and helium. The stars then had to explode, spreading all the elements far and wide to be used in new stars, planets and even life.

Other Ecosystem *Examples* Include:

Understanding Life

OUR LIVING GLOBAL ECOSYSTEM

Our world, life, and our society are a product of a universal ecosystem. Our planet maintains the right distance from the sun, protecting us and other life from deadly rays with its magnetic field. Our world has just the right mix of chemicals and minerals to support life in great diversity. The environmental systems of wind, rain, tectonics, rotation, tides, and magnetic fields all work together to make life possible here on our world.

Here is one example of our global ecosystem in action. The south Atlantic ocean plankton, which creates so much of our world's oxygen, is dependent on the rivers from the Amazon Rain Forest for all the food they need to survive. The rainforest is dependent upon winds carrying sand from the Sahara Desert in Northern Africa to provide the minerals and other elements they need to grow.

The example is of a desert, rainforest, and ocean working in harmony to support planetary-wide life. This process provides us with food to eat, oxygen to breathe, and is only one of many major ecosystems that we need to maintain if we are to not only survive but truly thrive over time. *Note:* At the time of this writing, our precious Amazonian Rainforest Ecosystem is being carelessly destroyed, which is jeopardizing our future.

We can even see the earth as an enormous spaceship flying through space at over 1 million miles per hour or 1.5 million kilometers per hour. If this is our spaceship traveling so fast, so far, for so long, isn't it prudent and wise to understand, maintain, and optimize all systems?

The Numbers: Earth Rotates on Axis: 1040 mph /1673.7 kph, Earth Orbits Sun: 67,062 mph / 107,925 kph, Solar System Orbits the Milky Way: 514,495 mph / 827,999 kph, Milky Way is moving through space and rotating: 600,000 mph / 965,606 kph. Totaling 1,182,597 mph or 1,609,344 kph.

Other Interesting Numbers: I don't have the space to cover all the interesting facts about our universe in this book. However, if knowing more about how our universe was put together interests you, check out these number sets: The Fibonacci Sequence, The Golden Mean/Ratio, and PI. Also, you might investigate "quantum entanglement" and "zero-point energy" for even more intriguing features.

REGIONAL ECOSYSTEMS

There are and were large areas of our planet made up of jungle, forest, desert, ocean, prairie, and swamp. Each of these regions is an ecosystem or habitat. These regions are dependent on one another. If we destroy these regions, the world's entire ecosystem can collapse. Many species, like birds, sea life, insects, and herd animals, travel through several different regions as part of their habitats.

LOCAL ECOSYSTEM

There are places within larger regions where conditions differ. These differences can work together to support life unique to that area.

For example, An oasis in a desert might contain plants and animals not found anywhere else in the desert or a stream in a forest may include fish, animals, and insects not found in the greater forest or anywhere else in the world. A yard in suburbia might be developed to support all kinds of plants and insects that the natural land around could not. Even your body or that of an animal is a local ecosystem supporting trillions of micro life forms that help the larger life form survive.

WE ONLY THRIVE IF NATURE THRIVES

In all cases, life is dependent on an ecosystem (except some extremophiles). Smaller ecosystems are dependent on the local ecosystems as well as the larger, regional, and planet-wide ecosystems. If the ecosystem is altered too much, life within must adapt, flee to a hospitable place or die. Most often, an ecosystem fails if conditions within are altered, or the range of conditions changes too much like being too hot or cold, too dry or wet, or too acidic or alkaline.

We destroy ecosystems through pollution, our thoughtless, uncaring "development," and by killing off or unbalancing the life within it. As in, if we kill off all the bugs, then all the life forms that eat them to survive will have to adapt, flee, or die. If we add in an invasive species that have no competitors, it can take over and destroy local life.

If we kill off an irreplaceable member of the food chain, like plankton in our ocean, then the whole food chain can collapse as all higher life forms are dependent on the lower forms of life (this includes us). Basically, if an ecosystem gets too much of one thing or not enough of another, the ecosystem will fail.

The fact that we can understand and affect our environment means that we can create and perfect our world's ecosystems large and small. Our economic development can work with nature to enhance our lifestyle and improve our health. This mastery will, in turn, allow life and us to thrive. For this to happen, we need a long term sustainable global environmental strategy and plan that we as a world can follow.

In the end, we must master our natural world, for we can only thrive within a thriving global ecosystem.

To ensure we achieve the goal of world mastery, we must respect life. This commitment requires all of us to take positive actions within our everyday life and correctly setup our societal systems. To know what actions to take and how to set up our societal systems to work with nature, we all need to understand some world care basics.

How Do We Care for Our World?

The natural capital that sustains us consists of all the metals/minerals, wood, food, and other resources our world produces. As noted, we need a healthy world if we are to survive and thrive. If we all do our part, the life around us will do most of the hard work for us by growing our materials and food, creating oxygen and energy, cleaning our air and water, and so much more.

The key here is to understand that caring for our world is often about leaving it alone rather than doing something to it. Life can be left to itself because it's active and can take care of everything on its own if the circumstances are right. So, if we set the stage correctly, leave it alone and don't hurt it, life will thrive and take care of us. In the end, the goal is to create global permaculture, which means that our global ecosystem is stable, growing, and sustainable long term.

Time is short, and if we are to survive, we must now work hard to restore and maintain our ecological balance, for if it gets much farther out of balance, we will create an environment that can no longer support us. The problem of our age is that we have harmed life and our ecosystems to such a devastating degree that to restore the balance, and set the proper stage for life to thrive, now requires all of us to work hard globally to fix the ecological problems that our ancestors and we have created.

Therefore, each of us needs to do our part, and this starts with the understanding of a few specifics.

WORLD CARE

In this section, we cover a few ways that we can all care for our planet, starting with the dirt under our feet.

SAVING EARTH: TURN DEAD DIRT INTO TOPSOIL

"Dead Dirt" is basically nonliving earth. Dead soil is most often uncovered, crusted over, and turns to dust and blows away. *For example,* see the American Dust Bowl America of the 1930s.

"Topsoil" is not lifeless dirt. Creating "Topsoil" from dead earth is key to our long-term survival. "Topsoil" is a thriving ecosystem that stores carbon, is home to trillions of life forms, and is the foundation of all land-based ecosystems. The "best" topsoil is called loam and clay loam, which is dark brown/black and rich with nutrients, micro life, insects, and all of what life needs to thrive. Living soil is also a communication network that plants and creatures use to communicate with each other about things like drought or insect attack.

Other soil types like clay and sandy can be amended (add organic matter, clay or sand, etc.) to create loam. Erosion (the removal of soil), desertification (growth of deserts), and the killing of our living earth are preventing life from reestablishing itself, which is adding to our environmental problems. We can help our world by creating good topsoil and planting correctly.

We kill our soil in many ways: by leaving it uncovered without trees, plants, or organic matter such as compost and mulch; by scouring it through the use of blowers such as those used by gardeners to remove every speck of organic matter, leaves, dust, and topsoil; by tilling the soil without adding organic materials; by not covering the ground after tilling; by the saturation of fertilizers, herbicides, pesticides, and insecticides.

Below we have outlined the fundamental steps on how to create living topsoil, help life thrive, and prevent erosion.

1. **Dig & Add Life:** Dig down where possible at least 2 to 3 feet. Mix in natural organic compost and other good organic matter. This can come from things like food waste, yard clippings, leaves, healthy micro life, and worms. Do not include thorns, toxic plants like oleander, unwanted seeds, and invasive plants). If needed, add some clay or sand to create the right consistency of loam.
2. **Seed & Plant:** We then native wildflower or plant seeds, ground cover, flowers, plants, bushes, trees, etc. When replanting forests and other areas, it's critical to use a mix of native trees, bushes, plants, and flowers. Including a diversity of edibles such as nuts, fruits, leaves, nectar, pollen, etc. it's critical to use a mixture of native trees, bushes, plants, and flowers including a diversity of edibles that are vulnerable to disease and which don't support a wide variety of life. The diversity creates a network of thriving ecosystems throughout the world and helps prevent other environmental problems from happening in the future. The planting of long-lived native perennials produces better results and is a more sustainable solution
3. **Compost:** After planting, add in a layer of compost. Compost is decomposed organic matter that went through a process called composting.
4. **Mulch:** Then add a layer of mulch. Mulch consists of organic materials like bark and rocks.

Covering the soil protects against erosion, helps water retention, provides nutrients, and more.

Mulch Note: Mulch is about covering the earth so that life can thrive. The best mulch has three layers.

- The first layer of mulch is a finer woody mulch that will act as a thin mat.
- The next layer of mulch is made of much thicker bark chunks, which will create a thicker longer lasting layer of protection.
- The next layer consists of rocks of different sizes. The stones help weigh things down and are a permanent part of the mulch. Rocks also help life thrive in many ways. If on a hill, it's good to dig in some larger and smaller rocks in strategic patterns to help prevent erosion as well as to provide perches for life.

The woody mulch will degrade over time, becoming part of the living soil. Only add more compost and mulch as this happens if required. When planting in the future, scrape back all the mulch layers in that area and plant. Then push back the mulch layer into place.

5. **Water as Needed:** Plants need more water in the beginning and for about a year as their roots grow. It's critical when planting most trees and bushes to water the root ball directly every other day or so for about two weeks. Using efficient sprinkler systems that provide water to the locations only when they need it can go a long way in preserving and using our water supply efficiently.

6. **Leave it Alone:** If not using the ground to plant food, then it should be left undisturbed. Here we do not dig it up and turn over the soil every year, for this will only

destroy the ecosystem below ground and will kill off many creatures who can't live at the new depth.

7. **Maintain:** Going forward, it just becomes a matter of removing the dead, trimming, and adding plants, bulbs, seeds, bushes, and trees as needed. It's key to ensure that our good soil stays covered with native plants or with organic matter such as leaves, compost, mulch, and rocks (do not use plastics or rubber as they leach toxins).

8. **No Poison:** We also need to stop the use and overuse of fertilizers, herbicides, and insecticides. Use natural controls like: microorganisms, spiders, other insects, worms (low, medium, and top diggers), natural compost and mulch, barrier plants that naturally repel unwanted pests/insects such as mint to repel mosquitos. Also, do not use rubber or plastics of any kind as mulch or soil additives. These are toxic and will leach harmful chemicals into the ground, killing life and tainting food plants.

Note: If the soil is saturated with toxins, there are certain trees and other plants that are good at soaking up these harmful chemicals. Once the job is finished, they can be removed and deposed of properly. Thus, allowing for a healthy ecosystem to be planted. This process is a way to restore the land to balance in stages.

GOOD FARMING & FOOD ANIMAL CARE

Using the land to grow food is key to our survival. To care for our farmland, we generally follow the good basic practices outlined above without adding rocks. However, with many crops, we need to disturb the soil every year to harvest and replant.

Also, because we are growing food, we are depleting nutrients in the soil as they transfer into the food. In this age, many farms have compensated for these needs by using a lot of toxic chemicals to kill off life as well as to fertilize crops. This practice has created a lot more problems as we can see with the rise of superbugs, weeds, algae blooms as well as the poisoning of the land and water to levels where no life can survive.

The correct long-term solution involves: adding organic matter to replenish the nutrients, growing alternative crops that can feed the land and support each other, planting barrier plants, adding in helpful microorganisms, insects, worms, and using other organic pest control methods. Always keep the soil covered with organic matter during off-seasons and at other times when possible. This helps let the soil recover and stay healthy. If using fertilizers, only use organic and just enough to do the job to ensure that they do not run off or seep into our water supplies.

One of the best alternatives to land farming is hydroponics and indoor farming. Indoor farming has many advantages over traditional farming. Some of these include the need for less water and other materials, as everything is precisely controlled. These alternatives provide longer growing cycles and growing times as we can grow food all year round and have access to 24-hour lighting. Also, indoor growing means our food is fresh and local as we can have buildings in every city and town that provide food for its citizens. This growing vertical approach also takes up less land and causes less pollution.

We must also take care when animal farming, when in close contact with animals, and when handling animal products. We need to follow these best practices globally because it's the humane thing to do, we want to be healthy, it will produce healthier food, and we can help stop the creation of more and more potent superbugs (viruses and diseases).

Some of the best practices regarding animal husbandry include: not overusing antibiotics, medicines, and chemicals on animals. Ensure that they and their environments are clean and healthy and that we don't put many different types of animals close to one another. *For example,* don't put bats, dogs, pigs, and birds together. Also, we must isolate the sick and the dead from the healthy and living. Our animals should not be continuously terrified for fear makes all animals unhealthy. They need space, good fuels, sunshine, and more, just as we do to be healthy and happy. We want our food animals to be healthy and happy because then the food is healthier for us and it's the right thing to do.

All people who are in close contact with animals also need to take extra care, so they do not pass germs back and forth. The best practices mean no kissing animals, especially on the mouth. After touching them, wash your hands and do not touch your face until you do so. See the "Life Manual: Fuel: Food: Preparation & Storage" for how to care for food made from animals in your home and business.

STOPPING DESERTIFICATION

Desertification is the process where a desert grows, destroying good land. This process can occur on occasion naturally, but in our age, many deserts are increasing because of human destruction and our lack of care. We allow deserts to grow when we destroy the environment (trees, plants, soil, animals, insects, etc.) and use or divert the water away from the land, especially in dry areas.

To stop the growth of deserts, we need to create buffer zones with substantial barriers close to and on the edge of the desert. These barriers are often stone, cement, and other large organic heavy objects without toxins like plastics and rubbers. Some of these anchors need to be high enough and strong enough to help break the wind and hold back some of the sand.

In some areas, barriers are needed, buried deep enough in the ground to help stop water from being pulled out into the desert. Next, we follow the process above to reclaim the land creating living earth behind the barriers. Excess sand can be used to create the barriers used in other locations, or even dumped into the ocean. Once an area is secure, the process can be repeated, pushing the desert back to its correct size. Note that extra water is needed in these areas during the process, and continued irrigation and care will need to be maintained to prevent the desert from growing again.

SUSTAINABLE WATER, FISH & OCEAN CARE

Part of our mastery of earth means caring for our water. The keys to caring for our oceans and waterways are relatively simple because life can care for itself if we correctly set the stage and don't upset the balance.

The Keys to Water & Ocean Care Include:

1. Do not pollute.
2. Clean up the pollution.
3. Do not over fish and restock as needed (more on this below).
4. Do not block fish/water life spawning grounds. This means that we may need to create fish runs up and down rivers that have dams and other blockages.
5. Restore health to systems by adding organic matter, missing life forms, and removing invasive species.
6. Become "Masters of Water" storage, movement, and purification.
7. Build to collect and utilize water and use porous materials in key areas so the ground can absorb water.

Overfishing and pollution is an issue that has been going on for many hundreds of years. As our rivers, lakes, and oceans are being polluted and depleted of life, all life suffers. If life in our oceans dies, we all die. We die because our oceans' photosynthesizers (plankton, seaweed, etc.) produce over half of the world's oxygen. The key to preventing overfishing is to create fish hatcheries and release more fish than we catch. We also need better fishing practices to ensure population sizes and balance within our bodies of water.

For example, we can add good organic matter to our oceans to help feed the fish and create more of an alkaline environment. In this way, we can turn our organic waste (plant and animal) into something good. We can remove the plastic and other pollution using robots. Our goal is to clean our water, so our fish populations grow every year, so eventually, water life can rebound and thrive. It's important to note that while our clean water sources are growing smaller, all the water we need is still here. It's just not in the right places or clean enough to use. A foundational human quest we share as a society is to become masters of our world's water and learn how to clean it and move it to where it's needed.

Being Masters of Water means creating systems where we refill our aquifers with clean water, move water from where we have too much to where it's needed, being efficient, caring for our oceans and other waterways so we and all life can thrive. To learn more about how you can make the best drinking water see the "Life Manual: Fuel: Water."

PROPER AIR CARE

Caring for our air means we need to stop polluting it, clean and balance it. According to WHO (World Health

Organization), in 2018, 90% of the world's population lives in areas with unsafe air pollution levels. Also, they found that our air is so polluted that it's a danger to the health and development of more than 90% of the world's children under the age of 15.

We can see our atmosphere and the air we breathe as a chemistry experiment. If we keep adding highly powerful chemicals like carbon dioxide and pollutants as we remove other key ingredients like oxygen, we change the chemical balance life has created to maintain itself. We live in an age where we have the technology to balance our air and stop pollution. The good news is that once we have a thriving eco global system, nature will do most of the work for us and clean our air and provide the oxygen we need. It's up to all of us to help fix things and maintain the balance. We can join with others and make our societal systems follow our demands for better treatment of our environmental commons.

The keys to fixing our air include:

- Stop cutting down rainforests and other old-growth forests, especially in places like the Amazon.
- Planting trillions of trees in all the areas that have been decimated over the last 7000 years. Look to where it rains enough, yet there are few trees or diverse ecosystems. These areas need replanting. Remember when replanting forests, it's critical to use a mix of trees, bushes, plants, and flowers that produce edibles (nuts, fruits, leaves, etc.), nectar, and pollen. This will ensure that we create a thriving ecosystem and not monoculture dead zones that are vulnerable to disease and which don't support a wide variety of life.

- Greenify our cities by planting rooftop and wall gardens, by lining our streets with trees, by building parks, greenways, and gardens here and there for everyone to enjoy.
- Buy products that do not pollute and are made responsibly.
- Expose companies that are negligent and force them to stop polluting and clean up their mess. We all need to ask why do big polluters (vehicle makers, energy companies, transport firms, plastic makers, chemical companies, meat growers, etc.) get to shorten people's lives, kill people, harm 90% of the world's children, destroy our world as well as jeopardize our future; yet they don't have to clean up their supply chain, be responsible for their product after use, pay anything or suffer any repercussions for their pollution nor even clean up or mitigate their mess?
- Proper use of our green and animal waste (clippings from trees, plants, food scraps, dead things, feces, meat, bones, etc.) can go a long way to improving our land and oceans in ways that all life can thrive. Ocean life would particularly benefit from our food waste.
- Do not personally pollute wherever possible.
- Switch to clean decentralized energy, high-efficiency standards, and electric transportation. Not only will clean energy provide us what we need to run our lives without polluting the environment, but it will also make us more resilient during disasters. We are more resilient because clean, decentralized power generation and energy sharing mean few, if any, will lose electricity during such emergencies. All the electric vehicles will allow us to get around and have a lot of backup battery sources available to draw on.

We just need to ensure that the creation of this energy does not create other pollution issues.

- Remove carbon, particulates, ground-level ozone, and other harmful chemicals through cleaner energy, industry, transportation and collection stations that store these chemicals in ways they can't cause harm.
- Purify the air within our homes and all our buildings. To learn more about how you can make the best air see the "Life Manual: Fuel: Air."
- Care for our oceans so they can recover, too, as they are a large producer of oxygen and cleaner of our air.
- See "Chapter 15" and learn how to join with others to create peaceful, positive change.

Living in clean, healthy air adds to our physical and mental health. Cleaning our air is imperative and must involve all nations as our air, like our water, is global and is something we all need to care for if we are to truly thrive as a species.

REAL RECYCLING

We find another key to planet care in the proper formation of our supply chains, product production, and waste systems. Here we need to ensure just about everything is reused or recycled. One person's trash is another's treasure, after all. The remaining trash should be carefully sorted and placed into safe locations that can be accessed so that when we learn how to recycle or reuse that material, it's available.

We find the key to cheap and effective recycling in how well we presort everything before it gets collected. Therefore, it's imperative to teach all people (especially children) how to recycle correctly. To help, we need standardized labeling that ensures the use of the same colors and logos on all signs and bins globally, as this practice will help everyone know what goes where.

Correct recycling also means teaching, not to "wishcycle" or to taint the batch. Wishcycling is when you mix things in a collection bin that you hope will work or that are very dirty like diapers/nappies, batteries, and other soiled items. Everyone needs to learn their local rules, push for advancement, and update practices as local systems improve. At this point, if it's questionable or you don't know for sure, it's better to put it in the trash than the recycling. In the end, everything should be made to be repurposed, and everyone should be educated to understand what goes where.

STOPPING BIO-POLLUTION

Bio-pollution is when life forms, such as plants (weeds, bushes, trees, etc.) animals (rabbits, cats, snakes, etc.), insects (beetles, worms, etc.) microorganisms (fungus, mold, etc.) from one part of the world are introduced into another where they don't belong. These invasive species did not grow up in the ecosystem, which means the local life forms often can't feed on the new life, can't defend themselves against it, or compete with it. This bio-pollution can destroy life and existing ecosystems that have taken millions of years to develop, very quickly, because the life form has no competition, and the ecosystem can't adapt that fast.

The species that become invasive are moved into an area normally because people move life around either intentionally through trade or because life hitches a ride with us like when marine life is sucked into the ballast tanks within ships in one location only to be released in another. Below is a basic list of how we can end bio-pollution.

1. End the transfer of life into areas where it can cause problems through fixing our import/export laws, inspections, and vehicles (see #2).
2. Fix all procedures, ships, and other vehicles that allow life to hitch a ride. This might mean stopping ships from different areas of the world from entering our rivers, lakes, etc. that are joined to the ocean. Instead, we could offload the ships and use trains, trucks, and local ships to move the cargo. It may mean creating filters so life can't enter the ballast tanks and more.
3. Aggressively find and remove invasive species as quickly as possible. Sometimes we can turn an invasive species like a fish into food as this can create demand and generate money, which will help spur the cleanup efforts.
4. Reintroduce native life to those areas and help reestablish the natural balance.

CONSERVATION OF OUR RESOURCES

Being conservative in our use of resources goes a long way to solving many of society's problems.

For example, saving energy also conserves water. Recycling everything means there is no waste and less need for new materials. Not letting our food go to waste saves both water and energy, as agriculture is the top user of water and energy in our world. Not eating as much beef allows us to be healthier, use our land in better ways, and cause less pollution.

Not buying excessive clothing and using sustainable fabrics saves water, human resources, and energy as making just one weeks' worth of clothes uses as much water as you drink over an entire life. Ensuring proper tire pressure allows you to go farther for less. Turning off the faucet when brushing your teeth, washing your hands and face, and while showering also saves a lot of water and money over time. There are endless ways to conserve and have a wonderful life. The key is to find real, sustainable solutions and then make them easy for everyone to do.

WARNING: A CRITICAL THREAT TO LIFE

We must remember that even though life is so plentiful and powerful, it can be killed and go extinct relatively easily. In fact, the human race is responsible for an ongoing mass extinction on a level not seen since the last massive asteroid hit our planet and wiped out most life. If we have an unhealthy environment, we all pay the price by being unhealthy, sick, and dying early and possibly horribly. In a real sense, we are living in an ongoing chemistry experiment, one which we have now been given great control over and must care for correctly, or we will die.

This warning is critical for our scientific, societal systems as it's often the scientists who work within them, who are sometimes like children marveling in their discovery, wanting to share what they found with the world, often without restraint or thought to consequences. One of our most revered scientists, Albert Einstein, expresses his regrets this way, "The release of atom power has changed everything except our way of thinking…the solution to this problem lies in the heart of mankind. If only I had known, I should have become a watchmaker."

We can see this problem today in the way companies disperse toxic and harmful chemicals or medicines into our lives while claiming their benefits, only to recall them later for causing so much harm. We can see this with the unfettered and easy propagation of the CRISPR/Cas9 device. CRISPR/Cas9 is a tool that makes editing all life easy, quick, and simple. A quick life editing tool means that anyone virtually anywhere can edit and create life.

For example, using CRISPR, we can work to cure cancer and other diseases, add vitamins to crops, and do other good things. However, it can also be used to create or modify diseases, so they can kill more quickly and be harder to stop. It can be used to eventually mutate and modify humans, combine us with animals, create intelligent animals, and any other type of life we can imagine.

If we are to avoid extreme problems, we must consider carefully if certain inventions should be created. If we decide yes, we then need to decide <u>where</u> they are to be created and <u>how</u> released.

This includes things like: genetic editing, the automation of work, mass animal farming, robotic & cyberwar, cloning, self-replicating nano-machines, AI, the creation of sentient and other life, the creation of human/animal hybrids (chimeras), deep fakes, fake news, surveillance overreach, cybernetic enhancement, the weaponization of space, etc.

The farther we go in science, the more imperative this becomes as any mistake with certain technologies on this planet can mean the end of humanity and life. In these cases, if the technology is needed, we can develop them in safe, closed systems somewhere in space or on other planets. To be clear, we are not science bashing or saying science is bad. Science is a key part of our society and helps us solve problems. However, as we go about our work to solve problems such as alleviating suffering, we need to ensure that what we are doing is right and truly safe before release.

This verification means certification by third parties and not the creators or those who stand to profit. Then after it's released, we need to monitor it to ensure that it's truly safe. Verification and monitoring are essential because some technologies, if mishandled, can create a catastrophe. While we have divided ourselves into countries, ideology, ethnicity, and so many other ways, we share and are all dependent upon the same world. Just because a few people can kill and destroy everything does not mean we should allow them to do it. We all share these environmental commons, and this global ecosystem made up of our air, oceans, and land. It's up to every one of us to do our part in its care.

REASONS FOR RESPECTING LIFE

"Reverence for life is the highest court of appeal."
- Albert Schweitzer

We are all living in an interdependent relationship with all that is around us, so respecting life and our environment comes naturally for many reasons. The reasons listed below can help us all gain a better understanding of why we need to respect life as well as be a source of useful information you can share with others who may need help.

HUMAN DEPENDENCE ON OTHER LIFE

We owe our health and our society to nature. Just about everything we create and need comes from our environment. We depend on all the ecosystems around us for clothing, food, housing, clean air, water, and so much more. It seems every week that someone discovers something from a plant, insect, or animal that we can mimic and use in other applications that enhance our lives.

There would be no medicine without plants. We have found more solutions by analyzing life than from any other source. Life is loaded with truths that, once understood, can solve many of the problems we face. Currently, we have only discovered a small fraction of life on this planet. We are also polluting, despoiling, and destroying life faster than we can learn from it, and often before we have even looked to see what is there. Without a healthy diversity of life, we lose answers to so many questions.

The goal is to work to coexist with nature, not dominate it out of existence. In the end, we are all directly affected by nature, and without it, we cannot live or find the solutions we need to thrive. To destroy our natural world's balance and diversity, we destroy ourselves.

WHAT KIND OF CARETAKERS ARE WE?

We have dominion over the earth and all creatures. Dominion means total control, and control does not mean destruction, but in fact, it means to manage. How we manage our natural world is a test of character for all of us as it determines our quality of life and that of future generations.

The tests of character are found in the question of what kind of masters do we want to be?

- Do we care for every life form within the food chain because we know that if one falls, the rest of the food chain can break down?

- Do we treat our farm animals with respect by providing a clean and healthy environment where they are not always scared, crowded, and confined? Where different types of animals are separated so they can't transmit and create more potent diseases?

- Do we want to treat life with brutality and disregard because we have the power to do so, or do we realize that life is extraordinary and offers us so much more through coexistence, fair treatment, and discovery?

- Do we see that a healthy environment consisting of clean air, water, food, and land means

we are all healthier people, and we are helping future generations to thrive?
- Do we realize animals feel emotions and suffer as we do and deserve to live without us tormenting and torturing them even as we use them for our purposes?
- Do we see our remote natural world of jungles, forests, deserts, lakes, rivers, and oceans as assets?
- Do you see our natural world as a resource, providing endless solutions for so many problems like providing life-giving oxygen, storing excess carbon dioxide, maintaining our weather, providing a place for nature to thrive, and giving peace of mind for so many more?

No matter how disconnected we are from the treatment of the environment or animals, we are all responsible for how our natural world is treated. We take part by using what is supplied through our societal systems such as food, clothes, houses, roads, buildings, and all the rest that is produced by our society.

At this current time, the uncontrolled global creation of pollution and the mismanagement of our environment is putting us and all other life on this planet in jeopardy. We are the cause of an ongoing mass extinction that has already exterminated all kinds of animals, fish, and plants from existence. This mass destruction without regard or plan is hurting all ecosystems around the world and threatening our very survival.

Our ability to manage our natural world gives us an excellent opportunity to shine as a species. Our global need forces us to cooperate on large scales. It's through cooperation and applying solutions worldwide that we can overcome or compensate for many of the problems that come with the human conditions we live under.

The human race must manage our world with care because it's the foundation on which our development individually and collectively rests. To be excellent caretakers, we must understand our world and apply solutions cooperatively as a species. Our working together brings many lessons and opportunities to grow individually and collectively.

Our goal is to create a sustainable symbiotic relationship with our natural world and our universe so that we and life can survive and thrive. Coexistence is possible if we are thoughtful, caring caretakers who truly cooperate. In the end, we are all diminished as our world is ravaged, yet we can prosper when our world is thriving.

LOVE & FRIENDSHIP

Appreciation for other life can come from the fact it allows us to exist. It can also come through appreciation and love as they naturally lead to respect. Respect through appreciation is the same process found in how children respect the caregivers who love and care for them.

On some level, we can all appreciate nature as a beautiful view or garden. Pet owners know the companionship and love that comes from sharing our lives with animals. Dogs are animals, but no one who has ever loved and cared for one through a lifetime would say the dog did not love, feel emotions, have hopes, suffer, and show signs of intelligence.

Sometimes human and animal relationships can be closer on some levels than any human relationship. These relationships can even heal us. "Pet Therapy" is when a pet is given to someone dealing with a serious problem. This type of therapy has shown to help all kinds of people, from very ill children to recovering veterans heal faster and with a better mindset.

Pets can help us recover from PTSD and help all of us avoid many health and mental problems. This is because often, pet owners are more active and gain peace of mind from sharing and caring for another living being. Pet owners are also more able to feel sympathy and empathy for others. The ability to love, feel, bond, find solace and companionship are traits of high value and mean so much to so many. These feelings and friendship are enough of a reason to have respect for life and our animals.

Some animals are also said to have intelligence at the level of a baby or toddler. Is a baby or toddler less lovable because they are ignorant, less capable, or less intelligent than you are? What if our child did not develop mentally beyond the level of a child? Do the less intelligent deserve to be tortured and killed without regard? Life does not have to be equal, super-intelligent, or even sentient for us to care for it, love it, and show respect.

We have a phrase called "humane" treatment that we apply to people and animals. We use a word to describe caring and treating something with respect, which is drawn from what we call ourselves, the human race. Humane is used because we know right from wrong, and "humane" treatment is the only treatment true humans can offer. To be "Humane" is to be Human. To treat our world and all life humanely is to show respect for our planet, ourselves as a species, and to God.

It's a fundamental human condition that we respect our natural world by accounting for this within the operation of our societal systems. This foundational coexistence is not optional and made so much easier when done out of love and compassion. At the very least, if you love and respect your family, friends, and others who do love nature, you can find respect for nature because you respect your loved ones and want them to be happy and enjoy their lives. Nature is a positive, meaningful thing that so many of us care about. Therefore, it should be meaningful to all.

Logic, Intelligence & Reason

"Look deep into nature, and then you will understand everything better." - Albert Einstein

It's logical, intelligent, and reasonable for us to know, understand, and control all aspects of our world as well as create and maintain its systems. Not only do we need them to survive and thrive, but because they are a value on so many levels, to so many, they are worthy of care and respect. Undeniably, caring for our world and all life correctly will not hurt us; it can only help. Therefore, it is logical to do so.

Survival of the Fittest?

In evolutionary terms, "survival of the fittest" refers to the ability for life to survive while competing and in a changing world over time. The adaptations life develops to cope with the natural world, dangers, as well as its' needs, are a wonder to us all. These adaptations range from a giraffe's long neck to another animal's claws, talons, tusks, fangs, thick hides, and walking and flying abilities. It is all so complex scientists are still learning from it all. Evolutionary development can be fast for a few, but the process most often is very slow, taking thousands of years. Gradual evolution is why quick, drastic changes in the environment or climate can kill off so much life so quickly.

The problem today is that "survival of the fittest" is being twisted into a tactic and used by those who could care less if the world is despoiled. The ignorant say things like,

"Well, if they or it can't survive, then it's their problem – it's "survival of the fittest after all." The problem with this way of thinking is that we are the ones who are causing the changes and expecting animals to adapt overnight to impossible things. Also, this is not a contest to see "who is the last left alive."

For Example: If we dam up rivers that salmon need to run up to spawn, they die out. If we pollute the environment, animals will get sick and die off. We can't expect elephants, lions, tigers, and other wildlife to instantly develop bulletproof body armor and invisibility so that our guns and scopes can't find and kill them. We can't expect fish and birds to start being able to digest plastic.

Giving life no chance and then saying they were not fit enough is not correct. The truth is, we are choosing not to give life any chance to survive; this is not "survival of the fittest." We are committing genocide, mass extermination, and extinction of most other life on this planet either through direct or unintentional actions. The key here is to realize that the survival of our natural world is not optional. If the human race wants to be the fittest, our environment must be thriving. If we push this too far, we will put ourselves on the chopping block through our mismanagement and become just another life form we exterminated from this earth.

THE GARDEN

Many refer to the place of our creation as "The Garden of Eden." A garden means someone has worked with nature and created something beautiful within a thriving ecosystem. There are profound and sacred reasons for this connection to nature.

For many, our bond with nature does not need a logical explanation as we feel the power, majesty, and connection to something more. Our bodies are of this world and universe. Nature can be a bridge to higher levels of being as well as a connection to our world, universe, omniverse, the divine, and God. To be our "True Self," there must be a connection and respect for nature. The randomness, curved, multicolored, textured, varying depth of the natural world helps us mentally, physically, emotionally, and spiritually in many ways. Conversely, artificial plastics, straight lines, unnatural lighting, ugly and closed spaces can lead to mental problems and even insanity.

For some of us, we innately feel the deep connection between nature and the divine. For others, this is something we can learn to recognize, often as a feeling that has always been there yet has gone unnoted. For those of you who do not feel any connection to nature but are believers in God, you can still respect it through knowing nature is part of creation and is needed for us to thrive. Respecting our world shows our love, faith, and is one way to worship God. Ultimately, we can find respect for nature because God created the human conditions that require it for survival and for us to thrive. We can also find respect because this was given to us by God as a test of who we are as individuals and collectively as a species.

BE FRUITFUL & MULTIPLY

For some of us within certain faiths, we were told that we are to be "fruitful and multiply." The key here is to understand both parts.

- To be fruitful is to be productive.
- To multiply is to have enough children to ensure our survival as a species. This means not just today but also going forward.

The idea behind being "fruitful and multiplying" is to build our society to support a growing level of population. Back in the day when this idea was first attached to religion, the human race's survival did not seem a sure thing, and our standards of living were very low.

In the past couple of thousand years, we have done well on multiplying our species as now humanity covers the globe in vast numbers. However, we have not performed well in being fruitful and developing the systems needed to support this level of population. Overpopulation without the systems of support leads to many negative issues such as desperation, war, disease, poverty, mass migration, ignorance, and destruction of our natural world. To understand population growth, let us go a little deeper and look at how we grow or shrink our populations.

Population Growth Example: We start this example using a couple of people, (2) and show how many children they have. We can express this in an equation. 2=0=-2. This means "2" (the couple) "=" (have) "0" (no children) = (this equals) -2 (Negative 2 population growth). 2=1=-1 the couple has one child, which is negative 1 growth, 2=2=0 the couple had 2 children, which is the breakeven point. 2=3=+1 the couple had three children, and here is where the population begins to grow.

As a society, some of us have many children, while others might have one, a couple, or none. Adding together the number of all the children born in a year contrasted with deaths is how we determine our yearly area/global population growth. Over time we can see the trends. Currently, an educated woman who has access to well-developed societal systems have fewer children, which means that highly developed countries experience a stabilizing or reduction of population.

Conversely, those of us living without good societal systems and who lack education most often have many more children. In these areas/countries, overgrowth strains the already underdeveloped society systems, which can lead to unrest, lack of resources, famine, war, and mass migration or flight from areas that can't support this level of human life. To honor God and the idea of "being fruitful and multiplying," we must realize that we have enough people and possibly even too many. Still, we have not honored the idea of creating a great society or caring for our natural world to support these multitudes.

The solution is found in the control of our population individually, the development of our societal systems, and the natural world collectively. A proper application will increase the number of children who are wanted and growing up in loving households with societal systems and a world to support them. Children with access to sound societal systems have a much better chance of living healthy, fulfilling, meaningful, productive, and joyful lives. Access also helps ensure that future generations will have the same or better opportunity as well as the chance to exist.

LAW 3: RESPECT LIFE - SUMMARY

We affect and are affected by our planet in many ways. Over the past couple of thousands of years, much of our world is deforested, water sources polluted and fished out, and our soil destroyed. Respecting life is at the core of creating a better self and society. We must understand our surroundings and act with thought and care. Nature has a right to exist, for it has been here longer than we have, and it's needed for all life to exist, including us.

Respecting life is a matter of creating a beautiful and sustainable world. Our respect means considering nature and animals as we construct our world.

We can do this by building parks, gardens, greenways, water/food access, animal crossings, sanctuaries, niches, hideaways, wild areas so they can feed, nest, and breed. At this point in our history, we need to put more back into our natural systems than we take out so they can recover.

If we are to be good caretakers, we need to fix what we broke and help replenish everything so nature can rebalance itself, recover, and once again thrive. Our renewed waterways, soil, and reforested lands will allow us to store carbon, create oxygen, and revitalize our global ecosystem.

Uncontrolled pollution and the creation of toxic products with no way to recycle or clean up their mess is an unsustainable system that will lead to our destruction. For all these reasons, respecting life and caring for our world is not optional. Instead, it's <u>required</u> if we are to become our "True Self" and for the creation of our "True Society" to become a reality.

We must evolve morally faster than our technology, or else our lack of caring will destroy us. Respecting life shows respect for each of us as it ensures our survival. We can see this as collective self-preservation. Caring for nature protects our future advancements. This human conditional situation provides us with an opportunity to prove our character as individuals and as a species.

Genuinely respecting our natural world and integrating this way of being into our society will allow us to gain so many benefits. Some include greater peace, happiness, better health, more self-awareness, and a more natural connection with our world, each other, our universe, omniverse, and God.

Chapter 5
Understanding People

Within this chapter, we continue with "Step 4: Center" and the "10 Laws" by exploring the remaining "Universal Laws" that cover how we interact with other people. Let there be no mistake; the laws covered within this chapter are critical to your success as well as our success as a species.

Law 4
All People are Equal

*"Respect is how to treat everyone,
not just those you want to impress."* - Richard Branson

People (high-level sentient beings of conscience) are equal without exception or equivocation. When we talk about people being equal, we do not mean that every person is equal in ability as clearly some of us are better able at some tasks than others. It does not mean that we have to like and agree with everyone. Clearly, we like and agree with some people more than others.

Equality often means being indifferent to things like ethnicity, gender, social status, wealth, and all the rest. Equality in this sense means each of us has the right to: life and a humane level treatment, respect, common courtesy, dignity, privacy, equal rights, justice, liberty, free speech, consideration, fairness, decency, tolerance, freedom, control over our bodies and destiny, access to quality systems of society, especially education, health care, and the other basics.

Also, everyone has the right to fair and equal pay for work, choice in most things, and to be generally treated well and not discriminated against. Equality includes the freedom to change our opinions, belief, and religion at any time without fear of reprisal. Equality also covers freedom from religious and political discrimination and persecution. The "level playing field" in the economic sense is to be set at the same level around the world and at a level that allows for the humane treatment of all people and our environment (See "Chapter 13" for more on how to level the playing field).

No person is deserving of more rights regardless of their position of power, access to the tools of power, or because of birth, family connections, skin color, gender, sexual orientation, age, mental or physical ability, or any other difference. Equality includes access to protection and justice without favoritism. In this sense, on the foundational level, all of us are equal in our society and before the law.

Side Note: If we ever discover other true sentient beings of conscience, they are also to be treated as equals in this sense.

PREJUDICE, DISCRIMINATION & XENOPHOBIA

The main factor preventing equality from being the norm in society is prejudice and discrimination. Prejudice and discrimination are a learned behavior whereby we form an irrational dislike, fear, or hate of someone or something. This type of negative thinking is typically passed down from generation to generation by role models.

We mainly choose to discriminate against those that are not like us. Often, this means those not of the same skin color, gender, sexual orientation, age, religion, political party, country, ethnic group, language, culture, or level of intelligence, wealth, beauty, or fame.

The extreme form of prejudice and discrimination towards other people is called "xenophobia." Xenophobia is an intense fear and hatred of strangers, foreigners, or anything strange or foreign.

Often prejudicial and discriminatory language will group all people of a type and uses a broad brush to disregard them. As in "you know _____ this is what they deserve." Or "all _____ are stupid and are made to serve us." Or "Those _____ are animals and deserve it."

Sometimes people dehumanize "other" people, groups, countries, and "their" ways of living, to make war, or to take what "they" have. We are taught to feel that "they" deserve what "they" receive and that "we" are superior. This superiority allows us to rationalize any action against "those" people.

To sum up this idea, it's the local society in which we are raised that shapes our founding beliefs and attitude regarding other people. Therefore, in most cases, the prejudice and discrimination that divides us is a learned trait. Because of this learned hate, some of us see small differences in people as indicating people are lesser and are therefore deserving of whatever horrible fate befalls "them." Also, some people use prejudice so they can feel superior to "other people," self-righteous, and then rationalize their inaction or hateful actions against other people as just and good.

Equality & the Tactics Used to Divide Us

"The price of hating other human beings is loving oneself less." - Eldridge Cleaver

There are many tactics used to divide us by the powerful, so they may use us to get their way. Tactics that pit one group against another are some of the most used as they are the most effective in manipulating us, "the masses."

Prejudice and discrimination are a tactic often used by those who want to control people for their gain by pitting "us" against "them." You can learn more about the tactics used against us in the "Life Manual: Fuel: Information and the Tactics Used to Lead Us Away from Collecting Good Information."

Those seeking power incorrectly look to divide us because there is a human trait that gravitates toward a tribe or team, the familiar and introversion. Also, because some people are not raised correctly, they have a malformed sense of empathy and sympathy. Being twisted in this way means some people either feel too much or too little or are twisted into feeling pleasure from the pain and the suffering of "those people."

All these factors push many of us to look at differences rather than our overwhelming similarities. Focusing on differences leads to confusion, and it's this confusion about others that gets twisted into something very negative like fear, prejudice, discrimination, apathy, hate, and violence.

We are One People

The key here is to realize these negative ways of viewing "other people" and work to change them individually and within our society. Those of us who get caught up in small differences are missing the vast similarities that unite us all. We all share fundamental similarities that prove our equality. These similarities are all based on our shared human condition and things like our desire for a good life for ourselves and our loved ones. None of us want our children to be treated as less than other people or to live horrible lives.

In fact, we are all one tribe and family. There are NO separate human races; there is only one human race. All of humanity can be traced back to the same two genetic male and female ancestors (Genetic Adam and Eve), who lived around 150 thousand years ago in what is now northeastern Africa. Our race, the human race, spread throughout the world from this single tribe.

We all share 99.9% of our DNA. The remaining 0.01% is what accounts for the differences we see in height, hair color, facial features, and all the rest. The ethnic differences we see have to do with environmental effects and breeding selection by those who settled that area of the planet thousands of years ago. In this age, as we come back together, share, and join, we are becoming stronger people, genetically, and as a society.

UNIQUELY EQUAL

Inequality, prejudice, and discrimination are being used to confuse and divide us and is preventing us from creating the "True Society." We need everyone helping each other to find all the solutions.

The fact is we are all equal yet unique. Our similarities bind us together, and our differences make life much more vibrant and society more fascinating. Unity of humanity does not mean sameness; instead, it means accepting, celebrating, and appreciating the differences and diversity.

Traveling is so much more enjoyable because everything is similar yet different. Our differences are what make us unique, interesting, and help energize each other and our global society.

There is proof that we are all equal found in the fact that people of every ethnicity and gender from all over the world have done great things and risen to positions of great power through merit. We can't let our past or those in current positions of power to continue to corrupt us and lead us from the truth.

If any of us are diminished, we are all diminished. It's through correctly formed systems of society, most importantly, quality public education, nutrition, and the correct raising of children that we end discrimination and prejudice.

However, it's essential to understand that as we view all as equals, it does not mean that we have to like or respect other people's words, actions, or choices. If a person is hateful, mean, prejudicial, corrupt, generally disrespectful, demeaning, mocking, or shows other bad qualities and vices, we can try to help them, and be respectful toward them. Still, we need not feel obligated to like them or respect their actions. In this case, equal means we "like" others equally as in we like people whose actions and words are respectable and who treat us well and with regard.

We are similar, yet unique. This uniqueness also means we all have different talents and interests, and yet when we add it all together, we become much greater than the sum of our parts. It's our diversity within our similarities that allows us to cooperate and find the answers to every question facing us. Because of this fact, we benefit the most when all people are equal, adding to our society in positive ways.

Law 5
Treat People as You Want to Be Treated

"We have committed the Golden Rule to memory; let us now commit it to life." - Edwin Markham

The law of reciprocity has shown up in just about every religion and spiritual path throughout time. It's known by many names but most commonly today as "The Golden Rule."

Basically, the golden rule states that we should treat others as we want to be treated, or at the very least, as we want our loved ones to be treated in that situation. Reciprocity is about fairness, a level playing field set at the fair level, and a two-way street. The golden rule also includes a firm grounding in the belief of human equality. See the "4th Law" above for more.

"Law 5" covers our interactions as individuals among one another. It also extends to all our organizations, clubs, businesses, governments, religions, teams, ethnic groups, clans, families, as well as all the systems and other groups within our society. At its core, the 5th Law is about being good and kind to one another. As we interact with people, we can ask ourselves if we are treating others as we would want to be treated and teach our children to do the same.

The idea of reciprocity is also something to be considered from a perspective of when our loved ones or we are at our worst. Like when we are vulnerable, helpless, fragile, weak, sick, traumatized, desperate, lost, very young, very old, or caught in an emergency or disaster.

We need to use the powers of empathy, sympathy, and conscience to put ourselves in their position and ask, "how would you want to be treated at these times?" How would you want your child or loved one treated? It's clear we would all want the best. Reciprocity guides our actions as individuals and the formation of our societal systems.

To honor the "5th Law," we must eliminate: inequality, prejudice, hate, discrimination, degradation, misery, implicit bias, corruption, desperation, poverty, slavery, torture, genocide, terrorism, war, murder, assassination, execution, honor killing, crucifixion, stoning, burning alive, maiming, human and animal sacrifice, abduction, sexual harassment, rape, sexual assault, branding, acid attacks, female/male circumcision, female genital mutilation (FGM), mutilation of any kind, incest, child abuse, child labor, child soldiers, child marriage, child molestation, sex with children, forced and unwanted arranged marriage, caste systems, unequal and unfair pay, the pink tax, counterfeit products such as medicine and money, malicious computer programs, blackmail, corporal punishment, kidnapping, hostage taking, extortion, fraud, slander, libel, hazing, bullying, theft, privacy abuse, adultery/infidelity, spousal abuse, false accusations and bearing false witness, false flags, deep fakes, spreading of false and misleading information, arbitrary and unjust arrest or detention or imprisonment or exile as well as all other demeaning and inhumane treatment of people.

In most cases, we should also not lie, steal, mock, manipulate, break our oaths and promises, threaten or imply force to get our way nor should we cheat, bribe, hurt others or kill. However, there are times when these behaviors can serve the greater good. They can help overthrow dictators, free people from the thrall of false leaders, expose corruption, and allow us to protect our loved ones and ourselves. Every situation is unique and should be judged accordingly.

Do not take this casually. We must understand that the use of these tactics is negative, and, in most cases, should not be used. They can lead to the abuse and corruption of our character. They must not be used lightly, but instead only as a last resort and after careful thought. These negative ways must not become a permanent way of doing things, for if it does, it means you and/or the system has been corrupted. To say it another way, corruption is acceptance of the unacceptable and the corrupt.

Bullying Note: Since child and adult bullies cause so many of these problems in our society, it's imperative that we fix this issue permanently. The solution is tied directly to how we raise our children, so how to end bullying is covered within the "Child & Family Guide: What Children Really Need: Bully Correction & Support for Their Victims."

POWERFUL MEN VS. THE WRONGNESS

Seeing others as equals and treating them as you would want yourself and your loved ones treated is key to life but can be difficult for men who are strong, independent, and want to be left alone to do what we want. Since independent and capable men are most often in control of the primary systems of society, these circumstances create challenges for those of us in these positions, as well as for those of us affected by them.

For men who are in this position of control and security, they may find it hard to view others with compassion. They disregard others because they are so capable and well off, it may seem that "equality" and "respectful treatment" means that everyone should just be left alone to care for themselves and do as they please.

The problem is that not everyone is the same, and no one is an island. In the case where we are independent powerful, capable men, it's good to view the situation from the perspective of someone who is not as powerful or capable.

For example, you can see the universal truth of reciprocity (treating others as you wish to be treated) in these situations by thinking about how you would want your less powerful and seriously ill mother, grandmother, or child treated in these situations. Think about the people you care about the most being in those bad situations without you to help and ask how you would want them to be treated by others who are there or by the society at large.

Think about how you would want to be treated if you were not well-off and independent but instead living in a horrible place, poor, ill, or hurt and uneducated. Think of yourself as weak and sick, lost and broken, old and confused, and without resources. How would you want to be treated then?

The men who are bullies, broken, and lost are a big deal because men only make up about 50% of the population, yet account for like 95% of the problems and horror in our world. Broken men commit the vast majority of murders, mass shootings, arsons, terrorist attacks, robberies, muggings, car jacking's, rapes, abductions, pollution, and other evil acts.

Additionally, throughout human history, all the billions of us who have been forced to give our lives in wars have done so, mainly because of a few male leaders. We can see time and time again, that they don't care for their people properly and therefore resort to stealing from others. They can't solve problems and disputes peacefully nor win a consensus because they are so greedy and feel so "superior" that it's their right to take from and subjugate other people. War, rebellion, and desperation are the outcomes when the golden rule and equality are not firmly part of the leaders' or countries' moral code.

Good people only triumph over evil by peacefully overcoming it while continually working to prevent it from rising in the first place. The reason this is true is that all good people will lose something valuable participating in war even if we "win" in the end. We fail and become lessor because if we are participating in acts of violence and destruction, it means we are <u>not</u> focusing on what is good or working to improve. It's this negative mental focus and process of taking negative action (killing, destroying, hate, etc.) that hurts and negatively affects good people no matter if we win the war.

For clarity, following *The Way* and the path of nonviolence does not mean we are pacifists who will never fight or go to war. It just means we see it as a last resort and a failure of our higher values and goals, for there may be situations when we must fight to protect and defend ourselves, our loved ones, and help those who cannot. We may even need to rise up in great numbers to take down tyrants, hate groups, and other twisted, unthinking people who have fallen to the dark side.

Also, undeveloped men tend to revert to more of a savage or barbarian level of behavior when dealing with other men seeing everything as a competition and a contest of dominance. It's we, the men, who form social tribes and teams that divide us into "us vs. them" and "win/ lose" situations. It's most often arrogant, self-righteous, and closed-minded men who disdain all people who do not follow them that cause most of the problems.

This imbalance in male leaders leads to mismanagement and all kinds of issues within our societal systems.

We have seen, throughout all of human history, a few men wanting to impose their will upon the rest of us versus those in power positions working to fulfill the will and needs of the people. This negative male tendency is compensated for by including women who are seen and treated as equals into the organizations and all meetings, as well as through other accountability efforts and proper checks and balances. It's also solved by raising our male children correctly (see the *Child & Family Guide* for more).

The problems surrounding powerful men have been with us since our beginning. However, the goal is not to rid our world of men who have these qualities. Instead, the goal is to raise them correctly, so they can use their power in positive ways to help our world. We, as a society, need to help them become better people as often the qualities found in powerful men are necessary to create order from chaos. If channeled correctly, this force can be a great boon for society and the world, but as we have seen, it can also create some of our most significant problems.

Therefore, it's imperative that men choose to help fix these problems by creating environments and organizational statutes that mitigate these issues from happening. We do this because we want to become truly successful as well as to do right by everyone. We also do it because we don't want to make mistakes and be corrupted. The solution is found in a firm belief in the "10 Laws" and a system of checks and balances that help us stay on our "True Path."

In the end, we men all need to be brave and call each other out for our misbehavior at the time it's happening. In the locker room, board room, backrooms, bars, clubs, and everywhere else. We need to do this when it's only us men hanging out as well as when we are in public. We can pull our friends aside or even call them out in front of everyone.

We need to stand together in groups to help those of us who are powerful yet lost so they can be corrected and learn to behave appropriately. We cannot sit by and be spineless toadies and sycophants. We need to be our brothers' keepers so that when the few of us men stray too far and are genuinely lost and a danger to others and society, we can help set them back on their "True Path."

POSITIONS OF PUBLIC TRUST

Reciprocity is also about honoring and showing a high level of respect for those who are doing a good job and serving at critical positions in our society. People like our parents, teachers, police, firefighters, servicemen, and women, emergency workers, doctors, nurses, National Guard, volunteers, guards, and those fighting for good causes and faiths. We honor these people because they are filling key roles within society that add to the common good.

Note that these are respectable positions, but we need only show high levels of respect if those <u>individuals</u> in them are respectable. To say it more simply, to be respected, each <u>individual</u> needs to be respectable. While giving respect to the respectable and not to others, it's very important not to lump all people working in a job together as being corrupt just because one or some of its members were found out to be. If the <u>individual(s)</u> in the position of public trust are corrupt and abuse their power, we need not show them the level of respect we do toward those who are in those positions doing a good job. *For example,* we respect all police even if we don't show respect for the few who are corrupt.

In fact, most often, it's only through our dissent that we can remove these negative people from the system and replace them with those who are positive.

Leaders can't demand respect and expect it to be given from the heart. Leaders must be worthy and earn respect through good deeds, righteous behavior, keeping promises and oaths, being a good role model and person, doing a good job, being productive, and by giving real compliments on a job well done no matter how small or large.

CROSSING THE LINE & BECOMING CORRUPTED

To be worthy of a position of public trust, we can't give in to temptation and false loyalties. As we work side by side with people, especially in very intense situations, over time, they can become like a family where we would die to help these people.

Those who are soldiers, police, emergency workers, and others working intense jobs often feel this the most keenly. The problem is that our sense of allegiance and duty towards these other people, taken too far, can hurt the person we love, our society, and ourselves.

For example, Police in America use the analogy of the "thin blue line" as a symbol to represent the police standing between chaos and order, between criminals and the innocent. It's often used to show solidarity among fellow officers. So far, this is all as it should be and a good thing.

The problems only occur when someone violates the rules of the organization, the law, or other virtues within their morality code, and it's not handled properly. To some, this "blue line" means you can never speak outside the organization and must cover up all problems. We also see this behavior within our religions, governments, and corporations.

In cases like this, not saying anything is condoning their behavior. We are not helping anyone if we do nothing or help cover up their corruption. To be clear, it's through you helping the fallen avoid consequences, cover things up and break the law that you become corrupt, and corruption spreads. You are doing right, being loyal to your loved ones, your job, and the true virtue behind your oath if you do the positive and do <u>not</u> become corrupted.

The truth is most of us in these positions of public trust have a higher code that we believe in (like these "10 Laws"), and often we have even sworn an oath of office to uphold the constitution, the law, equality, justice, or some other virtue rich commitment. These commitments preempt any obligation to the fallen and lost within your organization.

Your actual duty to your loved one is to help them out, not aid them in their negative acts. You need to protect your integrity and the integrity of your organization by outing and excising these problems, or else they will fester and become systemic corruption and "just the way things are done." You need to help your friends become better people, not aid them down this negative corrupted path. If you help the corrupt, you are corrupt.

Our goal as leaders, therefore, is to create fair and open systems so that "we the people" know what is happening, and only those of real merit are in positions of power. It's about ensuring those of us who are in control have the correct checks and balances to secure us from corruption.

All people and leaders need to work together to end corruption in all levels of society. Our overall goal as leaders is about helping to build a better society on all levels, free of corruption so all people have access to the well-run societal systems and can enjoy a wonderful life.

The Way | Step 4: Center - continued

Finding Forgiveness & Healing

"Darkness cannot drive out darkness; only light can do that. Hate cannot drive out hate; only love can do that."
- Martin Luther King, Jr.

Many of us are consumed in cycles of hate, destruction, and negativity. Some of you are caught up into situations that are truly horrible where others have done you a great wrong and/or you have done them a great wrong.

In these cases, for you to grow, you need to forgive them, and yourself or else end up in a spiral of negativity where your sole focus can become one of hate, revenge, and violence. No good person would want your life or a loved one's life to get caught up in this cycle of negativity. To say it another way, only the broken and twisted feel good about the misfortune and suffering of others. These people need help and are to be pitied.

The truth is hate begets hate; atrocity begets atrocity. Tragedy cannot be undone by another tragedy. There is no end to this cycle of hatred and violence if you work to avenge every wrong that has ever happened, and others do the same.

Forgiveness is about claiming your power by not letting a bad circumstance or bad people have power over you. You want to reclaim your positive power because if you focus on something negative, you become negative. If you hate, you become hateful. Evil, and those wishing you ill win if you focus on negativity.

For Example, if you continuously focus on hating someone, how they wronged you, and all the different ways you would want to take revenge, you become a twisted, unhealthy, and a negative person. The harmful chemicals released into your body, and your constant negative focus, will change you and lead you away from your "True Self."

All people can be good people. Good people twisted into negative people who are far from their "True Path" is how evil wins. Forgiveness does not mean you accept or that you don't want justice. Forgiveness is about not letting a person or circumstance hold negative power over you, twisting you into someone you don't want to be. You pity and forgive them and/or yourself for being human and making a mistake. You transmute the energy within the situation into something positive (See the "Life Manual: Our Practice: The Power: Transmutation"). You make amends, do your best, move on, and work to become better.

How to Let the Healing Begin

The way to heal all wounds and end the cycle of hate, atrocity, and revenge is through grief, pity, and forgiveness. Grief caused by a broken heart or a major shock is often the sharpest when it happens, but over time as you go through it, even if it does not ever go away or become acceptable, it does become bearable. However, it's in these sharp moments of grief and anger where you can typically see the great wrongness and injustice and find yourself wishing and praying for it not to exist.

Pity for those on the "other side" is easily found by feeling sorry for those who have been so negatively twisted. The reason for this is that all good people want everyone to have a wonderful life. Therefore, all those who are misled, ignorant, doing wrong, and lost need our help and compassion so they too can become their best. It's in this deep desire for an ending to the wrongness added to your pity and compassion that allows you to find your way to forgiveness, self-healing, and down your "True Path."

If you feel the horror and know, "this should not be," you have taken the first step. The next step is to realize that there are those on the "other side" who are also feeling these same feelings and desire for the horror to end. Because of this, those from all sides who want the horror to end can join together as a single group, a group of all those who have lost yet want something better for their future and next generation.

It's through our shared compassion, mutual empathy, and sympathy that we can bridge the gap between seeing "them" as the "enemy" and "other" to a place where "we" are in this "together," working to build a new path out from the horror of the past to a better future for everyone. These healing groups must then work to stop those wishing to continue the tradition of hate and violence by helping them see the way to peace and by actively preventing them from continuing to spread their hatred and violence.

THIRTEEN SACRED TEXTS THAT MENTION THE GOLDEN RULE

The "Golden Rule" is so fundamental to being human that below you can see it has been a part of all our faiths throughout history. The faiths listed below are in alphabetical order.

Baha'i Faith: Lay not on any soul a load that you would not wish to be laid upon you, and desire not for anyone the things you would not desire for yourself. Baha'u'llah, Gleanings

Buddhism: Treat not others in ways that you yourself would find hurtful. The Buddha, Udanavarga 5.1

Christianity: In everything, do unto others as you would have them do unto you, for this is the law and the prophets. Jesus, Matthew 7:12

Confucianism: Do not do to others what you do not want done to yourself. Confucius, Analects 15.23

Hinduism: This is the sum of duty: do not do to others what would cause pain if done to you. Mahabharata 5:1517

Islam: Not one of you truly believes until you wish for others what you wish for yourself. The Prophet Muhammad, 13th of the 40 Hadiths of Nawawi

Jainism: One should treat all creatures in the world as one would like to be treated. Mahavira, Sutrakritanga

Judaism: What is hateful to you, do not do to your neighbor. This is the whole Torah; all the rest is commentary. Go and learn it. Hillel, Talmud, Shabbat 31a

Native Spirituality: We are as much alive as we keep the earth alive. Chief Dan George

Sikhism: I am a stranger to no one, and no one is a stranger to me. Indeed, I am a friend to all. Guru Granth Sahib, pg. 1299

Taoism: Regard your neighbor's gain as your own gain and your neighbor's loss as your own loss. Lao Tzu, T'ai Shang Kan Ying P'ien, 213-218

Unitarianism: We affirm and promote respect for the interdependent web of all existence of which we are a part. Unitarian principle

Zoroastrianism: Do not do unto others whatever is injurious to yourself. Shayast-na-Shayast 13.29

In the end, treating other people as you would want to be treated in a similar situation should seem logical and a normal thing to do, for who does not want to be treated well?

THE 3 UNIVERSAL LAWS SUMMARY

It should be obvious; we all need to care for our world and each other in a very positive way, for this is our home, our nest, our womb. Humanity is dependent on each other, on all life and our planet. Because one person or a small group of people can ruin everything for the rest of us, agreement on all three Universal Laws is essential for us as a species.

Law 3: Respect Life.
Law 4: All People are Equal.
Law 5: Treat People as You Want to be Treated.

If you do not agree, then others may do as they want to you, your loved ones, and all you care about without regard. If you do not agree with these laws, you give up your freedom, the right to fair and just treatment for yourself, your loved ones, and our world. Instead, we surrender your life to anyone who can wield power over you. This is because if it's ok for you to hate, take, and destroy without regard, then, by your logic, it's equally right for someone to hate and steal from you.

There is no end to the justification of discrimination unless we end it for everyone. Ending the sickness of superiority that has infected all our societies throughout time is accomplished through the belief in the "2 Laws of Purpose" and the "3 Universal Laws." To be clear, there is no superior ethnic group, only superior <u>human</u> ways of being and doing. The different ways of doing that we see are of culture, not of genetics.

The key is to integrate all the best and leave the rest while you always lookout for what's even better. It's about raising our children correctly and seeking equality, justice unity, true education, and training.

Promoting harmony within our diversity is the goal and responsibility of all. We find our true humanity within well-balanced consideration, empathy, and sympathy. We express this through the creation of a kinder, more respectful, considerate, and just society.

We help everything run more smoothly if we are polite, have good manners, and treat others well. It's about providing and allowing access to key systems of society and truly educating people, so the knowledge they gain is applied in a way that aids them in their ultimate quest as well as our greater society. We must change the negative into positive if we are to succeed. Feeling that you would like to do right by <u>everyone</u> and then taking actions to make that happen is at the center of *The Way*.

Since we are all dependent on the wellbeing of everyone else, respecting the life, dignity, individuality, and the diversity of others is part of what it is to be your "True Self" and live within a "True Society." We are all of the same race, the human race, and if we choose not to divide, segregate, and work against each other, but instead cooperate, we can do just about anything. We can only reach our full potential as a race and as individuals if we honor these "3 Universal Laws" within our life every day.

Chapter 6
Understanding God

"God gave us the gift of life; it is up to us to give ourselves the gift of living well." - Voltaire

The God Laws

As part of "Step 4: Center" of *The Way*, we are covering the laws that make up our core value system. We have covered "The Laws of Purpose" and "The Universal Laws." Now we finish up the laws with a set of rules covering God. "The 5 God Laws" below provide a starting point where all those of faith and non-believers can find common ground.

The fact that God is possible and that so many believe are enough reasons to have a basic set of governing rules. It's also important because a lot of problems in society are created by the organizations we have built around faith and science. These rules will allow us to peacefully interact when dealing with the issues of God within our society.

I have found these laws and the virtue they express at the heart of all faith, philosophy, morality, and science. All is presented with the utmost respect and gratitude for everyone.

One way or another, we all have a code when it comes to God. A clear understanding and choice of a complete and positive core value system covering God is the way to become your "True Self," create the "True Society," and more fully connect with God.

The Name of God

If the reader has an issue with the word "God" or "Heaven," feel free to change them to any other positive terms that mean God, including ideas like The Creator, The One, The All Creator, Allah, Jehovah, YHWH, and Yahweh. Other words for heaven include things like nirvana and the afterlife.

Non-Believers/Atheists/Agnostics Note

The Way does not require a belief in God. We can be good people without the fear of God or even the idea of God as our guide or friend. We can choose to do right because it is right.

However, "the God Laws" can help all of us understand the faiths of our world. They can show us how we might all work together by focusing on the shared virtues found within all faiths, morality, and science. These insights can help us navigate this life more easily and help us build our "True Society." So, as a non-believer, it's important not to discount or skip over the information contained within "The God Laws" because the information within this section needs to be known by everyone if we are to create a world of peace and understanding.

Law 6
There is No God Other than God

To get started, we need to know who or what God is. To answer this question, at this stage, we need only look to one primary aspect of God.

God as the:
- Creator or Originator
- Prime Mover
- Unmoved Mover
- The nothing or non-nothing that begets everything
- First actor within the action-reaction cycle
- The "One" who started it all

PROOF OF GOD

We can't prove to everyone's satisfaction that God exists or does not exist. God may always remain a subjective truth so that we can have free will and therefore choose our destiny and fate. However, according to Science and Philosophy, a creator is possible. The possibility of God also allows for the possibility of heaven. At this time, it may be that we are not able to prove this truth scientifically because our tools are not good enough. The absence of proof is not proof of absence.

God, the originator, the prime mover in the action-reaction cycle, is the energy source and force that started "The Big Bang," which is the name for the start of our universe. From this originator perspective, "God" can be and is the only God. Using the word God to represent this first creator being does not mean you have to believe or have direct knowledge of God.

Even if there are very powerful beings that can perform wondrous things, or even if we can, it does not make them or us "God" or a "God." It would just mean they, or we, are powerful beings who can do amazing things. Regardless of ability, all who come after the prime mover are not the originator.

The word "God" is, therefore, only being used to describe the prime creator of everything. Because of this, there is no "your" God, "his or her" God, or "their" God. There is only God. The differences are found in our interpretations and organizations, not in the deity we call God.

> **WHAT IS HEAVEN?**
> Heaven is a topic, like God, that is complex. Here the key point to understand is that heaven exists as a section of the omniverse, spanning many universes and dimensions, where beings who are developed to a certain level reside and thrive. It's a place of endless happiness, discovery, challenge, fun, peace, development, and so much more.

RELIGION, SPIRITUAL PATHS, THE MESSENGERS, & GOD

For a more in-depth understanding, we need to look at how we have manifested the idea of God within our Society. Religion is a human-made organization that has a system of codified beliefs, opinions, customs, and rituals concerning the existence, nature, and worship of a deity (God) or deities, and divine involvement in the universe and human life. Some of what many name "religions" are instead spiritual paths. A spiritual path is a program used to better one's life that does not necessarily contain the idea of God. Buddhism is an *example* of this type of spiritual path.

God is a being and not a human organization. God is not bound by any religion. God is the "topic" these organizations are claiming to be talking about. Most religions were either founded by or created from the teachings of a "Messenger." Many religions are thousands of years old and carry traditions and world views of those times.

Religion is a major societal system that affects all our lives in many ways. We can see them as different vehicles, trying to get all of us to a better place, which is based on virtue. Religions most often operate as a business in that they own property, employ people, and offer products and services that are consumed.

LARGEST FAITHS AT THIS TIME: (listed by year founded)

Hinduism: Religion/Spiritual Path (depending greatly on sect) (Mainly found in India)
- o Founded Around 3500+ BCE. Existed in parts much earlier.
- o Founder: No one person, formed through collective writings often from unknown authors.
- o Books: The Bhagavad Gita, the Upanishads, Rig Veda, etc.
- o God: Within Hinduism's many writers, there is the idea that there is only one God, and all the other "gods" mentioned within this faith are but aspects/avatars/creations of The Creator God. There are also interpretations allowing for many beings of great power they call "gods."
- o Sects: Shaivism, Vaishnavism, Shaktism, etc.

Judaism: Religion
- Founded Around 1812 BCE
- Founder: Abraham, who was 75 years old when he heard a call from God to start his journey, which ultimately began the Jewish faith.
- Books: Torah (the law of God as revealed to Moses and recorded in the first five books of the Hebrew scriptures, Talmud (the body of Jewish civil and ceremonial law and legend comprising the Mishnah and the Gemara. Midrash (an ancient commentary on part of the Hebrew scriptures, attached to the biblical text.)

Nevi'im (the second part of the Jewish Scriptures which contain the writings of the prophets).
- God is only God
- Sects: Rabbinic, Karaite, Hasidic, etc.

Chinese & Asiatic Faiths: In the age of this writing, many see the dominant eastern faith, centered in China, as a combination of Taoism (Daoism), Confucianism, and Buddhism, which is then customized locally by adding in other ancient rights and traditions like ancestor worship.

Confucianism: Moral & Spiritual Path
- Founded 551-479 BCE
- Founder and Name: "Confucius" is a Latinized form of the Chinese K'ung-fu-tzu, "Master K'ung." Confucianism and Confucian are not meaningful terms in Chinese. They are western terms.
- Basic Books: The four books include the: Great Learning, Doctrine of the Mean, Analects, and Mencius. The five classics include: Classic of Poetry, Book of Documents, Book of Rites, I Ching, and the Spring and Autumn Annuals.
- God: God is only God with a great focus on Heaven.
- Sects: Mencius, Xunzi, Dong Zhongshu, Ming, Korean, Song, Qing, the Modern sect, etc.
- Information: Confucianism has never existed as an established religion with a church and priesthood. Although the ideals within what the west calls Confucianism became the official ideology of the Chinese state, Confucius was only honored as a great teacher and sage. He is revered and not worshiped, named God, nor did he name himself God. The basic teachings of Confucius are composed of a set of political and moral doctrines emphasizing self-

control, statesmanship, development, virtue, as well as social and political order.

Taoism or Daoism: Religion and/or Spiritual Path
- Founded: Around 500 BCE. Established as a formal religion between 400 to 300 BCE.
- Founder: Laozi is also known as Lao-Tzu
- Book: The key book of Taoism the Tao Te Ching (Dao De Jing or Daode Jing) or The Way and Its Power.
- God: One can say that Taoists do believe in God; they just call it the universe or cosmos. In Taoism, the universe springs from the Tao, and the Tao impersonally guides things on their way.
- Sects: Quanzhen (totally true) and Zhengyi (exact one) are the two primaries.
- Name and Information: The name Taoism is derived from the Tao Te Ching. What we know as the Tao grew out of shamanism, various religious and philosophical traditions in ancient China. It is a philosophy that advocates a good simple life, oneness with the universe, living life at peace with one's self, others, within a world of changes.

Buddhism: Spiritual Path
- Founded 460 BCE
- Founder: Siddhartha Gautama was a prince who was separated from all hardship, the old, sick, and issues of life. Once he was exposed, he was so moved, he "awakened." Buddha is a title meaning "one who is awake."

- o Books: The path is centered on the works of The Buddha that include "The 4 Noble Truths" and "The 8-Fold Path."
- o God: This faith is not concerned with God. It focuses on the development of self as a way to reach higher planes of existence.
- o Sects: Theravada, Mahayana, Tantric, Zen, etc.

Christianity: Religion

- Founded 27 CE. The first official organization formed about 397 CE.
- Founder: Abraham & Jesus Christ. The book and organizations, while based on Christ (0-27CE), were not directly created by him as he was killed before writing anything down or forming an official religion or organization. However, his first followers (apostles) continued to spread his message in speeches and writings/letters/testimonies. It's these writings that hundreds of years later became the basis for the New Testament and, eventually, the Religion of Christianity.

    It should be noted that the Catholic Church is the first organization to be officially recognized as the first church of Christ. They claim their legitimacy by linking the organization to the apostles who followed Jesus.

- Books: These first organizers of the Catholic Church canonized some religious writings about Christ into the New Testament. The Bible they created is made up of this New Testament and the Old Testament (which comprises thirty-nine books that are considered to be the Hebrew Bible or Tanakh). Since Christ was the fulfillment of a prophecy within the Jewish Torah, the "New Testament" was added to the

book and not substituted. Note that groups like the Mormons, while Christian, also use other books.
- God is only God
- Sects: Catholic, Evangelical, Protestant, Orthodox, Quaker, Methodist, Lutheran, Baptist, Mormon, etc.

Islam: Religion
- Founded 622 CE
- Founder: Abraham & Mohammad
- Books: The Quran: Mohammad spoke the words, and his wife (Khadijah bint Khuwaylid), wrote them down. Over time, their creation became the Quran. The Quran consists of surahs that cover many important topics, issues, and people, including surah 12 Joseph, 14 Abraham, 19 Mary, and more.

    There are additional books within Islam. One is the Hadith, which is a collection of reports about Muhammad's life. Another is Sharia or Sharia Law, which was a system of laws created in response to a very lawless time and the corruption found within Judaism, Christianity, and the society in general. The goal of Sharia was for it to evolve into a clear set of fair and just laws that reflect the virtues of peace and love that are at the heart of Islam.
- God is only God.
- Sects: Sunni, Shia, Kharijites, etc.
- Name: Islam is unique among the religions listed as the name "Islam" was created by Mohammed. He created it by working with the root of "*al-Silm*," which means submission/surrender and *al-Salaam*, which means peace. The name Islam, therefore, is a call for all to submit or surrender to peace.

Sikhism: Religion (mainly found in Punjab India)
- Founded about 1500 CE
- Founder: Guru Nanak and nine gurus who followed
- Book: Guru Granth Sahib
- God is only God
- Sects: Nirankaris, Nam-Dharis, etc.
- Name and Information: Sikh means "one who seeks after truth." The first word in the Sikh scripture is "Sat," which translates to the truth. Sikhism is based on truthful living.

THE CHILDREN OF THE BOOK

Many refer to Judaism, Christianity, and Islam as Abrahamic Religions as they all revere Abraham as the founding Patriarch, see God as the only God, and share other ideas. Because of this, we can see all Abrahamic Religions as different sects who look to represent God as brought to light by Abraham.

BALANCE VS. SUPERIORITY

To understand and improve our faiths, we all must be aware of a significant issue within our religious organizations. There is often little to no checks and balances on those in power positions. In many cases and especially within the Abrahamic religions, there is a tendency to propagate a feeling of superiority and righteousness over "other" non-believers, sects and faiths.

This deluded sense of superiority and righteousness is the same human failing found within isolated ethnic groups who feel their ethnic (white, black, Asian, etc.) background grants their group some superiority over "others" not of that ethnicity. Within these faiths, the feelings of superiority come from a belief system rather than ethnicity.

The feelings associated with believing that we are right, superior, and powerful separates us from others by leading us to see "other people," not as equals. Instead, this unhealthy fixation on self-superiority and righteousness stunts our growth. It makes it virtually impossible for us to understand any "<u>fact</u>" that does not align with our preexisting world view or feelings that we have been taught to think and feel by our faith.

Often, it's those who feel the most self-righteous and superior that gain power and take a hard line against genuinely caring for other people, our environment, and society. They do this because they have a false sense of their superiority, believe things that are not true, and are unwilling to examine their failings or challenge their authority figures.

Being sane, rational, and a true believer means that you are open to change when facts and science do not align with your religious, spiritual, or political desires, wishes, or wants. You choose reality and truth over what you want, wish, and thought was true because this truth leads to your ultimate goal. Willful ignorance, choosing to believe in lies, half-truths, and not challenging authority figures is not the way to your "True Self," our "True Society" or heaven.

Sects, Heretics & Cults Unmasked

To ensure our understanding and ability to manage our societal systems of faith, we need to go a little deeper into a few key aspects of their structure. Within every religion, there are different sects. A sect is a subgroup of a religion. These sects are often referred to as having liberal, conservative, literal, radical, orthodox, or fundamental views of the religious works. Sects interpret the books and other tenants of that religion in different ways, often emphasizing some ideas while diminishing, dismissing, or glossing over others.

Sects are often formed by those who feel they have a superior understanding or view. The main difference between sects is found in this focus and interpretation of the original messenger/message by the leader(s) of the sect.

Some sects fractured from other sects that were fractured from others. This dividing within a faith is how we end up with faiths and sects that focus on very narrow interpretations of "The Message," or even an elevation of part of "The Message" above all the others. Most of this is inconsequential as these interpretations conform to harmless traditions, virtue, or appeal to personal taste. In fact, true faith can play an important role and be a constructive part of life as they are peaceful, loving, good, and can help people find their "True Path."

THE REAL HERETICS

However, others have focused on part of a message or twisted the meaning so that they can hate and do evil yet claim it's good. I am calling these people heretics. To be clear, I have changed the meaning of the word heretic in this book. In the past, a heretic was used by those of a religion to justify killing or destroying the lives of anyone who spoke against them.

I am using "heretic" to describe all those who twist any of our faiths into a tool of negativity and evil. This is based on the fact that virtue, morality, goodness, and God are at the center of true faith.

Self-deluded superiority and fracturing have created sects within each faith that focus on passages and interpretations. This allows these sects to justify what the main body of the faith, and the rest of society, would call evil, radical, or extremist. These heretical sects operate more like tyrannical dictatorships oppressing people rather than being a positive virtuous spiritual organization that helps people.

In fact, most heretics revere men of the past above all others and worship an interpretation of a book that is thousands of years old instead of listening to the living God and the truth of the age. It's these extremists who hold the twisted belief that violence, hate, oppression, destruction, rape, slavery, murder, genocide, mutilation, misogyny, and other atrocities are somehow honoring their faith. They have been twisted into believing they are good even when what they do and believe goes against human conscience and all standards of humane treatment, virtue, and morality.

EXTREMIST SECTS & CULTS ARE STARTED IN 2 WAYS

1. **Fracture**: As outlined above, these extreme or radical faiths are often a product of a fracture within a religion or sect. These sects are led by someone who claims to have a better or clearer interpretation than others in the faith.

2. **Power Hungry:** Many times, the people who want power, fame, wealth, control, and wish to impose their will over others need justification, legitimacy, and followers to do so. They gain acceptance from their target group by claiming to be part of their religion. They say they are fighting for those oppressed, forgotten, poor, and desperate. They claim to speak the "true" meaning of the message or messenger and do favors for that group. Here the leader is not a believer, and they are just using the followers of that faith as a tool to get what they want.

CULTS & HOW TO KNOW IF YOU ARE IN ONE

Small fractured sects, especially when the members pledge their sole allegiance to their leader rather than the leaders and tenets of the greater faith, are referred to as a cult. You can tell if you are part of a cult because they often do not want you educated, have contact with the outside world, and work to incite feelings of anger, fear, violence, and hate toward "outsiders" or "non-believers." They also want you to give them all your wealth, time, and live within their community, doing only as the leaders dictate.

TWISTED FAITH & EVIL

This twisting of evil into good is how the most heinous and inhumane acts are justified by the followers of a twisted faith. The reason for this is few, if any, who do evil think they are doing so. They not only feel good about committing evil deeds, they feel justified, right, superior to all other people, and holy as well as the closest to God.

Anyone who understands why God created "Evil" can see this twisting of good people into evil is one of its primary goals. As there is no greater victory for the "Evil One" than to tempt "Good" people into committing "Evil Acts," thinking they are doing good, honoring their faith, and acting in the name of God.

Evil only moves in this world through humanity. In this way, we can see the "Evil One" as the great tempter testing to see if we will choose the good and hold to our "True Path" or give in to temptation, be broken, and turn to evil. Throughout human history, many millions, if not billions of us, have been murdered, tortured, raped, oppressed, while others of us are twisted into committing these atrocities in the name of someone's inhumane interpretation of only part of an ancient message.

It's imperative to understand that it's only people, and mostly men, doing all of these horrible things. The demons or devils walking our planet are humans who are twisted and lost. Our only solution is to help them, stop them, and prevent others from becoming like them.

TRUE FAITH & THE FALLEN

"True Faith" is about creating peace, harmony, unity, understanding, and cultivating the rest of human virtue, and a relationship with the holy, divine, and God. Therefore, any sect or cult that murders, rapes, hates, enslaves, maims, tortures, and oppresses in the name of (insert sect or cult here) is not part of a legitimate belief system or part of any religion nor honoring God. Instead, the followers of such a twisted faith are the lost and fallen.

For example, a group who names themselves "Christians or Muslims or Jews or Hindus" for "Peace & Freedom" who then go around killing, raping and oppressing are not part of that larger faith or even a legitimate sect of the central faith. They are power-hungry heretics using the religion for legitimacy. They are twisted, claiming to be good yet doing evil.

The original goal of religion may have been to reflect the virtues professed by their founding messenger(s) and to honor God. While inspired by God or enlightened people, we find the problem in the translations and interpretation of these ancient messages into modern language, formal systems, and institutions within society. The interpretations and structure become the problem because our institutions of faith have little or no checks and balances in place and are run by flawed human beings. They also often exalt their members and key leaders above the rest of humanity.

Throughout human history, we can find evidence of corruption, violence, division, destruction, hate, inequality, prejudice, discrimination, and dysfunction within all institutions of faith. The fact is that those who commit evil have fallen; it does not matter the position within a religious organization or society. We can love them and feel bad, but this does not negate the fact that if in a position within a faith, the fallen should be fired, expelled, and removed from any position of authority or power. All information regarding their crime needs to be provided to the civil authorities so that they may be stopped and prosecuted.

In all these cases, no one gets a pass just because they are considered "holy," or it might look bad. If those within our "holy" organizations are not held accountable for evil acts, how can these organizations claim any real virtue or serve as role models for anyone? How truly "good" is a "holy" organization if no one can question them; if they oppress people, ideas, and maim our children and us; if they condone child molestation and rape; if they teach us to hate and kill everyone who does not agree with or do what the "leaders" say?

Therefore, because our holy institutions and those within them are or can be corrupted, it's incumbent upon and the duty of all the members to ensure that there are checks and balances in place. We must also question and test all the ideals against conscience and morality as well as expose the inconsistencies and corruption within our faith to its members and leadership so they can be fixed.

THE SOLUTION

The solutions to all these challenges found within our religions are similar. Flawed systems are one of those universal challenges set by our human condition that we all must work together to overcome.

All "True Faith" is about the cultivation of virtue and connecting with the holy, divine, and God. Ultimately, it's the responsibility of all of us to ensure we are not participating in a twisted faith and that our faith has not been tainted or hijacked by heretics, the lost, the fallen, or evildoers.

For all of these reasons and for your personal development as an individual, it's essential to know what religious sect you belong to. Then to compare and contrast its beliefs with other sects within our religion, the "10 Laws, " other humane morality systems, faiths, and your sense of conscience to ensure that you are following a good and positive faith.

One easy way to tell if you are following a heretical faith is found in how it makes you feel about other people and faiths. If your faith makes you feel hateful towards "those other people" and wants you to commit acts of horror upon "certain groups" of people, you are following a twisted faith, heretic, or in a cult.

After you have taken care of yourselves, making sure you are in a positive faith, you can look to help free others under the thrall of heretics and heretical sects and cults. As a global society looking to dismantle these organizations, we must first stop linking crimes to faith. We stop relating crimes to faith to stop giving legitimacy to these heretics and cults that are seeking to twist our faiths into evil.

This strategy means our news and other media need to stop saying things like "Jewish, Christian, or Muslim terrorists killed…" There can be no true follower of faith that commits these heinous acts. These evil-doers are using these faiths to gain legitimacy, spread hate, and divide us. We only play into the hands of the fallen by making it seem like a particular religion is committing the crime.

Those in media who know those of true faith would not commit acts of evil yet continue to link crimes with religion are tainting those faiths in the eyes of those listening and creating more division. We must peaceably work to stop those linking faiths with criminal behavior.

We also need to ensure that we portray all criminal acts as something that goes against our faiths and human morality. In all cases, we do not publish their names, manifestos, photos, religious affiliation, or anything in their regard. We can just refer to them as just another person who had a psychotic break or part of a misguided hate group without naming their group. We can then mainly focus on helping the victims and solutions that fix the sickness in our society.

We can help prevent extreme negative fracturing within a religion by ensuring all the other societal systems like education are running well. We must blow the whistle, give evidence, and leak vital information on harmful plans and corruption as well as do everything we can to stop those who would do evil.

Ok, now that we understand the basics of how our faiths become fractured and hijacked, it's essential to understand a couple of other vital issues that have hurt our understanding of God and true faith over the centuries.

An Eye for an Eye &
Turn the Other Cheek (EETC):
Another of the main issues found within most religions and justice systems is the seemingly contradictory virtues of "an eye for an eye" and "turn the other cheek." This concept reflects the idea of "a velvet glove over an iron fist" and other metaphors.

Below are both virtues in short form:

- **An Eye for an Eye:** If you take something from me, I will or can take something of equal value from you.
- **Turn the Other Cheek:** As in forgiveness, the acceptance of rightful punishment or chastisement, or the willingness to accept a hurt to teach someone a more important lesson.

If either of these virtues (EETC) is taken out of context from the whole faith and all virtue, our conscience and a real sense of morality, as well as in relation to one another, it can distort our view of right and wrong, our sense of sympathy, empathy, compassion, and justice. This distortion can lead to many adverse effects personally and within our society. Only within the context of each other, combined with the higher ideals within the whole of the faith and human morality, can we understand that these ideals are not contradictory. Each has its place as they represent two extreme ways to respond to conflict.

There are times that just recompense, and even punishment are required. There are other situations where we must allow forgiveness if more significant lessons and peace are to be achieved. There may be situations that need a little of both. If we balance EETC with the ideals of equality and treating others like you and your loved ones would want to be treated (Law 1 & 2), we find EETC is relatively easy to apply correctly and fairly. This is because our goals as humans are to help everyone become their best and to create a wonderful world everyone can enjoy, not unjustly hurt, and take from each other.

Judgment Day, Ending Times, Apocalypse, Armageddon, Revelations, Etc.

Another common issue within most of our faiths concerns the writings that refer to the ending of all life or the destruction of our world. Within these apocalyptic writings, life usually ends in a very horrible way because the human race has failed.

The scientific fact is that our world will end. We know that billions of years from now, our sun will go out. Before it completely dies and if our earth is still orbiting our sun, all life, including human life, will be destroyed (possibly excluding some extremophiles). If we are to continue to be fruitful and multiply in a virtuous and sustainable way and continue to thrive over the truly long term, we will not only need to protect our world so it can sustain us but go even further. Long before our sun goes out, we will need to relocate to other worlds and/or move our world to a safe location and/or build our own solar systems where we can live in peace.

Prophecies of what will happen if we <u>fail to grow in a virtuous way</u> were very common at the creation point of these religions. They all serve the same purpose, which is as a <u>warning</u> of what will happen if we <u>do not succeed</u> in honoring God and living up to our potential. Within the Abrahamic faiths, the apocalyptic ideas are linked together and share many common points.

The fact that apocalyptic writings exist as a "warning of failure" is critical. The intent was to provide a <u>warning</u> of what would happen if we failed and as a motivator pushing us to do our best. The writers of the day made it seem so horrific that all people would want to work hard to avoid it. The problem is that over thousands of years, the interpretation of these writings has been twisted by some heretics and accepted by large groups to mean something completely different.

In our current age, there are good people of faith who have been twisted into longing for our destruction and the ending times to arrive by any means instead of working to honor God and live up to our potential. They see the destruction of humanity at our own hands as unavoidable and something to work towards and rejoice. Some have even gone so far as to see it as their duty to help bring on the end times.

God was very clear that our purpose is to survive and thrive in a virtuous and sustainable way. If God wants to end us or not, the choice is God's and not ours. To believe otherwise is to separate these apocalyptic writings from all other virtuous precepts and tenants of faith and then twist a good into evil.

It helps to realize that many of those in power perpetuate this twisted view because it means they can increase their control over us through fear and the claimed ability to grant access to a positive afterlife. It also allows those of twisted faith who are tainted by hate and superiority to feel it's good and right to actively work to create world wars, to kill and destroy us all.

In the end, all apocalyptic writings are accurate in one sense. Our world and universe will come to an end one day. As humanity, we must take these warnings given by our holy ancestors and the facts presented by our scientists seriously. We must work hard as anti-entropy agents and children of God to do our best to live up to our full potential as a species for as long as we are allowed to exist in this universe. This is because if we do our best and things end by an "act of God," we still honored God and did our duty, and this will be rewarded.

LAW 6: THERE IS NO GOD OTHER THAN GOD
SUMMARY

There is and can only be one God. Religions and systems of faith are flawed, as are all our human systems. It's up to us to see these flaws and overcome them. Flaws within our faiths are a challenge and test for all of "True Faith" to overcome. This challenge is built into all faiths through the human conditions we all live under because they serve as high-level tests of our character and willingness to live up to our higher ideals no matter the organization or people involved. In the case of religion, we need not accept everything said or written by the ancients or modern-day profits. All our religions, spiritual paths, and faiths need to fit in with our greater understanding of life, conscience, virtue, and morality.

Someone pointing to a passage in a book thousands of years old that has been translated and interpreted (often incorrectly) or saying that God told them so is <u>not</u> a reason to go against all that we know is right and good, moral or our conscience. These are tests of our character and our willingness to find "True Faith." These negative ideas should be shunned, not accepted, or embraced. We need to speak up, challenge, and not accept those who would twist our faiths into something hateful and negative. These are significant challenges within all faiths that, once overcome, will help us find the "True Faith" we all seek.

In the end, while we may not ever be able to prove the existence of God to everyone's satisfaction, the existence of God is possible. This fact, along with the other evidence you can personally find, is enough reason to believe.

Belief in God does not require belief in a particular religion or spiritual path. In these cases, believers can simply say they are spiritual rather than religious.Regardless, it has been proven that faith and belief in a positive God and virtuous precepts found within a religion and/or spiritual path can give direction, "lighten our load," heal, relieve pain, and grant access to all kinds of seemingly superhuman abilities.

Our faith can also mean that we don't fear death, are never alone, and have access to a reliable and inexhaustible source of positive energy and a catalyst that can help us go farther than we could otherwise. Therefore, even if God does not exist and there is no heaven, but you choose to believe, you could still live a happier, more virtuous, and healthier life with more energy and peace of mind than by not believing.

Chapter 7
Understanding Your Place

Within this chapter, we wrap up "Step 4: Center" as we finish exploring "The God Laws" that are at the core of "Our Code." Understanding the rest of these laws will help create more peace in your life and our society.

Law 7
We Are All Directly Connected With God and This Connection Cannot be Broken.

"We all have the same root, and are connected…To tap into this connectedness, we must go within." - Summerlyn Guthrie

All is created by God, and you are no exception. Since everything is of God, we are continuously and directly connected with God. It cannot be otherwise. To help visualize the basics within this truth in a purely physical sense, think about it like this. Whatever you are touching is touching something else, which is touching something else. If you go with this far enough, you get to the point where everything is connected.

A simple *example* is that your body is touching the air, the air is touching all the atmospheric layers, the topmost layer is touching space, and space is touching the rest of the universe, which is part of the omniverse (all universes and dimensions). All is created by God using God's energy. Therefore, all is part of God and connected to God.

This total connection is how you are physically connected with everything, including God. Since everything is one, there can be no separation.

We are also spiritually connected directly with God through our Soul. There is no requirement needed for this connection. This connection cannot be undone or broken. No person or organization can stand between you and God nor have any say in your fate/destiny or relationship with God. Ultimately, your destiny is between you and God.

Even though this connection is there, some of us may not feel it. Finding this connection for some can be like learning to hear a soft sound that has always been there but has gone unnoticed. If feeling unconnected, it only takes time and true intention to find it. If you are of faith and at times you feel alone or abandoned, you need to see these times as a test of faith and of your character.

In fact, no one is closer or farther from God than we want to be. If there is a block, shadow, or distance, it's of your own making, and only you can remove it. To be clear, you can choose to turn from God, believe you cannot connect, and even deny this connection. You can also choose to connect.

Ok, now that we understand the basics of this connection, let's go a little deeper into how we were created and our life span.

What are Soul & Spirit?

Your soul is like a unique "seed" created by God. Your soul grows a spirit around itself. The soul is not destroyed in this process; instead, it evolves. Your soul/spirit contains all of who you are. This soul/spirit is who you really are and is what directs your body.

The blueprint of who you are as a "Being" (soul/spirit) is not contained within our universe's observable dimensions nor within the temporary energy form (body) that you are using within this universe. Instead, because all is of God, as you live a life, you create a "master blueprint" that is continuously imprinted within God, and it's this soul/spirit that God joins to a body anywhere in the omniverse.

ONE LIFE & LIVING FOREVER

When we die, some believe that we go on to live many more lives. Others believe we only live one life. The truth is there is no difference. There is only one life in either case. The reason these are the same is that the first is a human perspective, and the other is the perspective of God.

From a human perspective, we see people being born and dying, which means if they do come back, they would be reborn and live a new life. From God's perspective, our life starts the moment we are created, and it's this life form that takes on many bodies as they live. We have "One Life," that lasts forever using bodies as needed.

From this perspective, your life lasts forever from the point of your creation. All your achievements help you develop through all of these "lives." So, what you do every moment does matter. Here you can think of your body as the temporary vehicle you are using in this life, and it's the only thing that is aging and dying. You can see aging and dying as another mental, physical, emotional, and spiritual challenge to help us develop as beings rather than the end of your life. Here, instead of seeing a life's ending, we see a "being" transitioning from this body to another and the beginning of something new.

CREATED IN THE IMAGE OF GOD

Our connection with God runs deep, as many have said that we are created in the "Image of God." "Image" in this case does not mean physical representation as in how we look. Instead, one aspect of the meaning is concerned with the fact that we were not given all knowledge and wisdom but instead given the innate need and capacity to know and understand. The characteristic of being a "truth seeker" and "mini-creators" is ingrained into the core of humanity. Therefore, to use God as a substitute for intelligence dishonors this great gift.

To be clear, the fact that God is at the start of everything does not negate our intellect. God created us and gave us so many excellent gifts, with our minds being one of the greatest. We must use it to show our appreciation and respect. Our desire and ability to observe and understand our wondrous universe to such a profound degree is fantastic. Taking human minds out of our society and keeping people ignorant does a disservice to the entire human race and does not honor God. In fact, it's profoundly disrespectful to our creator NOT to develop our minds and cooperate in the creation of the "True Society."

We, the "observer or witness" with the ability to truly understand, is very important and fundamental to the purpose of the universe. We can see this point of the observer within the age-old Zen "koan" asking, "Does a tree make a sound when it falls in the forest if no one is there to hear?" One of the main points within such philosophical exercises is to get us to consider if anything can happen or exist without an observer.

Intriguing Observer Side Note: An interesting scientific discovery points to how important the idea of the observer is to our Universe. *For example,* this "observer effect" is seen clearly in the "double-slit experiment" where one single photon of light is released into a tube with two holes at the end. When observed, the photon of light acts as a particle and comes through only one of the holes. However, when we <u>do</u> <u>not</u> observe the photon directly, it acts as a wave, and we see the light coming through both holes at the same time. - *End Side Note.*

To fulfill one of our primary missions of life of knowing and understanding means that we can't give up our free will and ability to think, reason, and know. This perspective is critical because sometimes we are told by our chosen authority figures or those in centers of power of a faith that to honor God, we need only do what they tell us or learn what is in books of their choosing. Some even force this state of ignorance on all the people of their country or faith except for the elites and those of the leadership's choosing.

If we surrender our free will to think, reason, compare, and question, then we are giving up a primary gift from God that makes us human. If others are taking this from us, then we are their slaves. Our vulnerability means that those in power positions must not give in to the human failing of thinking you know everything and, therefore, should control everything. A leader without checks and balances is depriving themselves of a critical component of the system they lead.

To say it another way, <u>not</u> developing our minds and abilities does not honor God, but instead is choosing to be no more than an ignorant slave submitting to the will and designs of another human. Our surrender in this manner dishonors God and yourself.

Progress & the Spiritual Challenge

To honor our connection with "God" and "True Faith," old flawed traditions that reflect misunderstandings of messages, inequalities, hatreds, and prejudices of our past can be disregarded without fear. We must focus on our living connection with God, conscience, and genuine virtue. We must not let unenlightened interpretations, bad translations, harmful traditions, and bad ideas held thousands of years ago shade our understanding of the living God, real goodness, truth, or our future.

The goal of faith and religion is not to perpetuate a human's understanding of God held a few thousand years ago or to worship a book. Instead, we are to live with God in the now and develop our systems as we gain understanding and perspective. This development is the challenge. Our success honors God as it shows that we are learning and capable of choosing and implementing positive changes within complex societal systems as a large group.

This human challenge of having to shed old traditions that do not adhere to higher standards of virtue, conscience, and morality have been with us throughout our beginnings. We have done away with many of them. To truly honor God, we must use our minds and conscience to question and test everything. If channeled correctly and joined with others, our minds are our greatest strength, and together we can improve our intuitions of faith, which will enhance our world.

The Children of God

Ultimately, all is One. We are all created from and by God. We are always connected to God because all is of God, and God created us. Therefore, we are all "The Children of God" and are thus a family.

A real family because, as we have learned, we also all share the same genetic male and female ancestor (Genetic Adam and Eve) and 99.9% of our DNA.

A flawed family true, but our flaw forces us into many challenges that lead to more significant advantages. Our imperfections, if handled well, is a great gift. Knowing we have these flaws (also named "original sin" by some faiths) and working to compensate for them is one reason we are worthy of consideration and an honorable species. Choosing correctly and working together as a family is critical if we are to truly succeed.

It's up to all of us to join together and not let anyone divide us in our collective mission. Every issue does not have to be turned into an "us vs. them," "zero-sum," or "win-lose" situation. We have the power to find real solutions and create consensus for we are family. Most often, reasonable people with the same accurate and complete fact base and who believe in the "10 Laws" can come to universally acceptable solutions.

LAW 8
GOD IS OUR SOLE AND FINAL JUDGE, & WE ARE JUDGED BY OUR TRUE BELIEFS, INTENTIONS, WORDS & ACTIONS

"People pay for what they do, and still more, for what they have allowed themselves to become. And they pay for it simply: by the lives they lead. " - Edith Wharton

WHY IS GOD THE FINAL JUDGE?

Your life is continuous and without end. You transition from body to body from universe to universe.

Your soul/spirit is imprinted on God as you live. God, as the judge, is like our parents or educational facilities teaching, testing, and judging us as we grow. As we do better, we get to go to different places and do more things. If we do not do well, then we go to less fun places where we work to learn the lessons we missed and are even punished.

Just like a loving parent, God cares about where you end up and wants you to succeed. To help, God has given us the great gifts of being unique yet similar, free will, consciousness, and the ability to create a world of our choosing. Because of this, your life can only be a competition with yourself, for you are the only one walking your path. There is no comparison between lives. You are literally in a unique place that no one has ever been and will never be.

Sometimes humans must be "burned to learn" as well as broken and remade for us to find our "True Path" because we are so clueless and lost. Some of us who have done and seen the worst can appreciate the best more than the rest. The main point is the lesson and not the event.

It's up to us as a species, globally, to create a more conducive societal system so all people can become their best and reach their full potential. Supportive systems will help more of us receive the best judgment from God as we go through life.

You as the Judge

We are here to work on ourselves and for a better world. Pointing our fingers and condemning others in mean, non-constructive ways does not use our conscience and inner judgment ability for its designed purpose. Those who use this ability in this way do so, so that they can feel superior or self-righteous and avoid dealing with their failings.

Our inner judgment ability and conscience are here to be used upon ourselves, others, and society to improve them in a good way. To do this, we need to understand our failings. It's through constructive self-judgment that we can learn to improve ourselves.

However, it's essential to realize that often our inner judge is harsher than God or anyone else would be. The key here is to find the balance and constructive solutions. Be good to yourself and don't beat yourself up. Look for the lessons and focus on solutions. Much of life is not a pass or fail but more a measurement of degrees of personal success. The key is to know the difference. You can learn something every moment.

Example: Pay attention to life's signs. Like your mother saying, "be careful, it's slippery out," as this can mean the difference between life and death. Or a fumbled screwdriver while working on a job may be a little sign to help us become better at our dexterity and focus.

To learn more about this topic, see the "Life Manual: Our Practice" as well as "Fuel: Information."

GOD IS FAIR

The fact is that God is fair and wants you to be your "True Self," live a "True Life," and go to heaven. God's purpose in creating us and moving us through life is so that we can evolve into wondrous beings of free will. The reason why God did all of this is a simple one. The answer is similar to what parents feel when they want to have a child and help them become "Truly Successful." You only need to play this great game of life in the right way to win. It's up to all of us to use our gifts to create what should be.

It seems harsh, but to God, we are children who need to learn, sometimes this comes with great trauma and drama, often of our own making. Being children means all the horrors we see around us are just things we need to learn to master, just as we expect our children to master sharp knives, crossing streets, driving, and so much more.

We, as the human race, have the drive and power to stop and mitigate most issues, even natural disasters. All our pains and problems are, in fact, tests and lessons we need to pass and figure out so we can evolve and move on. Knowing these facts shows us that we are judged on who we are as a person and our true character as well as collectively as a society.

How We Are Judged

"Happiness is when what you think, what you say, and what you do are in harmony."
- Mahatma Gandhi

This law states that we are judged by our true beliefs, intentions, words, and actions. Every day and in every way that we live, our lives reflect who we are as a person. In life, we are judged by the content of our true character. It's through our true beliefs, intentions, words, and actions in all situations that you reveal who you really are. They show if you are honoring the gift of life, your primary life's purpose, and your obligations to society.

Thoughts are Free

To be clear, we are not judged by what we think, for we can think anything. Thinking is how we explore and learn. Sometimes we may think things that are not good or positive. It's how we react to these thoughts and how we focus on them that matters. It may be that we have a negative or evil thought, and we dismiss it for an untruth and pass a test. It can also mean that we can learn something or do something positive with this negative.

Just because you can think something negative, or do not feel something as most others do, does not make you bad, wrong, or evil. It's what you do with it that makes the difference. Humans are Sentient Beings who can think anything, so it's natural for our minds to explore all sorts of thoughts and perspectives. A thought is not what makes us evil or good. It's our true beliefs, intentions, words, and actions (BIWA) that matter.

Note: Even those of us who feel little or nothing (sociopaths) can still choose the positive out of logic, self-preservation, and self-improvement. In case you were wondering, a psychopath is someone who has failed this challenge and gone over to the dark side.

For example, you might have an innate ability to understand crime and feel little to no reaction to horror. Here you can choose the negative path and become a criminal or the light side and work for justice. Working for justice means you can work in situations that would break an average person and solve crimes that would otherwise not be solved.

There is a lot more on how to master and understand your mind found within the "Life Manual: Our Practice: Mental Practice" and the "Life Manual: Fuels: Information."

Ok, now that we understand that our thoughts are not judged, let's go through the facets that are.

YOUR BELIEFS

Beliefs are a state or habit of mind in which trust or confidence is placed in some person, creed, or thing. Beliefs, in this case, are deeply tied to your core moral code because they form, affect and determine your attitude, intentions, thoughts, judgments, choices, words, actions, reactions, emotions, feelings, and other beliefs. It's vital to know what your core values are exactly, for they are at the center of who you are and determine who you will become. The "10 Laws" that cover all aspects of life are here to help you honor this law, the other laws, as well as win this great game of life.

Your Intention

The intention is what we truly want to happen. Here it's the intent behind what you did or said that matters.

Your Word

Your word is made up of how truthful you are as well as your oaths, promises, and commitments. Being honest and keeping your commitments shows a key facet of your character. Your word matters because it takes dedication and effort, to be honest, tell the truth, to live up to your commitments, and go the extra mile.

- o Breaking Our Word: How you respond when you break your word or are unable to keep it, even though you did your best, is equally important. If there were specific reasons or extenuating circumstances that prevented you from keeping your word, you need to handle the situation by letting everyone know who is involved as soon as possible. You need to seek forgiveness by apologizing and making amends for your lapse.

- o Honorable Word Breaking: In some cases, the honorable thing is to break your word, commitment, or bond. *For example*, it's honorable to break your word when it was given to corrupt organizations or people. Once you find out this truth, you can help them fix the problem if they are willing, and/or blow the whistle, and/or turn them into the proper authorities if the situation is that grievous.

Breaking your word or commitment in these circumstances is the honorable thing to do as it's through acceptance of corruption that we become corrupt, and corruption flourishes. A true friend will call you out when you stray. If the circumstances are unjust, you do greater honor to yourself, other people, our society, and God by staying true to "Your Code" than by accepting the unacceptable. If you don't say or do something, who will? How do you help without speaking up or taking action? You can fail many of life's tests by doing nothing. You will learn more about how to effectively break your word/oath in these untenable situations yet make a positive difference and protect yourself within "Step 6: Unite."

YOUR ACTIONS

Actions, doing, and deeds cover all you do and do not do. Every act matters from the smallest unseen to the greatest and public. Here your "doings" include an understanding of your intent. You can ask yourself, "Do I honor my code ("The 10 Laws") in word and action in every circumstance?"

EXAMPLE SITUATION

Here, we are using a dropped glass as an example. In this first example, the person sees others as equals and treats them as they want to be treated. They intended to hand a person the glass. However, as they gave it to them, it fell, shattered, and cut the other person. In this situation, the action of dropping the glass had a negative consequence of the cut.

However, because that was not the intention, it's not judged negatively. This event does not end here. Also, the actions we take after the mistake matter. Do we provide help, get help, make amends, or just walk away?

If you make a mistake, it's how you react and respond, and it's the lesson you learn that matters. Are you owning up to your mistakes and dealing with the consequences reasonably and rationally? Are you fixing your character flaws and mistakes? Here you can see mistakes as tests of character and opportunities to improve. You must learn from such circumstances so you can become better and evolve as a person.

In another example, it might be that someone hates "those people" and intentionally drops a glass to cut someone. If they drop the glass and the cut does not happen, the person is still judged negatively.

Here what happens after also matters, as in do they feel good that it did not cut them. This positive feeling might help redeem them if they realize their first belief, intention, and action were wrong. Or do they feel like they missed the opportunity to hurt them and want to try again? Here the intent is still negative even if the action did not materialize.

Law 8: God is Our Sole and Final Judge, and We are Judged by Our True Beliefs, Intentions, Words, and Actions Summary

"Don't compare yourself with anyone in this world…if you do so, you are insulting yourself." - Bill Gates

You now know the basics of how each of us and humanity is judged and how that determines where you go in the future. Anyone can be redeemed. This knowledge allows you to take steps so you can get a favorable judgment.

Therefore, you need not compare yourself to another or beat yourself up for your failings. Instead, you must focus on doing your best, learning the lessons, overcoming the challenges, passing the tests, making amends, implementing solutions, and getting to the next level.

While God's goal is to provide us with a life that allows us to achieve our ultimate goal, we still must make a choice, walk the path, and take action. We can fail. Our environment can help or hurt us on our path. In the end, we need to create unity of purpose, belief, intent, word, and action if we are to be "Truly Successful." *The Way* is a system designed to help you achieve the true goal of life and receive a favorable judgment from God.

LAW 9
RESPECT GOD

"Men are respectable only as they respect."
- Ralph Waldo Emerson

There are many reasons for respecting God. However, it's important to note that choosing to respect God does not mean you have to believe in God. Also, it's important to note that we are talking about only God and not any religion, spiritual path, or people that claim to represent God.

The primary way that we all show God respect is by caring for all that we have been given, such as our life, other people, society, our world, and the universe. We show respect when we work to be our best, care for each other, and our planet. We show respect through our care because these are great gifts, and if we don't care for ourselves, each other, and our world, we are being discourteous and not honoring these great gifts. Following the Golden Rule and treating others as equals is also very respectful as we are all the children of God. In this light, we can see that following *The Way* is a way to respect God. We also respect God by not disrespecting God.

THE THREE PRIMARY WAYS WE DISRESPECT GOD

1. **The Curse:** One of the ways we show disrespect is by saying things like, "God (curse word)" or "(curse word) God." Disrespecting God (swearing, mocking, imagery, etc.) can be offensive to many people.

    For example, swearing, in general, is offensive to many, but bringing God into it brings things to an entirely different level as if the insults are directed at our loved ones such as children, mothers, fathers, brothers, sisters, or wives.

    Think about if a close friend brought us home to meet their family, and their very religious grandparents are there. Would it be appropriate to use foul language or mock God in front of them? How about if you brought someone home and they mocked your family? Of course, that would not be ok.

2. **The Images:** Imagery of God is Disrespectful. The fact is that images can limit and bar us from knowing the fullness of God. This is because an image cannot contain the full truth of God, and therefore, all such images diminish God.

    For example: Often, God is rendered in Human or Animal form. In the west, most often as an old white man with a beard. God as a "him" or "her" or as an "animal" avatar have also been depicted in many religions throughout history. God, in some of these images, is even made to seem aloof, unreachable, unknowable, stupid, uncaring, mean, and confused.

The fact is all imagery representing God diminishes God. It can taint the perspective of God by those viewing such imagery, especially impressionable children. Such imagery can also be used to separate and segregate us.

The answer is not to deface or commit violence against these images, the people creating them, or those viewing them. Instead, we peaceably make our objections known and use logic, reason, and love to create change. Eventually, when there are enough of us, these images will disappear and be seen in museums and as ancient ways of thinking.

3. **Fraud:** It's also exceedingly disrespectful for people and organizations, claiming to be directed by God, or working for the good of society like our holy people, police, doctors, nurses, teachers, firefighters, politicians, government and charities workers, etc. to be corrupt and not fulfill their primary mission and uphold the virtues within the oaths they swore.

EXCLAMATIONS OF HOPE & FEAR OK

Saying things like "My God!" or "God is Most Great!" (Allah Akbar) or "Jesus Christ!" or other exclamations using God when great things happen, either good or bad is ok. The intention behind these calls is out of appreciation, love, happiness, or even fright or fear. We are calling out to bring God into our lives during an intense moment. The feeling behind this type of call is more of a call to a loved one or friend to thank them or to ask for help than a curse.

FIVE REASONS WHY TO RESPECT GOD

1. **It's Possible:** We can't be sure there is no God, and since God is possible, it can't hurt to show some deference to "The Creator." What if you met God later and you became friends? How would you feel about what you said and did in the past?

2. **It's Part of Your Goal:** Your goal is to be a positive person. It's a good practice to remove offensive behavior from your actions. Disrespecting God is a negative way of being. The fact that it's a negative way of being is enough to eliminate it. This practice helps strengthen your mind, builds character, and develops self-control.

3. **It's Offensive:** Since disrespecting God is offensive to so many, removing it can help improve your relationships with others.

4. **You Don't Want to Block the Flow:** You don't want to turn from God or interfere with your connection with God. Disrespecting God is one way you turn from God. So why complicate the issue with this destructive behavior?

5. **You are Good:** Your respect for God flows naturally by wanting to do right by God. It can also come out of profound respect and appreciation for the "Being" who created all of us, this fantastic place, and for giving you a chance.

In the end, respecting God shows self-respect and respect for one another. For non-believers, God could exist, so by showing respect, you are simply ensuring that you are not damaging this key relationship. Also, by eliminating this negativity and false perspective, we will help create a clearer perspective of who and what God is and less friction within our society.

Law 10
Worship Only God, God Does Not Require Worship, & God Can Only Be Freely Worshiped

Worship is the feeling and expression of reverence and adoration for God. Worship is not asking for anything other than forgiveness, and only at times of real feeling. The spark or cause of worship should solely reside within the worshiper as a true expression of a deep desire to say thank you, express love, and appreciation or to be at one with God.

How we express these feelings can vary. If focused correctly, this energy and expression are healthy and can be very motivating. When a lot of people worship together, this effect can be greatly magnified. Ok, now that we have the basics, let's go a little deeper into what these phrases mean.

- **Only God & Not Required:** Worship is a type of devotion reserved <u>solely</u> for God. To be clear, this means we do not worship relics, images, symbols, animals, people, nor other life or things. Worship is thanking, loving, and appreciation, as well as being at one or at peace with God. Additionally, God being the source of everything, God does not require nor demand our worship as God is self-sustaining.

- **Freely Worshiped:** Worship of God is something we can only do out of a free will and true intention for only then is it meaningful. We cannot worship God by going to a building or location, performing any ritual, or reciting words without the true belief, feeling, respect, desire, and good intention to back them up.

Worship is not a requirement or a primary focus of our lives. In fact, it's disrespectful to neglect your life, responsibilities, and other people to worship God. This is especially true when there is no real desire backing it up or if you are doing it out of fear or to evade your responsibilities.

We can't force or coerce anyone to honestly believe in or worship God. Nor can we force anyone to believe in a particular religion, spiritual path, or faith. For even if we do force others to say the words and perform the ritual movements, it does not mean there is true belief and understanding within them.

Formal religious and spiritual worship is only one way to show respect and love for our creator and friend. For those who know that God is ever-present and that everything is "The House of God," then following *The Way* is continual living worship of God. This is because, by following *The Way,* we strive to honor our creator by living rational, positive action every day, in every way. Within this flow of life, we then naturally make time to worship God spontaneously and through reasonably planned occasions out of deep respect, sincere desire, appreciation, and love for our creator and friend.

Ultimately, God can only be freely worshiped because this level of appreciation is reserved only for our Creator, and for it to mean anything, it must be sincere. To do otherwise is disrespectful and a waste of time. True worship of God is demonstrated by living a good life and by expressing sincere gratitude here and there. In the end, whatever you do, do it because you really want to, and don't let it take away from the primary mission God has given you.

STEP 4: CENTER - CONCLUSION

*"Better than a thousand useless words is
one word that gives peace."* - Gautama Buddha

You now know that your core belief system determines your attitude, intentions, thoughts, judgments, choices, words, actions, reactions, emotions, feelings, and other beliefs. Add all of this together, and it's essentially who you are. Any belief system that is worth having must not be forced upon you, and it should be complete, able to stand up to others, reason, morality, and your conscience.

The "10 Laws" just covered comprise a complete core belief system, covering all areas of life, that once confirmed within you act as a compass heading, helping you to judge life moment by moment to ensure you are moving in a positive direction.

To briefly sum up, "The 2 Laws of Purpose" show us that our purpose and the meaning of life are found in making ourselves and everything their best. "The 3 Universal Laws" show us how to care for each other, all life, our world, and the universe in positive ways. "The 5 God Laws" show us how to have a great relationship with our creator as well as develop our religious and spiritual systems, so they bring peace and help all of us.

Together, these "10 Commandments" help us to "live rational, positive action" in critical areas of life. They show us the way, bringing clarity, peace, and moving everything in a positive direction. The deeper your understanding and commitment to these core beliefs, the more they will help you navigate life.

Your choice to live by this code will change your future and our world for the positive. This is because all evil needs to win is for good people to do nothing or to do the wrong things. Armed with the "10 Laws" and *The Way*, you will know what actions to take. It's through centering on these fundamental core values as a species that we can truly unite and make a real difference now and for future generations.

ALL 10 LAWS

"You don't have to teach people how to be human. You have to teach them how to stop being inhuman." - Eldridge Cleaver

Below you can see all the laws in two forms. The first is without the headings, and the second shows them as positive statements. You can see the laws with headings above in "The 10 Laws Defined." You can also get these lists and others on our site as a free download, www.7Way.Me/wd.

1. The Primary Purpose of Life is to Be Your True Self, Live a True Life, and Go to Heaven.
2. The Primary Purpose of Society is to Create Our True Society.
3. Respect Life.
4. All People are Equal.
5. Treat People as You Want to be Treated.
6. There is No God Other than God.
7. We are All Directly Connected with God, and this Connection Cannot Be Broken.
8. God is Our Sole and Final Judge, and We are Judged by Our True Beliefs, Intentions, Words, and Actions.
9. Respect God.
10. Worship Only God; God Does Not Require Worship; God Can Only be Freely Worshiped.

THE 10 LAWS AS POSITIVE STATEMENTS

1. I Know My Primary Purpose is to Be My True Self, Live a True Life, and Go to Heaven.
2. I Know the Purpose of Society is to Create the True Society.
3. I Respect Life.
4. I Know We are All Equal.
5. I Treat Others as I Want to Be Treated.
6. I Know God is the Only God.
7. I Know I Have a Direct and Unbreakable Connection with God.
8. I Know God is My Final Judge, and I Am Judged by my True Beliefs, Intentions, Words, and Actions.
9. I Respect God.
10. I Worship Only God Freely.

Chapter 8
Living a Meaningful Life

"No other version, no matter how perfect it is, would ever feel better than being your True Self." - Edmond Mbiaka

Step 5: Be

The Way directs us to "Live Rational Positive Action." Within the last step, we learned of a core belief system covering all aspects of life with the first law of our code, directing us to become the best person we can.

Therefore, within "Step 5: Be," you will learn how to create your "Daily Way," which is a map that allows you to ingrain essential virtues and foundational best practices within your everyday life very quickly. This knowledge will enable you to take another critical step down your "True Path" toward your "True Self."

Within this step, you will gain an insight into the "Art of Life," the "2 Keys of Time and Ritual," and learn how to master the "Foundations to Life" that will help you be your best physically, mentally, emotionally, and spiritually. It's important to realize on a deep level that the real goal of your "Daily Way" is to teach you to simply "Be" the person that lives these best practices every day naturally without having to try. In this way, your life is a personal journey.

It's your unique positive expression within the commonality of our society, that can have the most significant positive impact. Within *The Way*, the idea is to first focus on critical virtues and best practices that center around several fundamental human conditions we all share. As we firm up our foundations, we will improve ourselves and our world. This strategy also allows us to go farther in all other areas of life.

THE ART OF LIFE

Human society has labeled the highest level of human accomplishment "Art." Art is something that goes beyond the mundane and ordinary. Art is good and can be fun. Also, it can be transcendent and bring our bodies, minds, emotions, and spirit to higher planes of existence. Because of this, we need to explore this concept a little more deeply as it's at the center of everything we strive for and do.

Everything we do can become art if enough care and consideration are applied. Buildings can be just square boxes that are ugly or great architectural works that take our breath away. We often refer to those who have achieved exceptional levels as artists, as in "she is an artist in the boardroom," "kitchen," or on the "court." We say things like, "Wow, he brought that to an art form."

"Art" applied to public and shared places makes all our lives more fulfilling. If our environment is inspiring and beautiful, it naturally helps us be more positive. The use of "Art," media and entertainment can certainly lighten our load and provide much-needed relief.

Life would be much less bearable if bearable at all, without the "Arts." Music, paintings, sculptures, plays, beautiful architecture, pictures, videos, gardens, and other entertainments can lift us, allow us to escape, and help us in many ways. It can help us feel things we would not otherwise feel. Art can help broaden our perspective and aid in understanding. It can inspire us to realize the nobility of human nature and aspire to higher levels of accomplishment. Art can be funny yet compel us to think about profound and meaningful issues.

Art also helps us escape from the drudgeries of life for at least a little while. However, if abused, media and entertainment can be a distraction leading us away from our "True Path," accomplishments, and productive interests and be a massive waste of time. The key is to know how to find the balance.

In essence, Art is the creation of beautiful and thought-provoking works. "Art" and beauty are subjective. We find this sentiment in the saying, "beauty is in the eye of the beholder." This means that not everything is beautiful to all people, and a few things are only beautiful to some people. However, some things are beautiful to most people like flowers or a good view. The benefits of "Art" in our society cannot be solely quantified in terms of wealth or production because the real value to society is so much more significant than either of those measurements.

LIVING AN ARTFUL LIFE

The "Art" of just about anything is found in the journey toward its perfection. We can see *The Way* as a guide to "Living an Artful Life." All we do can be done artfully, in a way that is more thoughtful, mindful, caring, and considerate of how things are done and look. The benefit to society is found when we add everyone's artful positive lives together, for here is where we start creating something really wonderous.

Take the Japanese Tea Ceremony, *for example,* we find the art in every movement, the words that are spoken, the arrangement of everything, to the final product of the tea. However, it goes much deeper into how the tea was grown, the way the workers live and do their jobs, and the mindset of everyone involved and more.

In the end, you can be "Living Art." Searching for the art in all things is natural for us as we strive to be our "True Self" and create our "True Society." Our artful way of being is an expression of the divine found within us, after all. It's through this divine connection and artful human expression that we can transcend to higher levels of being, life, and society.

THE ART OF LIFE CREATES WONDERS

Human life, work, and cooperation at its best is an Art. It creates opportunities for more positive coincidence, harmony, providence, synchronicity, serendipity, and synergy within everyday life and society. These are more than just words; they have the power to change everything very quickly. So, let's quickly go through each one.

- **Positive Coincidence** is something that happens by chance in a positive, surprising, or remarkable way, linking to something in your life.
- **Harmony** is an orderly and pleasing arrangement — existence without destruction and a lack of conflict.
- **Providence** is the wisdom, care, opportunity, and guidance provided by God. Providence encompasses all the others on this list yet goes far beyond them. Providence imparts a sense of the divine and existence of God as in miracles.
- **Synchronicity** is the simultaneous occurrence of events that appear significantly related and have a corresponding positive effect on each other yet have no readily understandable or discernible causal connection.
- **Serendipity** is an aptitude for making desirable discoveries by accident or is a set of circumstances

that align just right so we may gain insight, truth, or understanding.
- **Synergy** is a cooperative action where the effect is much greater than the sum of its parts.

The effects of these positive happenings within our life and society are more significant and inspiring than can be imagined. They open us up to empathy and sympathy, where so many of life's lessons and answers are found. The better the society we create, and the people we become, the more of these positive happenings will naturally occur everywhere. More positive happenings will help us become happier people and provide us with positive energy and more solutions that will help us go further than we could have otherwise.

MASTERING YOUR DAILY WAY

"You'll never change your life until you change something you do daily. The secret of your success is found in your daily routine." - John C. Maxwell

So, if our goal as humanity is not just to live but to live artfully, how do we do that exactly? The "Daily Way" is a customizable basic plan, outline, framework, roadmap, guide, or routine that helps you build positive habits around key virtues and best practices so you may thrive and create an artful life.

WHY WRITE IT DOWN?

Creating your "Daily Way" allows you to get a quick start on developing yourself because mapping out critical parts of your life to a certain level will enable you to reference it, learn from it, and make improvements. This diligence will also allow you greater freedom to find the artful way you can express yourself while doing your best.

Living your "Daily Way" helps keep you focused on your larger purpose, and goals of life, for it keeps all the basics in mind and you on track. Here you will build a solid foundation for your body, mind, emotions, and spirit, and many other vital areas of life as you gain deeper insights along the way.

Basically, in order "To Be" your best, as in having all the good habits integrated within you, you need first to train yourself ingraining essential best-practices as habits. Training requires focus and concerted effort over time. Having your "Daily Way," which is an outline of your life, in a form and in a place that keeps it in mind and easy to reference is key in forming positive habits.

Add in a "Habit Focus Sheet" to help you focus on new or problem areas, and you have a complete basic daily to-do list on how to become a better person. This strategy allows all your life plans and critical information to stay present in your mind. This strategy makes it easier for you to follow along and improve as you go through your day.

HOW LONG DOES IT TAKE TO GET RESULTS?

"Goals give us direction. They put a powerful force into play on a universal, conscious, and subconscious level."
- Melody Beattie

In the end, our goal as people is to simply live a positive rational life without having to try. It takes about 90 days to build a habit. So, within every 90-day cycle that you follow your "Daily Way," you will create lasting positive change and get better and better. You will see some results immediately and more over time. Change is possible; you just need to do it.

Over time, individually and as a society, more and more will become second nature, and you will "Be" without a thought given to its execution. If you were taught the best practices to the basics of life since you were born, it would be just how you do things. In the end, your "Daily Way" is just that, yours. You are the one who sets the goals and the pace using best practices as your example.

CONTROLLING TIME

"Dost thou love life? Then do not squander time, for that is the stuff life is made of." - Benjamin Franklin

Before constructing your "Daily Way," it's crucial that you understand the "2 Keys" of "Time" and "Ritual." They're important because they will help you make everything more efficient and fun. We start with Time as it may be the most precious thing we have. While it's infinite, once gone, it can never be retrieved. The better your use of time, the more productive and fulfilling a life you can have. Time is a deep subject, but we don't need to know everything. We can get started by looking at a few key aspects. Let's start with how we tell time.

Time is a social construct and has no value other than what we agree on. We are all familiar with the standard clock, however, for us to use time effectively within our "Daily Way," we need to understand the phases of the day and how to count "Our Time." Because of the human condition of the day and night cycle and our dependence on sleep, each day is broken up into two primary phases, "awake and sleep." Our Awake period has 4 significant stages, and sleep is noted as one.

- **Morning:** Includes all you must do to get the day going like awakening, eating, and cleaning. Even if you start your day at 11 pm, you still call this your morning phase. Morning is based on when you get up and how long it takes you to complete this stage.

- **Day:** The Day is when you are most active and do the most work. The day starts after your morning is complete.
- **Evening:** Your evening is when you typically wind down from the day, ensuring all is done and that you are ready for tomorrow. It can be a time of cleaning, relaxing, food preparation, entertainment, socializing, uniting with others in common cause, and more.
- **Night** is the time you start to slow down and disconnect and separate yourself from what happened during the day and evening. Here you also perform all the before bed tasks like cleaning our teeth/body, locking up, checking to make sure you left no fire burning, etc.
- **Sleep:** There are different phases to sleep; however, for right now, we need only understand that this is the time we have allocated to be asleep.

COUNTING TIME

As adults, we are generally awake between 15 to 17 hours each day, which means we need about 8 hours of sleep to be healthy. See the "Life Manual: Sleep" for the exact numbers and sleep guidelines and the "Child & Family Guide: Healthy Discipline & Rules: Sleep Rules" for baby, toddler, child, and teen sleep times and help.

Within the "Daily Way," we look at time as starting from when we awaken and then track how many hours we have each day. Tracking allows you to know exactly how much time you have and, therefore, can use it more effectively. Think of it as a countdown timer for your day. Colors are used to indicate the different phases of the day and are noted within the "Daily Way" example below too.

We can write "Our Time" using three numbers. As in 05:12:17, which indicates you are in your 5th hour, and you have 12 to go in your 17-hour day. You can also do it in short form by just using the first number or first and second.

For example, "I'm on my 5th hour." Or "I'm on 7/10," which means you are on the 7th hour and have 10 hours left to go today.

The example below lays out the phases of the day indicated by colors and a 17-hour day that starts at 7 am.

World Time	Our Time
7:00am	01:16:17
8:00	02:15:17
9:00	03:14:17
10:00	04:13:17
11:00	05:12:17
12:00pm	06:11:17
1:00	07:10:17
2:00	08:09:17
3:00	09:08:17
4:00	10:07:17
5:00	11:06:17
6:00	12:05:17
7:00	13:04:17
8:00	14:03:17
9:00	15:02:17
10:00	16:01:17
11:00	17:00:17
12am-7am	Sleep

Phases & Colors

Yellow: Morning

Green: Day

Pink: Evening

Blue: Night

Grey: Sleep

Publishing Note: In some versions of this book color was not included to in order to lower your cost. Please visit 7Way.Me to see & download the color versions.

THE NOW

The crucial next facet of time to understand is how humanity uses it. The flow of time never stops for us. Within the flow of time, there is the past, now, and future. However, it's only in the "now" that we can do anything. Actions in the "now" create our future, and those actions become our past. The "now" is not a point; it's a flow. The flow in the "now" is when we live. The "now" is when our heartbeats, we breathe, think, and do. It's also when we make plans for our future actions.

All "happens" in the "now," and because of this, we need to make the "now" count. For it's only what you do and think in the "now" that becomes your past and creates your future. Within *The Way*, life is seen as continuous, a never-ending exercise, dance, sport, lesson, challenge, test, flow, and stream of the "now," which you are molding to your will so you can end up in a place of your choosing.

As you take control of time in your life, you can get in tune with the rhythm and use it to flow from moment to moment gracefully using transitions to help improve yourself. Luckily, the flow of life includes a repetitiveness that allows you to improve how you act and react from day to day and from moment to moment.

BASIC MOMENTS & TRANSITIONAL MOMENTS

The next key to time mastery is to understand how moments work in the flow of time.

- A "basic moment" is when most things happen. *For example*, being in a conversation with someone or working on a project for a time or getting ready for work or eating lunch.

- "Transitional moments" are the times we spend getting to and from one moment to another.

For example, a transition can be short, like when we walk from our bedroom to the kitchen, or from a meeting room to our desk. It can be a long interval, such as an hour commuting or traveling to get somewhere or to do something.

It's the "go-to and from" and the "times in-between moments" that are considered transitional moments. Transitional moments are essential to master because they allow us to connect and realign with ourselves mentally, physically, emotionally, and spiritually. You can use these transitions as "My Time" (see "My Time" below under the next section). Also, to get the most out of every moment, it's imperative that you understand the information within the "Life Manual: Our Practice."

You can see your "Daily Way" is broken up into moments and transitions as in moment-transition to moment-transition to moment-transition. The moment and the transition are both equally important. Within your "Daily Way," you work to master these moments and the transitions to get the most out of them.

My Time

Now that we understand some of the basics, we need to turn time to our advantage. There are times that we need to set aside and dedicate to ourselves. No matter what is happening in the world, how many troubles you have or work there is to do, you need to be able to take time for yourself. You need separation because you can't perform at your best and be there for your family if you are overstressed, tired, worried, dehydrated, malnourished, and run ragged.

To begin, you need to agree that to tackle all the challenges of life in the best way possible, you need to be at your best, and to be at your best, you need some time to yourself. A prime *example* of "my time" that is absolute is Sleep. The reason for this is that without the right kind and amount of sleep, your mind and body do not perform at their best. You can use "My Time" anytime you need a moment to balance and realign.

Other notable "My Time" moments can include times of fun, self-care, daily tasks, workouts, work, as well as relaxation.

KEYS TO MY TIME

The mental techniques taught within the "Life Manual: Our Practice: Mental Practice: The Skill" will help you to achieve this state of temporary separation and deep mindfulness instantly.

The critical element in "My Time" is what you are thinking and feeling. During "My Time," you can feel good and focus (be mindful) on what you are doing and just let <u>everything</u> else go. "My Time" can be just a ten-second moment to make it all go, purge all negativity, realign with what is real and meaningful, and refill with the positive. It can be a period at night where you relive great happy moments of your past to help find peace before sleep.

At its core, "My Time" is about focusing on what you choose, bringing in good feelings and thoughts as you unwind or do a task. It's being mindful and letting go of all the worry, future jobs, negative feelings, and bad energy. It's about being in that moment fully while you align your body, mind, emotions, and spirit with the positive.

TRANSITIONAL PHASES OF LIFE & TRYING TIMES

"Transitional Phases of Life" are times of trauma and/or great upheaval that can be of longer duration and be very intense. However, even though they are longer, they are still only temporary. Transitional phases can be many things: recovering from an injury or illness, a breakup, rebuilding from a disaster, being out of work, moving to a new location, getting married, having a child, or losing someone.

We are going to take a moment to explore this phase and how you can overcome negative consequences. Extra help can be found later within "Step 6: Unite: Overcoming Negative Thinking, Depression and Suicidal Thoughts" and "Overcoming Negative Addiction."

The key at these times is to:

- Remember, this is only temporary!
- Do what needs to be done so the phase can end in the best way possible as soon as possible.
- If you experience an adverse life event, look for ways to mitigate the negative effects from happening now and again in the future.
- During this trying time, it's imperative to follow our "Daily Way" by keeping the foundations intact. Your routine will allow you to get through it in a better state of mind and body. It will also give you a grounding and sense of accomplishment that is needed during these times and afterward.
- You must also continually remind yourself that it's not going to be this way forever – that this is a temporary phase. You need to take it one day at a time, working hard with your eye on the future goal. You can focus on the small things that can be done now that are all part of your real purpose for being here.
- Having hope and keeping your eye on the objective of getting through this phase while learning all you can is critical. If you do a good job, once you are out of this phase, all the good work done will make you a stronger, better person.

In the end, your ability to master time largely determines your fate/destiny. Remember, you don't know how much you have, and once it is gone, you can never get it back. So, don't create regret by squandering your most precious asset. Use it to its fullest and wisely while you have it!

UNLOCKING THE POWER OF RITUAL

"There is a comfort in rituals, and rituals provide a framework for stability when you are trying to find answers."
- Deborah Norville

Now that we have covered time, let's look at the second key of ritual, and how to use it to your advantage within your "Daily Way." A ritual is an established formal behavior associated with moments and the tasks we do. They are a system of procedures and actions. A ritual is a set, ordered way of doing something that can even have spiritual aspects.

A ritual takes a task to another level by clearly thinking out and implementing a formal way of behavior and action. Rituals can be in the form of activities that do not change to actions that are creative and are rarely, if ever, repeated in precisely the same way.

We all perform rituals within our daily life, some more formal and thought out than others. We can see them in religions, dojos, offices, schools. Rituals are found in ceremony and the way some people shake hands or bow or hug and kiss. It's found in the way we rise in the morning and go to sleep and in how we brush our teeth or eat.

The key to ritual within your "Daily Way" is to use it and not let it use you. Rituals taken too far can become superstition. Rituals do not control you or mean anything other than what you believe. You should never feel that if you don't do a ritual in a certain way or time that something bad will happen. You can always take them or leave them and change them at any time.

Do not create rituals that require you to perform some elaborate series of steps that detract from your life.

RITUAL BENEFITS

Within our "Daily Way," we use "Rituals" within key activities to make them easier, more enjoyable, and fun. They can help us more easily achieve more significant results. They can provide energy, a clear focus, as well as help to bring us to a higher state of mind, body, and spirit than otherwise possible.

You can create rituals to help you with any part of life and join them in moments of "My Time" for an even more substantial effect. Within the "Daily Way," you will build and optimize rituals into your life's critical foundational tasks and transitions to make these tasks more beneficial and fun.

RITUAL PARTS

Rituals generally have up to 8 aspects that include: Physical, Sound, Affirmations, Smell, Sight, Mental, Religious/Spiritual, and Fun (gamification). We can use them separately or combine all or a few to create powerful and effective rituals to enhance any experience.

PHYSICAL

The physical aspects of ritual include our body, what we wear, and touch. To really understand what they mean, lets quickly go through each one.

- **Body:** Here, we can consider every movement and position of our body or move in a free form. *For example,* all actions of your body can be considered down to the finest details such as how you move and breathe, your positions of sitting and standing. Or you can move creatively and freely, letting things happen naturally as we use all the best practices covered within the "Life Manual: Our Practice."

- **Clothes/No Clothes:** Within a ritual, you can consider what to wear as well as other adornments and how they are put on. It can also include how you prepare and clean yourself before dressing. You can also consider performing the ritual without anything covering you.
- **Touch:** You can consider what you touch, and when you touch it. Contact includes the fabrics on your body and those you interact with. *Example*: you can think of purity and the symbolism of touching things like a sacred or special item, pure water, or sunlight.

SOUND

Sound has power. Hearing different sounds can help us all focus, relax, get us energized, and more. Sound within a ritual can come in many forms like music, chants, singing, bells, gongs, nature, listening to someone read a book or speak and more. We can create different playlists for different rituals.

For example, you can have a playlist for peaceful nature meditation music without words to go to sleep and high-intensity music to get going in the morning. *Note* that there is music specifically designed to help us relax or become energized.

Note that using the same sounds throughout our life for some rituals can be useful as the sounds become part of the habit. *For example*, if you use the same music as part of your sleep ritual, it can help bring you to the point where you can sleep as soundly as a child throughout your life.

It's vital when choosing music to ensure the words of the song work well with a positive mindset.

Listening to music with negative connotations can affect us consciously and subconsciously. If you like a song, but the message is negative, try to find an instrumental version of the song. Then you can enjoy the music and even sing your own positive lyrics.

AFFIRMATIONS

An affirmation is a short positive statement that confirms our attitude or goal. The key to any affirmation is found in the three P's as they are always Personal, Present, and Positive.

- **Personal:** All affirmations refer directly to you. You use the pronoun "I" to denote this. Starting an affirmation with "I am" makes it personal and present. "I know and believe I am" is another powerful *example* of how to start an affirmation.
- **Present:** All affirmations must be spoken of in the now as if it's happening in the present flow of time. Affirmations are expressed in the now so that when they take place, the affirmation matches. All affirmations need to be realized in the now of that moment.

  For example, if you say, "I will be happy" or "I am going to make a great speech," you are putting this positive event off into the future where it will never happen.

- **Positive:** Affirmations are always positive and good as they confirm a virtue and/or best practice and/or outcome.

Examples of Affirmations that are Personal, Present, and Positive include: "I Am Positive," "I Am Giving a Great Speech," "I Know, and Believe I Am Happy." You will learn more about how to use this and other powerful techniques within the "Life Manual: Our Practice: Mental Practice."

SCENT/SMELL/AROMA

We find a scent's power in its ability to bring us to a state of mind or stoke a memory instantly. Controlling aroma is a potent tool you can use to change your mood, set the tone, and more. The study of aroma and the effects on your body and mind is called aromatherapy. There are many different scents and effects to experiment with. You can search "guide to aromatherapy" online to find what scent is good for what actions and to promote what feelings as there is limited space here.

- **Which One to Choose?** When choosing a scent for a ritual, think of how common it is. Will you encounter this smell often in life? It's better to pick a scent that you can associate only with your ritual, or at least to avoid a conflict. Usually, it's good to choose a pleasant yet uncommon fragrance for this reason or a scent that common for that purpose.

    It's important to note that certain smells can trigger effects within our body, so you want to make sure you pick something that matches the goal of the ritual.

    For example, for most people, lavender is relaxing and can help us sleep better. Peppermint/spearmint and lemon can stimulate the brain in many positive ways, helping with attention, clear brain fog, and even provide an energy boost.

- **How to Use:** We can release these scents into our environment in many ways. However, it's essential to use natural oil or dried flowers. Stay away from burning incense, candles, chemical-based products, or those required to be plugged in as they can release harmful toxins into your environment and may start a fire.

One of the best solutions is to put a small strip of cloth in a small jar. You can dab or soak scented oil(s) on the piece. The jar can be opened and closed as needed, thus giving you more control of what you smell at what times.

You can spread the scent by merely leaving the jar open or by removing the scented cloth and waving it about the room. You can even place it near a fan or intake for an HVAC (heating, ventilating/ventilation, and air conditioning) system to waft the aroma around the space. You can create a travel size like a little jar or plastic bag with a scented little cloth or cotton ball inside. You can then open it in the car or now and then throughout your travels to give you a lift.

Simply adding a few drops to a bowl of hot water can also work. You can even heat and boil flowers, spices, and herbs on a stove to release a scent into your whole home or workplace.

Another way to spread the scent is to add a little scented oil to purified water in a spray bottle and use it to mist the room. *Note* that there are problems with this method as you are spreading the actual oil into space and not just the scent.

Over time this can permanently affect the smell of that space. Also, oil on surfaces can collect dust, be harder to clean, and may cause damage and/or discolor fabrics and artwork. Therefore, if using this method, be careful where you spray. Pick places that air circulates like corners, unseen carpet areas, the underside of chairs, and other discrete locations.

SIGHT

Everything you see affects you on a conscious or subconscious level. During a ritual, you can focus your vision on images that can help you.

For example, during your meditation ritual, you could be looking at a pleasing environment, picture, mandala, candle, or even a blank wall.

What you see can change as you can start by looking at one thing and add in others as you go along. You can even include inspirational words that you look at and say out loud. As you think about what to look at during rituals, it's important to remember that colors evoke feelings. The color feeling relationship is a personal one. So, consider this when choosing colors for all rituals, workouts, meditation sessions as well as life and workspace.

MENTAL

The mental aspects of the ritual concern your thoughts and include things like purifying "Your Power" and using "The Skill" or meditation techniques such as focused, unfocused, clearing, and visualization during any ritual. You can focus your mind through images and by repeating or chanting key phrases, virtues, and affirmations. You can play mind games and more. You can learn more about the mental aspects that you can add to your ritual within the "Life Manual: Our Practice: Mental Practice."

SPIRITUAL/RELIGIOUS

You can add a spiritual aspect to any ritual by using everything in this section in a way that opens you up to higher levels of existence, our universe, nature, the divine, holy, sacred, and God. Pick things to say and do that inspire and help you connect. Find what works best for you.

GAMIFICATION & FUN

Gamification is the application of typical elements of gameplay. *For example,* point scoring, competition with self and others, rules of play, rewards, and fun. The idea of gamification is to help incentivize activities to make them more fun and less tedious.

Gamification helps add more happiness to your life. Gamification can mean adding in things like listening to books and music, combining dance and martial arts with our chores, and so much more. The possibilities are endless. Gamification can be applied to our personal life as well as work within the systems of our society.

Gamifying and adding fun to your life is a way to encourage yourself to work harder on things that are important to you. It can make things easier to accomplish because of the energy created through the incentive of having fun. Achievement is rewarding and creates positive energy that can be used to push yourself even further. The accomplishment of goals promotes a positive self-image, which helps you become your "True Self."

Adding gamification to our lives and systems of society helps everything become more fun and productive. Serious tasks don't always have to be done in a serious way. In fact, scientists have created games out of problems they have, like sorting and finding ways to put things together. Some problems they have worked on for years only to have them solved in a few days by people playing a game.

Gamification Caution: Gamifying your "Daily Way" so you can compete and challenge yourself is excellent.

However, it's not a good practice to compare your progress on your "Daily Way" to others. Your life mastery is not a competition between people as we are all on our own path, and these things can't be truly compared. However, there are parts of our "Daily Way" that can be shared and even made into a game. Take extra care when you gamify and include others.

It's essential to make sure the process stays focused on you and your growth. Gamification is about developing your character sheet, stats, skills, and leveling up. Here you are joining with others to have fun, receive encouragement, and help each other not to compete against each other.

A Special Note on Sound & Smell: Both sound and smell are very powerful, and together they can bring us to a mental state instantly like nothing else. *For example,* as noted, if you use the same scent and playlist from birth, you will be able to more easily enter sleep throughout your entire life, regardless of circumstance.

RITUAL SUMMARY

In the end, "Rituals" integrated within the "Foundations of Life" make life easier, efficient, and more enjoyable. Our primary purpose for integrating rituals within each of the "Foundations" is so that they are more deeply rewarding and enjoyable as well as something to rely on during hard times. This is because it's these ingrained habits that will get you through.

For example, in a crisis, automatically eating, sleeping, and doing the other "Foundations of Life" well means you can do a better job handling that crisis and will ensure that once you come out of it, you are still in a good position, if not a better one.

THE FOUNDATIONS OF LIFE

The key is to take what you just learned about Time and Ritual and apply that to each of these foundations as you go through your "Daily Way" every day. This application will allow you to enjoy and get more out of everything.

The "Foundations of Life" are covered in detail within the *Life Manual*, and they include:

- **Life Tasks:** Within this section, you will learn how to do everything more effectively and efficiently, allowing you to achieve more with less effort in all areas of life.

- **Sleep:** Within this section, you will learn how to get the best healing sleep and how to awaken correctly. Mastering sleep will not only set you up for a great day; proper rest will also help you feel better, be healthier, and achieve more throughout your life.

- **Our Practice:** Within this section, you will learn the basics of good practice sessions. You will learn how to properly train your body, mind, emotions, and spirit as well as how to refine your power, develop your skill, and how to have fun during it all.

- **Fuels:** Here, you will learn how to get the best and correctly consume light, air, water, food, and information, as well as how to make them all work for you and not against you.

- **Self-Care:** Within this section, you will gain the keys to caring for your body correctly, optimizing your health, healing, healthcare, and extending your active years through learning longevity techniques.

These are named the "Foundations of Life" because, as you can see in the "Daily Way," these are the foundations that human days are built around. These are things we all do and/or should do if we are to be our best.

As humans, we all need to master the basics in all these foundational areas of life if we are be our "True Self." Mastery of the foundations is one of those undeniable truths of life. The reason is that you must balance and maintain many critical aspects of life to a certain level if you are to be the best you can be. Balance in many areas is essential because if any part breaks down or gets damaged, it can divert your focus and take everything else you are doing down with it. To say it another way, you are only as strong as your weakest link.

DAILY WAY EXAMPLE

The image below is an *example* of the "Daily Way" in a basic spreadsheet format showing how it looks when filled out. The goal is to customize yours to fit your life. You can get a customizable version and App on www.7Way.Me/wd.

In this example, the top row starts on the left with "World/Our Time," then the next column is "The Foundation of Life," and finally, the last column lists the phase of the day and tasks that need to be done. Everything is color-coded to match the time-period and foundation type. The 1st hour of the day in this example starts at 7 am with a morning wakeup, warmup, practice session.

Publishing Note: As noted above, color may not be included in the "Daily Way" examples or other images within this version in order to lower your cost. Please visit our website to see & download the color versions.

Living a Meaningful Life

My Daily Way (1 of 4)

World / Our Phase	Foundation	Morning
7:00 Am 1:15:17 Morning	1st Practice Awaken	**Awaken Slowly:** Eyes Closed. (Note: Quick or Slow based on Need and Time Available) If Ok (i.e. quick check for pain, critters, time) 1. Do not move 2. Play with Consciousness 3. Dream - Remember and Record / If Bad change if and was gone. I won, did not get hurt, was not lost **Awaken Warmup:** Mind: The Way as Light, I believe I have a PL JA/PPMESSA, Our Code The Art Power and Skill 1. In Bed: Primary Warm up Breathing Exercises - Deep and Others as needed - Tongue Twisters Straighten, Lengthen and Flex/release, Potato Ankles, Wrists, Joints, Isometric others as needed 2. Exit Bed: Careful: Slide off to Floor if needed - Drink water / Standing Warmup / Make Bed /Open Blinds
	Transition	Body: Stretch arms walk using mesa steps Mind: PPMESSA / Consider next actions - Choose Food or Bio Break
	Self Care	Bio Break: Pee rules - Don't rush, learn to hold. Other go asap and don't delay. Read, Stand or Sit properly - Finish cleanly
	Transition	Body: Stretch arms walk deeper lunging steps Mind: The Way As Light - Consider next Step
	Fuel	**Food/Drink:** Water/Minerals 1+ Large Glass, Apple or other. Start Tea. Take Supplements
	Life Tasks	1. Start Music 2. Check Other House/Outside Todo Lists. Also Cleaning, Watering, Laundry, Vacuuming, etc. 3. Use Tray: Collect Dishes / Other that needs to go down - Ex Water. 4. Go Down: In Hall. Set Tray. 5. Get Newspaper, Put Mail in Mailbox 6. Hang Upside Down. 7. Open Blinds 8. Collect Tray from hall and bring to kitchen and unload. 9. Prepare Blast: Mixed dark berry's & ground seed/wintermax, seed, and dry. 10. Go Outside: Look at Sun w/Closed Eyes - Feel body - Check Weather for outside or inside morning practice. 11. Clean Kitchen etc 12. Bring Tray Up to Office. Put Breakfast in place.
	Transition	Body: Stretch arms walk using ninja steps Mind: PPA / PMA / PPMESSA / I am happy / I am having fun Remember: The Power, The Skill - Shazaamm! Prepare for Workout

My Daily Way (2 of 4)

World / Our Phase	Foundation	Morning Continued
7:30 Am Morning	2nd Practice	Remember sound book music, & Aroma. Do face/eye/voice/tongue/yell/ exercise too. Observe to Refine not Judge **Body:** Warm/Stretch, Yoga, FastFeetFists(FFF), Weapons (sword) (katana, 2wasashi, 2gladiator), hammers, tomahawks, nunchaku, sticks), St, TaiChi, PBags, Swim, Ride bike, Parkour, Back, Dance, MMA, Aikido, KravMaga, Belflex, Treadmill, Rowing - Handstands, Hang pull ups on bars/rings, Isometrics/Flexing, etc **See Mini Workout and Meditation Sheet. Observe/Do:** Breath, Balance, Speed, Strength, Endurance, Accuracy, Slow motion, Position, Focus. **Mind Meditation:** Roundabout &/or focus: Affirmations, visualization, realization & integration **Remember:** Still beginning of day so go into clear and focused intensity
	Transition	The Art of The Transition
8:00 Am 2:15:17	Fuel	Eat Breakfast: Mix dark berry's & ground seed/winter max mix. 1 Large glass or 2 of water after - little during. Sun Break. However if needed separate close protein/carb
	Transition	The Art of The Transition
8:30	Self Care	Clean Body. Get Ready for Work / Do other stuff as needed / Teeth: Floss, Brush, Scrape Tongue
	Major Transition	Go to Location to do Our Work

World / Our Phase	Foundation	Day
9:00 Am 3:14:17 Day		**Our Work of the Day:** Choose - Job, Life Tasks, Family, Hobbies - Jousting with others (vote, take poll, give time, etc.) See end of day for more. Day Review: Compare BNWA with The Laws, Code, Goals. Review Lists, Do Most Critical Items when Fresh. Check for or local combination Mail/electronics/phone First Refresh Day-Plan/Projects/Tasks: Computer, Outside, Inside Tasks. Sunday Fasting/Cleanse if time.
	General Work Practice	**Work:** Focus on doing a great job. Draw on Power and use The Skill - Balanced body **Body:** Follow 5 Min Rule - If sitting for hour stand and move for at least ¼ If standing sit/lie down/hang upside down. Check Body Position and Breathing working jaw "N". **Stay up on Hydration / Snacks as needed** **Mind as opportunities permit:** Our Time, Our Practice, PPMESSA, The Way Light, My Code, Other Affirmations, The Power/My Skill, Mind Games (memory, strategy, puzzles, etc.) Learn from The 4 Pillars

The Way | Step 5: Be

My Daily Way (1 of 4)

World	Our Phase	Foundation	Day- Continued
	General Work Transition	Look for Transitions, bio break, water, snack, making copies, going to meeting, etc. **Look for Mini Training Opportunities:** Extra deep sweat picking something up, stretch while making copies, etc. **Brain Development Training:** Play mind games here and there. Think on The Way, Our Code, PPMESSA. Learn from The Book: The Way and 3 Pillars.
10 Am 4:13:17	Mini Fuel/Practice	Sun Break / Workout / Meditate Hydrate
11 Am 5:12:17	Fuel	**Snacks:** Nuts/resins/fig/dates, Tomato (ES), Citrus (ES), Melon (ES), Avocado, Green Drink, Tea, Apple, Banana, Sprouts, Moringa Oleifera. Phylum shake, herbs/spice shots. **Hydrate:** Pure Water/Minerals, The Drink. (ES) Eat Separately.
12 Pm 6:11:17	Fuel	Sun Break / Hydrate
12:30 Pm 7:10:17	3rd Practice	Choose Practice. See 2nd Practice. Do new body move mind if dressed. Sun: 5 to 10 - Gardening, cleaning, minor outdoor / Learn more of The Way
2 Pm 8:9:17	Fuel	**Food/Water:** Yam /Potato or Grain or Protein. Add greens/sprouts, other vegs asparagus, Brussel sprouts etc. Green drink. No Caffeine after 12. Sun
3 Pm 9:8:17	Fuel	**Snacks:** Nuts/resins/fig/dates, Tomato (ES), Citrus (ES), Melon (ES), Avocado, Green Drink, Tea, Apple, Banana, Sprouts, Moringa Oleifera. Phylum shake, herbs/spice shots. **Hydrate:** Pure Water/Minerals, The Drink. (ES) Eat Separately.
4 Pm 10:7:17		Wrap day: Make lists, tasks, plan tomorrow etc. Sun Break.
	Major Transition	Finish Work move to evening activity. Choose from list or other.

World	Our Phase	Foundation	Evening
5 Pm 11:6:17 Evening	4th Practice	**Evening Consider:** Social, Get Outside - Sun. Stay In. Socialize (friends, family, and new) Time with friends/family, Life Tasks Check Lists, Refine Life, Clean/Tidy/Organize, Hobby, Write/Record, Learn something new, Join with others (vote, take poll, give time, etc.) Entertain: Reading/Listening, Music, News, Projects, Gardening, Deep Practice (meditation and/or body), Spiritual Pursuits, healthy rewards, Job stuff if need, Journal, take Pictures, Get out of Comfort Zone. **Things to Do:** If energy high be sure to burn and store to sleep is good. Prepare for next day / The Way
	Fuel	**Dinner:** The soup, Kale/other deep green, onion, steamed garlic, carrot, avocado, artichoke, olives etc. as needed. Add Hot pepper & other herb/space for health as needed. H2O little during more after. Tofu/Chicken as needed for protein.
6 Pm 12:5:17	Life Tasks	Close up house, get mail, lock, clean/tidy/organize. Day Wrapped !

My Daily Way (4 of 4)

World	Our Phase	Foundation	Evening - Continued
7 Pm 13:4:17	Fuel	**Water:** Ensure fully Hydrated 1.5 Hour Before Bed / After only little. **Food:** Night Snacks: Nuts, figs, raisins, dates, carrots, other veg, green drink, phylum shake, night time teas.
8 Pm 14:3:17		Daily Review: Compare BIWA w/Laws, Code, Goals. How did I do? Follow Daily Way? Lessons, refinements, do better? Make notes for tomorrow.
	Major Transition	From Evening to Sleep Prep Time. Adjust timing to work with day.

World	Our Phase	Foundation	Night
9 Pm 15:2:17 Night		**Ensure Day is Wrapped:** Next Day Planned, Tasks written and Sorted, Tidy Rooms. **Start Winding Down.** Focus on relaxing and no doing to much work. **Begin Ritual:** The Music/Aroma/ Actions. Peace/Relax	Our Time. **NOTE:** Begins early to ensure have time to close and do. Can start anytime. Reward Self w/Early Sleep if needed.
	Fuel	Ensure Hydration at least 1.5 hours before bed // Light Snack and Sleep Tea if needed
10 Pm 16:1:17	Self Care	Cleansing: Face, Skin, Teeth: Floss, Brush, Scrape Tongue.
Night Preparing to Sleep	5th Practice	**1. Before Getting in to Bed: Start Music / Aroma Therapy** **Body:** Warm down. Lengthen (ground and hang upside down), realign, stretch as needed. Face, tongue, eyes, BackBar, Arms and hamstring deep stretch and hold. **Mind:** Let Go of Day. Write notes. Use Skill to be at this moment facing toward our dreams. **2. In Bed: Our Time: Locked Down** 1. **Body:** On stomach and/or back. Straighten, lengthen and Rotate joints. Get comfortable. 2. **The Drill.** 2 Step Mind Light/Deep Breath/Flex/Relax 1. Same Time Image Accepting Light/Breath In/Flex whole body 2. Be Light / Breath Out / Relax Mind/Body TOTALLY. Repeat until wont dream sequence. 3. **Begin Dream Sequence** and also repeat "I am asleep" as needed. Image letting go, jumping of dragons. The Place, The Plan, The Power - make the best fantasy.
11Pm-7Am 8hr		Sleep

As noted, the "Foundations of Life" are represented within the second column in the *example* "Daily Way." The goal is to understand the fullness of each of these "Foundations" so you can optimize your life, health, and longevity.

World	Our Phase	Foundation
700 Am 1:16:17 Morning	1st Practice Awaken

The "Foundations of Life" have been separated into little mini-guides within the *Life Manual*. This information will help you master each of these critical areas of life. The goal is to gain a general understanding of all the foundations as well as to review them anytime you need help with these essential areas of life.

Your deep understanding of each of these foundations means that the small references within your "Daily Way" will trigger a more profound understanding. This connection between the small references and the more profound meaning will allow you to get more out of everything, and this is what will enable you to keep getting better and better over time.

It should seem obvious that optimizing how you do all your tasks of life, sleep, train yourself, consume fuels, care for yourself, and more will help you become your best and in all other areas of your life.

To be clear, understanding this information is <u>critical</u> if you are to be "Truly Successful." This is because to master the wholeness of you (mind, body, emotions, and spirit) requires vital knowledge. The *Life Manual,* along with the *Child & Family Guide,* brings you these keys of information so that you can create greater happiness within your life as fast as possible.

HABIT FOCUS SHEET

*"Without goals, and plans to reach them, you are like
a ship that has set sail with no destination."*
- Fitzhugh Dodson

Another helpful aid in your quest to ingrain essential virtues and best practices is called the "Habit Focus Sheet." As you go through each 90-day cycle following your "Daily Way," more and more virtues and best practices will become a habit and second nature.

Use of the "Habit Focus Sheet" can help you master best practices that are new or that you are having a difficult time. Here you list each one and then check off your completion of those best practices throughout the full 90-day period. The use of the sheet helps you stay on track and provides a sense of accomplishing something difficult. In the end, if successful, you will be well on your way to building permanent best practice habits. Go to www.7Way.Me/wd for a downloadable customizable version and app.

To use the sheet, you need only list a few habits you are trying to build and having difficulty. You can then track every day by placing a mark on the chart. You can use a check or x to indicate success or not, or you can use colors such as red to show a miss, a blue for an ok job, and a green for doing it well. Using this will aid you through every 90-day cycle, transform your life, and create a better self. The key is to keep working at it.

You can only fail if you stop. It's also essential to view this as a temporary process, a "Life Transitional Moment," that will not last or always be this way. You are working to implement permanent changes that will make things better. Once each cycle is over, you will be making more and more progress toward your better self.

The first image is an *example* of the blank "Habit Focus Sheet," and the second *example* shows how it could look when filled out. The goal is to customize yours to fit your life and current goals.

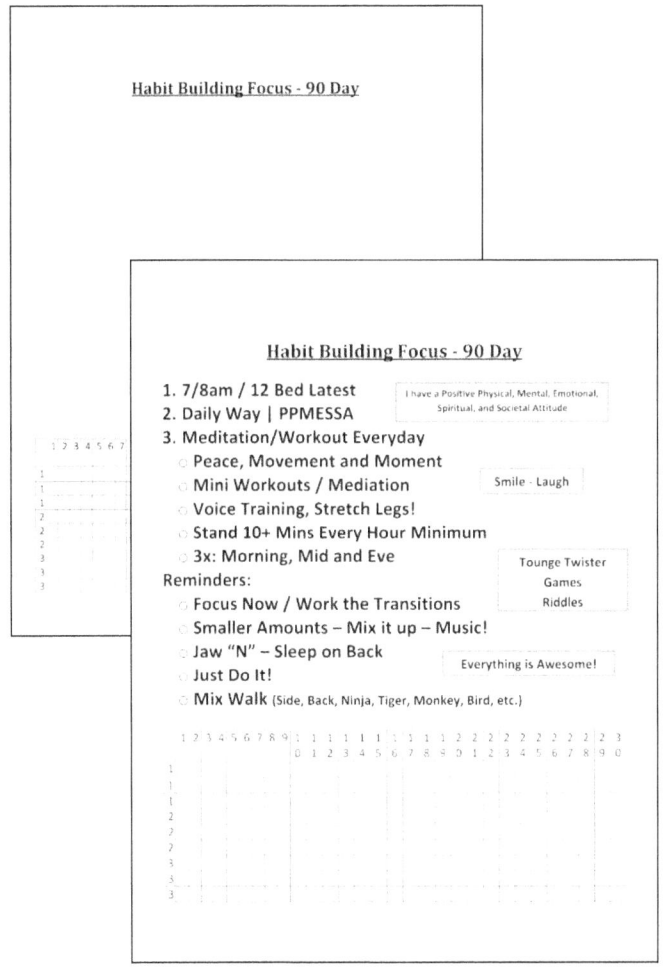

THE WAY | STEP 5: BE

DAILY WAY IMPLEMENTATION STRATEGY
1. **Learn:** First, seek to understand the whole of *The Way*.
2. **Construct:** After you understand enough, create your own "Daily Way" to fit your life.
3. **Follow:** Now that you have it created, you need only follow and refine it as you go forward.

You can start building your "Daily Way" right now if you feel a great need, or you can wait until after you have finished the rest of *The Way*. It's important not to let building your "Daily Way" at this stage distract you from finishing *The Way* if this is your first read.

This strategy is recommended because there is information in the later steps that you may want to integrate into your "Daily Way." Also, gaining the knowledge within the *Life Manual* associated with each of the "Foundations of Life" is key as it allows you to master each foundation and your day. Be sure to include an understanding of the *Child & Family Guide* as it contains more information that will help with your relationships and children.

To get results, you have a few ways to approach implementation.

- o **Slow & Easy:** For some, it's better to start with the easy and small than to make drastic changes all at once. You can pick all the things you feel you can implement now without much of an issue then work towards the others as you move forward.
- o **Powerful:** For some, it's preferable to jump in with both feet. Here you make a drastic change that encompasses everything you can. This strategy, if implemented correctly, can yield the most benefits in the shortest time frame. This strategy works because

many virtues and best practices work together, allowing for the easier forging of habits in more areas at the same time.

- o **Moderate:** Some of you will like a mix where you implement some drastic changes and take small steps in other areas.

The key, in the beginning, is to start with the way that allows you to get going as quickly as possible. Even if that means only one thing, it's better than nothing. If the method you choose is not working, you can try the other. If you are working at it, you are following the strategy.

More Than One Daily Way

When creating your "Daily Way," it may be beneficial to create more than one. When I started, I created two versions and updated my main version all the time. The first version I called "The Perfect Day," which reflected how I wanted to live. The second version that I called my "Daily Way" accounts for all the restraints in my life yet also all that I could do now. As time went on, I worked to change my lifestyle so I could integrate more of the "Perfect Day" into my "Daily Way."

1. **The Daily Way:** You can have one general "Daily Way" that covers every day and/or create some for weekdays, others for weekends, holidays, and vacations. If your life varies a lot, you can even create one for each type of day you live, as in-office days, at home days, travel days, meeting days, writing days, and more. The key is to find what works best for you.

2. **The Perfect Day:** This version of your "Daily Way" reflects the ideal version of how you would like to live every day if you were in complete control of your life.

3. **Other Daily Ways:** You can also create "Ways of the Moment." Think of these as mini-best-practice or how-to lists covering the best way to do something. These lists can cover what order and how to do certain tasks while incorporating all the best practices described within *The Way* and its *Life Manual* and *Child & Family Guide*." Think of them as shortlists of how you would optimally like to do something. The mini-ways can cover daily, relatively complex tasks to tasks you do occasionally.

For example, you might create a mini-way of the steps and actions you take when going to work or the gym to ensure you to it as efficiently as possible without missing anything or for when you cook or clean your living area. You might write up all the things you do before, while on, and after a trip to be prepared, safe, enjoy it while there, and to get back into your routine after you return.

You can share your "Ways of the Moment" how-to lists, pick one for something you are doing, vote for the best, and help improve them all through the app and our site: www.7Way.Me/wd.

DAILY WAY TIPS:

- Remember, following your "Daily Way" will become more natural; the more successful you are overtime for within every 90-day cycle, you will be building habits that will be your natural way of doing things.

- If you join with other people who are also working to follow *The Way*, the whole process will become easier, especially if they live with you.

- Review your "Daily Way" and "Habit Focus" throughout the day to ensure that you stay on track.

- Refine everything as you go for it's through the refinements to your life that you can reach even greater heights of "True Success." Knowing this is key to see your "Daily Way" as a living document and be sure to add all the refinements and little things you find missing as you go. It's in this process of perfecting your life that you will naturally begin to live artfully.

THE ANTI-DAILY WAY

The Way and your "Daily Way" are all about helping you be your best and balance your life. However, you can't forget that you can get stronger through occasional stressing of all these factors.

For example, learning how to "fast" helps you deal with hunger more effectively and allows your body to clean itself out. Stressing the low and high temperatures allows your body to regulate temperature more effectively.

You can work stresses of all kinds into your life to help make you stronger. It's important not to overstress yourself too often without recovery, as it will have a negative effect. The key is to find the balance, for, without this stress, you can't become stronger. You can take this idea of stressing yourself and add it to the fact that you also learn from the negative and the new. Then apply this to your "Daily Way."

For example, sometimes you need to do what you want, and that might be nothing, or it might be to break every one of your "Daily Way" plans and go do something else.

First, it's essential to understand that this is natural. Sometimes you need to be free and do something else new to find answers. We, as a human race, generally need direct experience, and often we need to be "burned to learn," too.

Sometimes we must take a negative path to find our "True Path."

Occasionally living the anti-way can be useful, so if you go off the plan, do not beat yourself up. Look for the lesson and integrate it. It can make your "Daily Way" better. Often going off your "Daily Way" can make you appreciate it even more. However, don't use this as an excuse to do it too often, especially in the beginning, while creating essential habits or else in 90 days this "Anti-Way" could become a habit you live.

PROBLEMS FOLLOWING OUR DAILY WAY

Some issues preventing you from following parts of *The Way* come from the environment and society in which you live. Sometimes, communities are not conducive to you becoming your "True Self." In the end, it does not matter what your challenges are; challenges exist. Your only option is to overcome and show the rest of us that the problem exists or be hurt, distorted, or crushed. We all need to help create a better world so that the path to "True Success" is not blocked for anyone.

Also, even if you can't show any outward sign of positive change, you can still do something profoundly meaningful. Real change starts from within anyway. You can change from within and hide it away until you can be free. You can do this while you make plans, bide your time, and be patient while looking for opportunities.

THE WHOLE POINT

You can integrate much of *The Way* into your life through your "Daily Way" and "Habit Building Focus Sheet." Your "Daily Way" is your customized roadmap that is reflective of your "True Path," which leads to your "True Self," and "True Life." The whole point of your "Daily Way" and "Habit Focus Sheet" is to help you focus on the integration of crucial virtues and best practices into your life so they may become second nature as soon as possible. This focus is how *The Way* helps you achieve unity of purpose and your ultimate goal in life.

It's through integrating the complete core value system outlined in "Step 4: Center" with the "2 Keys of Time and Ritual" applied to the "Foundations of Life" within your "Daily Way" that fixes and focuses most of who you are in mind, body, emotion, and spirit.

The effect of your effort, focus, training, and nailing down the "Foundations of Life" to a high level or even at a decent level will have a synergistic effect that is much greater than the sum of the parts. As you go through training yourself and focusing on all these positive ways, over time, your life and our world will change for the better.

Your journey can include positive changes that you don't even intend. As you become more positive, fit, and healthy, new possibilities and opportunities will open to you. The effect upon your life, those around you, and within your society is profound and is not to be underestimated. We are the power; we all are the leaders and followers that make up "the masses" of this world. This means if we are all focused on the positive, this will reflect within our life and the society we create.

STEP 5: BE - CONCLUSION

"Be yourself, but always your better self." - Karl G. Maeser

In the end, it's important to remember you are living *The Way*, not living <u>for</u> *The Way*. You are <u>using</u> your "Daily Way," it's not forcing you to do anything. You are only competing with yourself. The goal of *The Way* and the "Daily Way," "Habit Focus" and other tools is to create a "Constant Mental Focus" (CMF) or a state of mindfulness on "Living Rational Positive Action" (*The Way*) every day so you can be the best you can be. Living *The Way* is an ever-present state of being that you can always come back to if lost. Your choice to live rational, positive action is your attentive spirit, subconscious, and higher self-getting in sync with every moment of your life.

CHAPTER 9
FINDING UNITY

"Unity is strength... when there is teamwork and collaboration, wonderful things can be achieved."
- Mattie Stepanek

STEP 6: UNITE

So now that you have a complete and positive core belief system and daily life plan, for you to be truly successful, your best, happy, and to have a positive effect on significant issues, you must unite with other people. Unification allows us all to offer and receive happiness, help, motivation, inspiration, as well as participate in solutions. Note that "Step 6: Unite" starts here in chapter 9 and goes through chapter 15.

Within "Step 6: Unite," you improve how you interact with others and your society by learning how to put your best foot forward, how to nurture friendships, how to communicate better as well as how to handle and improve all relationships, both negative and positive. Note that you will also find more relationship-focused best practices within the *Child & Family Guide*. Much of the advice about healthy and happy parenting, relationships is also applicable to any loving relationship.

This step also includes the keys to how you can unite to manage power, government, business, wealth, and other systems to peacefully create positive change within our society. It's through this foundational knowledge on how you interact within society that will allow much of the rest of what you need to fall into place naturally.

Humanity's need for other people is our greatest strength but also our greatest weakness. You need positive relationships (friends, family, role models, guardians, mastermind group, etc.) with different people to attain the virtues of happiness, hopefulness, health, wisdom, security, and so many more. This dependence on your society and other people to be happy and positive means you need to ensure that these relationships, and your part within them, are the best they can be.

Ideally, relationships are synergistic in that all those who participate become better people. To do your part, you need to know the keys to interacting with other people. The goal is to support, reinforce, comfort, push, and help each other on our journey. To get us started, let's look at what unity really means.

What is Unity?

The idea of "unity" is a state of oneness and harmony between people and other life. Unity does not mean that we are all the same. Its unity within diversity. Unity is joining together based on our values and a common cause.

For example, we might unite in many different ways to ensure that our societal systems such as water, food, government, education, and business are running well.

The problem is that most often, when things are going well, good people focus on their lives and do not actively engage in large numbers as much. This balance only really changes when there is something very positive or negative happening, for here we join together to celebrate or protest.

The key to the "True Society" is that we all need to be continuously united in some key areas to ensure that our societal systems are running well. Remember, just because things are going well right now does not mean it will continue or that it's going well everywhere. So, by uniting, you can be vigilant in critical areas of society and ensure that everything keeps improving. Remember, without the good being active, entropy, and evil win.

In the end, uniting with other people who are looking to better themselves and our world in positive ways will allow you to have better relationships, build a better society, and help you become your "True Self." To be clear, this is not optional for as we said uniting with others allows you to offer and receive happiness, help, motivation, inspiration as well as participate in solutions. You need to find "your people," "your tribe," "your family," "your true friends" to really BE happy and your best for it's through these interactions that you find happiness, companionship, learn, can become better and make a real difference in the world.

ROLE MODELS, GUARDIANS & MASTER MIND GROUPS

"Setting an example is not the main means of influencing others; it is the only means." - Albert Einstein

To go deeper into how we interact within society, we need to understand three key groups. They are Role Models, Guardians, and Master Mind Groups. The reason these three facets of how we interact within society are listed first is that all of us are affected by our role models from birth. We need to help, protect, and defend each other. We all also need help at things we are not good at doing.

If you stop and think about having positive role models and guardians looking out for you and a mastermind group to help you along, I think you can understand why these are an excellent place to start.

As a force in your life, the three are much more beneficial when positive and working together.

ROLE MODELS

Those you spend the most time around and are influenced by are your role models. It's important to know who your role models are as they have a profound influence on who you become.

In the beginning, these people are chosen for you by life circumstances and those raising you like your family and teachers. As you get older, however, you have more of a choice with whom you spend your time. It's essential to try and spend time with those who help you become better, and with those, you can help.

The key here is to look at everyone you choose to spend time with, such as your friends and family. Even consider your heroes, leaders, and the famous people you admire, follow, watch, listen to, and read about.

Consider the influence these people are having on you.

- Can you see how they shape your views, mannerisms, ways of speaking, and thinking?
- Are they helping you become a better person?
- Are you just interested in them because they are powerful, famous, wealthy, and good looking or because they are really doing something positive in the world or for you?

Once you know if your role model is a positive or negative influence, you can decide if this person is worthy of adoration or emulation or even your time. Time spent following the doings of famous people should be for short bursts and only to get knowledge, inspiration, and energy that you use to do things within your own life the best way possible.

High Expectations: Having an inspired leader or role model motivates people to become and do more than they could otherwise. Being an inspiring positive role model is vital for all of us but especially for those in role model positions such as parents, teachers, police, faith, business, and government leaders, and all other leadership positions. You, as a role model and authority figure, can inspire people to greatness through your positive actions and words as well as by having high expectations. Our leaders' high expectations can really help us as individuals and as a group, to work harder, go farther, and behave better than we could otherwise.

GUARDIANS

We must all be guardians and keepers of each other. We must be guardians because, as you know, any of us can go astray, get lost, make mistakes, be corrupted, and go along with corruption if enough other people are participating. We are our brothers' and sisters' keepers, as it's often the lost, lonely, and desperate who do the most harm and need the most help.

You need to be vigilant, for sometimes it's only someone from the outside that can end the cycle of abuse. Often, an insider blowing the whistle is how great hidden wrongs perpetrated behind closed doors are brought into the light and fixed. Without people being called out and corrected, offered aid, help, or advice, some of them will not walk the positive path and will be or remain corrupted. It's all of our duty, as part of this human societal web, to be there for each other. The consequences for not taking care of everyone can be cataclysmic as we have all seen the atrocities the lost and broken inflict upon us.

Their ability to kill and destroy will only get greater as we advance. This is because it's the lost, corrupted, isolated, misguided, angry, enraged, desperate, hated, and lonely who fall under the influence of evil, heretics, and false leaders. The lost are the ones who join hate groups, who unleash the horrors upon the rest of us. We must <u>All</u> be the guardians of peace working to create and preserve all that is good if we are to reach everyone. Being protectors of the common good is not optional. Therefore, we must all work to ensure the lost are found.

Master Mind Group

As you grow and learn, you usually find your strengths and weaknesses. An excellent practice used to compensate for your weaknesses is with a "Master Mind Group." A "Master Mind Group" is made up of people that have skills, knowledge, and wisdom you do not have or don't have to their level. The best mastermind partners are those who complement each other, as they each offer the other something they need.

For example, you are a high-level businessperson who has no talent or interest in high-level math or fashion. While you do not have a facility in these areas, you need access to this knowledge when you are doing accounting for your business or when choosing clothes for work and socializing.

Today, your mastermind group can be part digital as in the tools and apps we use as well as with connections you make all over the world. You can form mastermind groups that last for a lifetime to very short periods to cover a project. To this end, as you move through life, it's important to develop friendships and relationships with people that have skills, information, and contacts that you do not have and to be there for others looking to do the same.

HOW TO CREATE POSITIVE RELATIONSHIPS

"All for one, one for all, united we stand, divided we fall!"
– The Musketeers

Ok, now let's talk about how you can become a better friend, family member, citizen, role model, guardian, and be a contributing member of a productive mastermind group. To start, we need to go into how to create lasting positive relationships.

The benefits you can attain from positive relationships and by living within a positive community are innumerable. In fact, loneliness and high-stress relationships are toxic, and if prolonged, will hurt you physically, mentally, emotionally, spiritually, and shorten your life.

Conversely, positive relationships help you grow as a person, cope better, and allow you to receive a hand up when you need it. Being a good person and around good people enables you to give and receive motivation, encouragement, inspiration, and help. You can find and be a positive mentor, coach, and role model. Thus, you can be a positive influence as well as be influenced by other positive people. Only through unity with other people can you influence and manage large societal systems and issues.

THE WAY TO AN ATTRACTIVE PERSONALITY & LASTING POSITIVE RELATIONSHIPS

To help you nurture positive relationships, it's essential to put your "best foot forward." You do this by cultivating an attractive personality and by being a nice and good person. Here you are not changing yourself to become someone you are not. You're working to be your best when interacting with others. These are skills that you already have; you are just developing them.

It's imperative to note that this only works if your real intention is a positive one. To be clear, you are not acting or pretending to trick, fool, and manipulate others, or hide who you really are. Instead, you do this through your genuine and honest intent to make friends and follow "Your Code." In the beginning, this might be something you have to work on to develop the skills, but like all training, you will learn, and it will get easier and even become second nature.

TO BE GENERALLY ATTRACTIVE, A TRUE FRIEND & TO NURTURE A POSITIVE RELATIONSHIP YOU:

- **Keep Your Word:** If you make plans or say you will do something or have the responsibility for a chore, do it early or on time.

    If Can't Keep Your Word:

    o You tell the person that you gave your word to as soon as you know you can't keep it.

    o Apologize and even try to make up for it in some way.

    o You note to yourself that you broke your word and ensure that you don't do it again, especially to this person.

    o It's also crucial that you only break your word rarely, which means that you don't break your word unless it genuinely can't be avoided. Sometimes keeping your word is not convenient or comfortable. In these cases, there are often lessons to be learned and tests of your character.

    o **If Late:** If you know that you are going to be late, first you contact everyone that is waiting as soon as you know you will be delayed, letting them know when you will arrive or when you will finish the work. The key is to contact everyone before you are late, so they are not waiting or wondering what is happening.

In the end, keeping your word and living up to your oaths are a crucial part of how people learn to trust and like you.

- **Give Real Compliments & Be Kind:** You can usually find ways to give compliments to your loved ones and friends. It might be a choice of clothing or the way they care for something. It can be very small or large. The key here is to be kind and give compliments regularly. We all tend to like others who show us kindness and notice our doings with real interest.

- **Express Gratitude:** Say thank you and express gratitude to others. Showing gratitude is done in small ways by just saying thank you when someone does something for you or sending a smile emoji when someone sends you a link. The goal is not to let their positive efforts toward you go unremarked.

- **Listen:** It's essential to listen to everyone. There may be times when someone needs to be heard and sympathized with without receiving any advice. Work with your friends so that you understand when it's essential to listen and when it's time to problem solve. Listening can be especially significant with close relationships between men and women. We cover this topic in more detail a little later within this step.

- **Communicate Well:** Learning to communicate well is a crucial facet to most healthy relationships.

We also cover this topic in more detail a little later within this step. For now, know it's essential.

- **Be Interesting:** Share and talk about interesting things. Be into what they are into by adding to it in some meaningful way. You can do this in many ways in person and through social media.

- **Give a Gift:** You need not wait for a birthday or holiday to do something special for or with someone. You can give a gift, plan an outing, and send a letter or card anytime. Share things with them that they might be interested in or might find helpful because of their interests.

- **Be Honest & Trustworthy:** Don't just tell your friends what you think they want to hear. You don't need yes-men and toadies as close companions. You need people who tell you the truth and those you can trust. Trustworthiness is what all people need from you too. So be honest, trustworthy, and honor your word. Demand that of all that you hold close.

    For example, a real friend will tell you if you have food in your teeth rather than let you talk to everyone that way. They will also do it in a diplomatic way that helps you avoid any embarrassment. Or if you are told a secret, you don't share it with anyone.

- **Look Out, Defend & Protect:** Defend and protect your friends, loved ones, and their interests, regardless if they are present or not. Stand up for your friends and their "stuff" when they are not there.

    You do this as you would like them to do for you. You should talk about your friends to others as if they could hear what you were saying. Do not gossip about them, spread rumors, or share confidential information, even in secret with other loved ones.

- **Ask Questions, for Opinions & Advice:** Asking other people questions and for their advice is a great way to bond with others. If you have friends that you respect, ask them for their thoughts on "things." They will appreciate it, and it may help you.

- **Plan Times:** Sometimes, you might drift apart due to work and other life issues. To keep a friendship alive, it's good to reach out here and there to say hello and to make plans. Even sending an emoji here and there is better than nothing.

- **Do a Favor & Offer Help:** If a family member or friend reaches out and asks for help with something, it's essential to respond. Take it seriously; get back to them. If you forget or cancel or don't show up, it will be taken as a sign that you do not care or value that person. Also, sometimes people don't ask for help but would like to have some. If you know, they can use help, offer, be there, or just show up.

    It's also essential to help in the way they ask. Your goal is to be the assistant, only taking over if they ask or with their permission. Listen to what <u>they</u> need, offer advice, and work <u>with them</u> on accomplishing <u>their</u> goals in the best and most fun way possible. Offering to help even if not asked, just being there sometimes is a great way to strengthen a friendship.

- **Be Polite & Have Manners:** Being polite is about addressing others with respect, being kind, and about how you would like to be addressed if the situation were reversed. Having manners is about how we do things, usually with a focus on cleanliness, grace, and respect. It also means asking instead of commanding as well as thanking people for their help and work.

For example, do you say thank you, and you're welcome? Do you ask or command? Are you nice or rude? Wash your hands before eating? Stuff food in your mouth and drop pieces everywhere? Chew with your mouth open or talk with your mouth full? Wipe your hands on your clothes?

Do you push through a crowd bumping into children and the elderly without care? In both cases, the elderly and children are unsteady. Therefore, being bumped can mean a fall that can cause severe injury and even death.

Being polite and having manners as well as all the other niceties that we do for one another is what makes social interactions more comfortable and pleasurable for everyone. We can think of having manners and being polite as the grease that makes our social interactions run smoothly, which will, in turn, help all of us be happier and have more energy.

This cycle of positive energy transference by the vast majority of us will have an even more significant positive effect on the whole of our society. Therefore, do not take your closest contacts for granted for using these skills with them and everyone in your life will help you maintain and build better relationships and make the world a kinder place to live

- **Have Sense of Humor:** Cultivating a positive sense of humor is also essential as it's often at the top of the list of desirable traits in friends, mates or partners. Positive in that it's not something that conflicts with the "10 Laws." Being funny does not mean mocking, cutting people down, being sarcastic, lying, hurting, scaring, demeaning people, or by using other negative actions or comments as depicted within a lot of current media. Positive humor can come in the form of jokes or just silly and fun comments. Learning the difference between negative and positive humor is essential for us as individuals and as a society.

- **Enjoy Silence:** Enjoy quiet times with people you care about. You do not always need to fill the air with talk. It's ok to be quiet when around others. Often these moments can be some of the most special, especially for people that are around each other often or that don't talk much. Camaraderie is found here because sometimes merely being together in peace is what is needed most of all.

- **Smell Good:** In most cultures around the world, if your breath or body odor is not correct, you can put people off. This includes things such as too much natural body odor, not enough natural body odor, or too much or not enough perfume or cologne. If wanting to be more accepted, it's good to try to conform to the local customs.

    Eating correctly, sweating, and cleaning yourself regularly and adequately goes a long way to creating a pleasing healthy human scent. You must be careful using antiperspirants and other products that contain toxins and toxicants like aluminum. You can also add a little pleasant scent such as a nontoxic scented oil, cologne, or perfume. See the "Life Manual: Self-Care" for more on smelling good naturally.

- **Acknowledge Suffering:** If you know someone is suffering that is close to you, it's important to acknowledge this, so they know they are not alone.

    Most people don't like to admit they are in distress so the moment might come fast by them saying "oh my back is hurting" or "boy, I twisted my neck last night" or "gosh, I miss her" or "yea it's been really difficult lately" it might be just a look or deep sigh. Here is your opportunity when you might ask, "Hey, are you ok?"

    The key is not to ignore it or say, "I know what you are going through" unless you have actually gone through it. You can say something like, "I know that must really hurt, can I help?" or "wow you are going through a lot" or "you have suffered a great loss," and "I want you to know that you are not alone and that I am here for you."

    You can call them now and then to see if they would like some help or to get out and spend time. The key is to let them know you are there for them and to do it in a way they don't feel it's a burden or obligation, but a sincere wish of yours to help them.

    Personal Suffering Note: Suffering is a part of life, and most of us will experience it at some point. There are many types of suffering, but all share the same characteristics. Each situation carries challenges and learning opportunities, as well as a lot of negative energy that needs to be correctly processed if you are to use it for positive ends. The key is that it takes time to really feel and work through it. Taking time is important as denial can prolong your suffering.

In the end, the goal is to face it, feel what you need to, seek the lessons, and make your way out the other side where you have used the experience and energy for something positive and become even better. We will go deeper into this topic in the next section.

- **Be Positive:** You want to be positive and for people to have a positive experience around you. *The Way* is your guide toward Living Rational Positive Action, so following *The Way* will help you be positive. Being positive also means you don't gossip, spread lies & rumors, fake news/information, nor participate in other negative behaviors.

    Being positive also means overcoming things like negative thinking, depression, suicidal thoughts, and negative addiction. Within the next two sections, we learn the basics of how to deal with these aspects of our human condition.

OVERCOMING NEGATIVE THINKING, DEPRESSION & SUICIDAL THOUGHTS

"Very little is needed to make a happy life; it is all within yourself, in your way of thinking." - Marcus Aurelius

To help us put a positive foot forward, we need to understand the consequence of some of the human conditions under which we live. One of the most significant problems facing humanity is how we deal with negative thinking, depression, suicidal thoughts, and addiction.

Below we cover these topics and show you how to deal with them effectively. This information has been placed here to help those of us who are suffering from these issues right now, as well as to protect you from future harm. You can also use this knowledge to help your people when they have trouble.

What You Really Want

The fact is you do not want to feel depressed, have negative thoughts and feelings, or kill yourself. What you really want is to be happy and have a wonderful life. What you really want is to overcome depression, an attachment to negative thoughts, suicidal thoughts, and all the rest, so it takes you farther down your "True Path" toward your "True Self" and "True Life."

What are Depression & Suicidal Thoughts?

Depression is a prolonged period of feeling sadness, hopeless, worry, and despair. These are negative feelings that are persistent and may feel like they will never go away. Suicidal Thoughts are a response to these intense negative feelings that we think or feel we cannot continue to bear.

Negative feelings are things like feeling sad, hopeless, desperate, lonely, fearful, worried, distrustful, ashamed, hated, hateful, worthless, desperate, enraged, reckless, unmotivated, or even suicidal. Note that each of these negative feelings naturally has a positive opposite.

It's also important to know that you are not alone and that the majority of us would like to be appreciated and admired for something good, yet we are often overly critical of ourselves. We all have weaknesses yet want to learn to compensate for them. We have unused capacity and skills that are not turned to our advantage.

We all sometimes or often doubt that we have made the right decisions or choices and wish for more clarity. We can hold ourselves together, but at times, can be worried and insecure on the inside. We can be a very independent thinker yet sometimes accept questionable things without proof. Most of us would like some positive change in life; however, we are hemmed in by restrictions and limitations of our own making.

KEY INSIGHTS

First, you don't want to kill yourself, feel depressed, or think negatively. Next, the definition of depression and negative thinking clearly shows us the crux of the issue and leads us to the solution. The fact is harsh negative feelings over time lead to a downward spiral ending in suicidal thoughts.

EFFECT OF NEGATIVE FEELINGS

All feelings are different mixtures of chemicals our body releases in response to something. Extreme negative feelings come from a specific combination of chemicals that, in the short term, can help motivate us, create focus, and can provide energy. However, this cascade of detrimental chemicals over time will do damage to us mentally, physically, emotionally, and spiritually. Negative feelings can create a physical reaction like feeling a tightness in your chest or an upset stomach, inflammation, clenching, restlessness, and sleeplessness, all of which add to the problem.

Positive feelings have the opposite effect. Positive emotions help improve all aspects of our health, including eating, sleeping habits, energy levels, motivation, and more. Positive feelings even flush out the harmful chemicals caused by depression and negative thinking.

WHAT CAUSES NEGATIVE FEELINGS?

Generally, negative feelings are caused by 1 or any combination of 3 situations.

1. **Negative Self Judgment:** You have a negative belief about yourself.

2. **Negative Happenings:** You have negative beliefs concerning things that either have happened, might happen, or will happen to you, your loved ones, or in your society or world.

3. **Negative Place:** If the environment in which you find yourself is depressing, unpleasant, or not conducive, it creates negative feelings. Sometimes depression is caused by this lacking in our home life and society. In these cases, especially when extreme, you must focus on getting help and making things better. This focus is important because HOPE is a very positive force that can get things moving in the right direction, even against the toughest of odds. See "Step 6: Unite" for more on how you can help change negative places into positive ones.

WHY DOES THIS HAPPEN?

Intense negative feelings, thoughts, and even depression and suicidal thoughts are normal and natural and are here for a reason. Most of you have had or will have times when you are hurt deeply in one way or another. Most of you can see there is a wrongness in our world, and sometimes it gets to you. You are human.

What you are experiencing is a human conditional effect. The fact is in this universe, positive needs negative and vice versa. We have seen this expressed throughout the ages as yin and yang. Within this universe, feeling bad means you can feel good, seeing the wrong means you can make it right. Our challenge as a species is to realize that the great gift of being able to see and fix the wrongness was given to us for a reason. It's our action or lack thereof regarding this gift that determines much of our fate/destiny.

Negative feelings are designed to make us focus on something, to learn, and give us energy so we can deal with it and solve the problem(s). If we handle it correctly, these situations develop skills that can make us better people, create a better society, as well as expose all the wrongness.

The fact is that someone has gone through something like you are at some point in history. There are many *examples* of people who turned a small or great wrongness, tragedy, or hardship into good. Turning the negative into the positive and good is what you really want to do. The key is to know that you can prevent and overcome negative thinking, depression, and suicidal thoughts (NTDST) as well as negative addiction.

To be clear, it's our <u>belief</u> in negative thoughts that create "negative feelings." We find the <u>key</u> in the word <u>belief</u>.

HOW TO OVERCOME NTDST

So, if believing in the negative is what causes the problem, then how do you get what you really want instead of being self-destructive during these desperately challenging times of life? Your challenge is to find a way to know the issue, learn, find solutions, and move on in a positive way. As we have noted, NTDST is tied to our shared human condition. The wrongness of life and the trials you go through generally focus on three areas: self-control, self-creation, and societal development.

The fact is that negative feelings are a mixture of chemicals your body released in response to your belief, and they will do damage to you over the long term. Since we build habits in about 90 days, we need a solution that works fast, and that will also work even if we have developed a negative habit.

THE SOLUTION

Understanding what was just covered makes the solution clearer. You must have specific thoughts, believe them, and then take certain actions over time to overcome NTDST. So, what are these key thoughts to believe and actions to take? There are a number of them. The key is to know them all for together they make a total solution.

FACE IT

Bad things happen. You may have a negative thought, have horrible things happen to you, your loved ones, and in our world. You might be in a terrible place or have done something very wrong. It might be that what you think is a big deal is actually nothing. Whatever the issue, you do not run from it, push it down, or deny it. You also don't languish in your dealings with it. You need to face it, deal with it, and then move on.

So first take the time and really look at it and deal with it. You are allowing yourself to think the thoughts and feel that pain and sadness. Is it the truth? Sometimes, when you focus on what you are depressed about, you find they are meaningless, superficial things, and they evaporate quickly.

If this situation is tied to a loss of someone or another great event, you may also need time to grieve and be in this moment. So, take some time but don't languish too long. All good people would always want you to learn, recover, and move on to have a wonderful life. So, face it, and let yourself feel what needs to be felt, make amends if need be, for this will allow you to move on faster.

LEARN LESSONS

Now that you have faced it and are going through it, the next key is to look for the lessons, challenges, and tests that you can find (See the "Life Manual: Our Practice: Mental

Practice: Learning" for more.) These insights might be in the form of a list of things not to do or to do. It might be some essential point or change that needs to happen within your life or society.

Here you are looking for perspectives and paths where you can change this event into either being nothing because it was meaningless or being something that you can learn from and become better. You need to ask yourself, what are all the things that you can do to get through this transitional moment of life that would make you better? Write these things down as they can be used to improve yourself, find direction as well as implement solutions. See "Step 5 Be: Time: Transitional Phases of Life & Trying Times" for more.

In the end, regardless of what you are feeling depressed about, these feelings are caused by a specific belief. You can think about anything and believe what you want. It can help to believe that all situations like this are character tests and challenges as well as spirit building exercises, that once understood and are past can't hurt you anymore or at least will be bearable.

You can use these situations to make things better or let them destroy you. The solution is tied to your choice in thinking, belief, and actions. All the trials that you overcome will become victories and an endless source of positive energy that you can use for good and during the other trials of life. See the "Life Manual: Our Practice" for more.

KNOW CHANGE IS GUARANTEED

The next key is to know that we all live in a world of change where nothing stays the same. Entropy is part of our human condition. Change is happening right now as time passes.

You will not be like this forever. It may seem overwhelming in this transitional moment. Nevertheless, this too shall pass, and you don't know what will happen.

When people say, "it's darkest before the dawn," they do not mean this literally, as it's not true in our world. Darkest before the dawn means that at the bleakest and hopeless time, there is something that could happen to change everything for the positive. This is hope. The critical insight here is that if you do a good job following all the solutions found within this section, as time passes, you are creating the positive change that will get you to where you want to go.

SEE THE WAY OUT

While you are facing it, learning lessons and know that change is guaranteed, you still need to know the way out. Here you need only find the desire for NTDST to end. This desire can come in the form of wishing this situation did not exist or that it never happened. This desire for it to stop allows you to make choices and take actions where you are mindful of the moment, working on the solutions and not focusing on the problem.

It's this sincere desire for this situation to end that becomes the starting point that you can use to get to a better place. It's like a bread crumb trail for it's through your desire for something to end that something new can start. It's this desire for the positive that leads you to make new choices and take different actions.

Knowing that change is guaranteed and that your desire will lead to the way out if your thoughts and actions are correct during the process still means you need the power to make it happen.

KNOW YOUR POWER

What is the power you need? Say your best friend contacts you and says, "(insert loved one's name) was just hit by a car and taken to the hospital, and I don't know if they are going to live." How would you feel at that moment?

Maybe you feel devastated, afraid for them, worried, sad, and desperate? Then they say…ha, just joking. What do you feel now? You certainly might be mad at the person for that mean joke, but you also don't feel devastated, worried, or sad as you did a moment before.

In fact, all those negative feelings just fade away in an instant. You may even feel good. Here you can have the same thought or see the same thing that caused negative feelings, yet now you feel nothing or even positive about it. So, what happened? The context changed or to say it another way, "change happened."

    I.   You believed a thought (thought 1).
    II.   Then you had another thought and believed it instead (thought 2).

Think about it like this. When you had an intense or bad dream that you woke up from, you were able to go from an instant state of panic or fear to believe that the dream was not true and then go right back to sleep.

These extreme *examples* are being used to illustrate how this basic human process works. Understanding the workings is very important because it works the same way in all situations, including depression and negative thinking. It's the chain of belief, unbelief, and a new belief that allows us to overcome NTDST. Even if you are truly oppressed, you can think what you want. No matter what you show on the outside, you can keep a part of you safe and for yourself.

USE YOUR POWER

You have the power to think something, then change your feelings through your belief. Therefore, if you think and believe the right things, you can turn the negative into not existing or into good feelings. Here you are turning a negative into positive.

For example, you can use this energy created by these negative times as a catalyst to create positive change. Others have turned great problems, tragedies, and hardships into good, and so can you. It's possible that you can even come through this better than you were before or do some great good.

You can use your power of belief to change yourself in this very moment, and any time you truly believe. You can see any issue as a life challenge, lesson, or test that you are to learn from so you can become better. No good person would want you to suffer; they would want you to rise. You can only become better if you let yourself. Simply believe you have the power and then use it as needed anytime. See the "Life Manual: Our Practice: The Power" for more.

MOVE ON

If you are having a hard time, don't stop, or you will end up there. To put it another way, if your current path has led you into hell, don't stop, keep going and make it through for if you stop, you will stay in hell. As stated, you can see any negative situation as a significant life challenge that, once overcome, will mean you are stronger and better for it. It might be hard to see it at the time, but afterward, it will become clear. Just do what needs to be done and move on. No guilt.

Moving on does not mean the situation is ok, desirable, or even acceptable. It does not mean that it was right and that you agree or even that it's over. You can be hurt, damaged, and even broken. Moving on means that you are dealing with it in a positive way and healing. Remember, all good people want you to recover, learn, and move on. So, punishing yourself is not the answer. Punishing yourself unduly does not right any wrongs or make a positive difference. In fact, it makes a bad situation worse. Only making peace and taking positive action will accomplish the real goal.

HELP PEOPLE & GET HELP

Unite with other people in positive ways. We all have needs that cannot be fulfilled entirely on our own. You need people to help you become your best. You can look for support groups where people are going through the same or similar things, coaches, trainers, and other positive activities where you will find positive people.

If there aren't any groups like that, look for any group helping people with trauma. They might be able to help. The participation and camaraderie with others can help you greatly. You might help others who are going through something similar. You might find that helping others actually helps you too. You might also join a group doing something positive and fun that you enjoy. Find your people, your tribe, and they will help lessen your load as well as enable you to reach higher levels.

BOND WITH ANIMALS & NATURE

Both animals and nature can be a significant positive boost. *For example,* A dog, if treated well, is always glad to see you and is an excellent source of joy. Being in a beautiful natural environment can lift your mood by merely sensing it. Plants around your living space can bring in a sense of peace. Our bountiful world is a never-ending source of good feelings and positive energy. Bring it inside and get out there and enjoy it!

HAVE FAITH

Belief in God, knowing you have a purpose and are here for a reason is also a great resource. Remember, you are never alone, always connected with God, and that God is your friend. The meetings, ceremonies, rituals associated with a positive faith can help you through hard times.

FIX OUR SOCIETY

As you have learned, some of our society is broken, and this wrongness can create negative feelings. Here, even in the most desperate places, you can have a positive effect by working to fix these problems. Your good works can help you recover and move on. Hope and positive action are very powerful and lead to the implementation of real solutions. Hope is also a great source of positive energy that lifts people up. Many of us are willing to sacrifice to fix big problems. Through hope and action, we can improve generation by generation. The more of us who join together, the easier it is to fix significant societal issues. So, get out there and help fix something, you might find you also fixed yourself.

REPLACE REPETITIVE NEGATIVITY WITH THE POSITIVE

You don't stop or do without; instead, you replace and crowd out with something good. This constant positive focus is an essential point for you to realize. You are not trying to stop any negative thing.

For example, you don't try to quit smoking. Instead, you live a healthy lifestyle.

The focus is not on stopping the negative; it's doing the positive. Focus on the solution. Choose what defines you.

Living rational, positive action in all critical areas of life naturally crowds out and immunizes you against negative thinking, depression, and suicidal thoughts.

So, if you catch yourself thinking something negative, immediately say something positive like an affirmation instead. You can even pick affirmations that are the opposite of what you were thinking. If you have a negative thought, you don't have to agree. Fighting against them, denying them, countering them with something positive can be effective in changing your belief system. You can think of it like your subconscious is testing you, and it's your answer back that matters. Do you agree and accept the negative or do you reject it and throw it back, replacing it with love and goodness?

For example, you do something wrong and say, "I'm such an idiot." You answer back. "No, I am not. I am working hard, just made an error is all, to err is human after all. I am learning and will do better the next time, so keep that negative unconstructive comments to yourself because they have no place here."

The same attitude applies to worry. To worry is to be anxious about something that may have happened or may occur in the future. Worry is here to help us focus, prevent and fix issues if possible. It's a damaging and fruitless behavior when there is nothing to be done. It's detrimental, as is all negative thinking, because it releases harmful chemicals in your body and occupies your thoughts and actions. It's fruitless because it does not affect what may or will happen. Instead of worry, replace it with something positive like a positive action to prevent or help, a creative act, a mind game, cleaning, or working out. After you have done what you could, you can realize it's meaningless, a bad habit, and then drop it and go on with your life.

FOLLOW THE WAY

The Way is "Living Rational Positive Action" and is designed to help you find and create a meaningful life. It enables you to fix and focus all aspects of your life in positive ways. The primary virtues that help us all overcome NTDST are to be positive, hopeful, peaceful, happy, optimistic, grateful, humble, mindful, resilient, persevering, disciplined, determined, persistent, dedicated, motivated, productive, responsible, controlled, centered, and patient.

Living *The Way* every day over time will ingrain these key virtues and others into you. All of which will allow you to overcome challenges, and the trials of life naturally. These virtues will fortify and immunize you against negative thinking, depression, and suicidal thoughts. The younger you build these critical coping skills, the better you will do during these transitional moments of life, for you will be prepared for life's ups and downs. See the *Child & Family Guide* for more.

While the whole of *The Way* will help, here are some things to focus on fast. The first key is to follow a complete "Daily Way" that covers all the foundations because keeping on top of all these foundational areas allows for a smoother transitional period. See "Step 5: Be" and "The Manual of Life" for more. Take special care with:

- o **Physical Workouts:** A good workout can lift a mood because it releases positive chemicals that make you feel better. It also washes out the harmful chemicals. Increasing the intensity and frequency of "Your Practice" in all areas, mental and physical, can be very helpful.

    So be sure to do some good longer workouts that wear you out and allow you to sweat, just don't push too hard and hurt yourself.

You can use your workout to help keep you balanced, as well as, when you are at your lowest, to get a lift. See the "Life Manual: Our Practice" for more.

- o **Sleep:** Sleep is your time to escape, recover, and heal. See the "Life Manual: Sleep" to get the best.
- o **Fuels:** Fueling your body correctly with "Light, Air, Water, Food, and Information" during these times can go a long way to helping improve everything. See the "Life Manual: Fuels" for more.
- o **Supplements:** St John's Wort, The HTP5, KAVA, correct levels of Vit B and amino acids - all can help promote a better mood. For more, see the "Life Manual: Sleep: Other Sleep Aids."
- o **Transmutation:** Use transmutation to change negative energy into positive. See the "Life Manual: Our Practice: The Power: Transmutation" for more.
- o **Meditation:** The mental practice part of "Our Practice" includes meditation. Increasing the frequency and session length of meditation during these times can be very helpful. Going through all the different techniques is an excellent way to get and stay on track. See the "Life Manual: Our Practice: Mental Practice: Meditation" for more.

Other Parts of *The Way* that can help:

- o **Unite with Other People:** This is mentioned above and here because of its importance. We all have the power to change the negative into the positive, and this is made even stronger when you join with other people.

    Friends, family, support groups, and events are all ways you can join with others. To be truly successful, your best, happy, and to have a positive effect on significant issues, you must unite with other people. Joining with others allows us all to offer and receive happiness, help, motivation, inspiration, as well as participate in solutions.

- o **Moral Center:** Understand the "10 Laws" covered in "Step 4: Center" in detail. There you find your purpose, the meaning of life, and more. Knowing all of this helps create a perspective on what is truly important, and this allows you to focus yourself appropriately.

OPTIONAL HELP: THERAPY & DRUGS

The use of therapy and drugs are not a requirement or even a recommendation. This information is provided so that you know your options.

- **Therapy:** If you are having trouble handling things on your own, seek professional and volunteer help. There are toll-free phone numbers, groups, and doctors who specialize in helping people just like you.

  There is no shame in this; sometimes, our minds need help just like our bodies do. So do not hesitate. If you need assistance, reach out. There are caring people ready to help you. Do not underestimate their abilities or your ability to get better, for often true healing can only take place with people who care.

  Just be careful, some therapists, as with many doctors, only get paid if you continue to see them, so they may not be working to help you as fast as possible. Therefore, it's recommended that you seek treatments that work toward real solutions, and only for the shortest time as possible.

  These sessions should be working to give you the power to control your own life and mind, ideally not create a dependency on the therapist. If you just need to talk over your life with people, to be validated, then make friends instead. It's a lot cheaper and a lot more rewarding.

- **Prescription Drugs**: There are prescription drugs that claim to help with depression. Be wary of only treating symptoms with drugs. The caution here is that most prescription drugs often only mask symptoms and do not address the cause. The side effects can also be problematic on their own. They also can do other long-term harm and cause dependency. The problem is that you still have the underlying problem and are adding a drug dependency on top of it, so be careful and check the side effects.

- **Natural Drugs:** There are plants that humans have used throughout history that can help you gain a positive perspective at these trying times. Plants like marijuana, peyote, ayahuasca, and certain mushrooms are used at critical moments.

    With all drugs, there are risks, and they all need to be understood before trying them. These are listed as options because of the fact many people suffering from PTSD, fears, loss, and other traumas have significantly benefited from the experiences associated with these substances and others like them.

    The key is to use them as an experience, learn and integrate the learning into our life, not to use them all the time or to escape problems. If ever using them, be safe, do not smoke them if possible, and ensure that they are of the correct dose and have never been exposed to herbicides, insecticides, or other poisons.

7 Reasons Why Not to Kill Yourself

"Believe that life is worth living and your belief will help create the fact." - William James

Ok, now that we have covered the way to overcome this type of negativity, for those of you who are thinking about killing yourself, please consider these facts. These should also be shared with anyone you feel might be at risk.

1. **BECAUSE IT'S NOT WHAT YOU REALLY WANT:** Read above. What you really want is for things to get better and to live a wonderful life. You don't really want to kill yourself. Instead, seek to understand and follow the information above and within *The Way*.

2. **BECAUSE IT'S NOT NEEDED:** You don't need to kill yourself because there is a way out. Change is guaranteed, and you have the power. See how above.

3. **HURTING OTHERS:** Know you will be hurting others who care for you. They will never get over it. It can even cause depression and suicidal thoughts in them. Do you really want to inflict that on people who care for you and that you love?

4. **NO GOOD PERSON:** No good person would want you to end your life. They want you to get better, move on, and live a wonderful life! This includes you! So, forgive and forget those who would want otherwise.

5. **LOST LOVE ONE?** If this situation is caused by the death or loss of a loved one, even a child, know that the person would NOT want you to feel bad, hurt, or kill yourself because of them. Honor them by using the energy from the event to become a better person and do good in our world.

6. **FAILURE:** If you try to kill yourself, it might not work, and you can end up worse off like be damaged mentally or physically, in jail or a mental institution.
7. **FAITH:** Most faiths put a penalty on suicide when not at deaths' door. Fear of this negative consequence on this level should make any believer stop and reconsider.

In the end, you can learn the skills needed to overcome negative thinking, depression, and suicidal thoughts (NTDST) no matter your stage. Together we can work to create a better world that will naturally help us all avoid many of the situations that cause these problems.

Believe you have the power and deserve to move on. If you are looking for permanent change, look for help in *The Way* as the steps are designed to help you create positive change within your life throughout time. Remember the keys: Think! Believe! and Act! You can do this!

OVERCOMING NEGATIVE ADDICTION

"The unfortunate thing about this world is that good habits are so much easier to give up than bad ones."
- Somerset Maugham

Our shared human condition fills our lives with many challenges, with negative addiction being one of the most challenging. Since negative addiction is tied to our human condition, we know that there are key lessons we need to learn. Once negative addiction is mastered, we can more easily evolve as individuals and as a species.

You are addicted to something that you can't live without and will do almost anything to attain. An addiction is something that can never be sated or satisfied as it can always come back. Addiction can be tied to habits that stimulate the pleasure center of our brain, which releases dopamine and is commonly called the "feel good" chemical.

Addiction can be positive or negative. It's important to understand addiction because we are all predisposed to negative addiction as a fundamental human condition. This is because of our human need for food and sex, both of which stimulate the pleasure center of our brain. These human conditional needs force situations of temptation, choice, self-control, and self-development.

For example, the human condition of being addicted to food can be a virtue when managed correctly but becomes the vice of gluttony when taken too far.

Negative addiction is frequently associated with drugs, tobacco, and gambling but also includes overindulgences in food, sex, entertainment, social media, etc. Most often, harmful addiction is not made by a reasonable choice but is one of circumstance.

For example, as many become reliant on pain killers like morphine and fentanyl for the treatment of an injury, this addiction becomes hard to stop even after our injury is healed, often leading to the use of illegal drugs like heroin.

Others of us are given tobacco and drugs by our role models or elders before we understand what is really at issue. Parents sometimes allow unmonitored and unrestricted use of electronics and social media that are designed to be addictive or that present images, sounds, and situations that children can't understand or deal with effectively.

ADDICTION PREVENTION

The best practice in dealing with addiction is to prevent it from happening in the first place.

We do this by:

1. Teaching the young self-control using delayed gratification (a.k.a. impulse control) with food and other things they like. For more, see the *Child & Family Guide*.
2. Ensuring that the young are not exposed to addictive products.
3. Ensuring that all know which products and drugs are addictive and harmful before use.
4. Helping those who are addicted to recover.
5. Stopping the design and creation of addictive foods, electronics, and other products.
6. Filling your life with the positive is also crucial. Here you can follow *The Way*, filling your lives with positive habits, exercise, training, and positive daily doings. Your practice can include delayed gratification/impulse control and self-control exercises to ensure that you keep yourself under control.

    For example, at work, instead of looking at your phone, you engage other people around you. You might place a snack you really like in front of you and wait to eat it for a long time or even give it away. You can do mini-workouts instead of that bad habit. The choices are endless. Find what works of you.

ADDICTION RECOVERY MINDSET

It's essential to keep recovery in mind as you go through the process of breaking a negative addiction. Remember that it's a transitional moment in life that will not last and that once you are on the other side, you will be a stronger and better person.

HOW TO OVERCOME ADDICTION

1. The first step for any negative addiction is first to realize it exists. You must acknowledge there is a problem before you can get help. Acknowledgment can be something you become aware of personally or by others bringing it to your attention.

2. Next, you need to find the desire to end it. Without the willingness to fix the problem, the problem will most likely persist or come back. The higher your motivation, the better chance you have.

    You can find great motivation by understanding why you are here, your primary purpose, what you should be doing every day to be your best, as well as how to live a meaningful life and make a real difference in the world

3. The third step is to create a plan to end your addiction.

    - This plan should include help from others as needed. There are support groups that help with ending every form of addiction.

    - Adjust the plan if it's not working to find the right balance for you. Note that there are commonalities when fixing addiction, but in the end, the program needs to be customized to fit the individual, for, while similar, we are not all the same. You might require different approaches.

        For example, exercise and meditation are part of everyone's plan. However, how you do it, when, and what you do can be very different.

- Your plan should also focus on adding positive elements to your life rather than only stopping something. The goal is to replace the negative with the positive. *For example,* you can do mini-workouts and meditations instead of the bad habit.

- Prepare for withdrawals. Regardless of whether you quit drugs fast or slow, you will go through withdrawals. Depending on the addiction, some withdrawal symptoms can be quite intense, involving severe fever, tremors, hallucinations, and desires to die or do the drug at any cost. Others might be just a prolonged sense of unease and want. Remember, other people, hobbies, work, workouts, games, and more can help here.

  You may go through tremendous emotional, mental, and physical anguish as your animal body fights off the addiction. After the withdrawal period is over, it's critical to heal and recover with proper nutrition as well as positive mental and physical exercise. You need to work to transmute all the negative and positive energy that comes with this event into building good habits that make your life better.

- Regardless of your situation, the key, as stated above, is to know that this is a transitional moment that will not last. Change is happening as time passes. You need to go through this so you can move on. It's a test of your will power and your ability to make hard choices and so much more.

4. Once you have beaten the addiction, you follow your life's plan, stick with it, and get help and support as needed. Having a well developed "Daily Way" to follow helps here.

- Be sure to train your body and mind hard during difficult times. Workouts will help rewire your twisted sense of pleasure into something more positive. So, if you play mind games, meditate, and work your body hard, you will stimulate the pleasure center of your brain, giving you some relief and creating positive feedback naturally.

- Continue to focus and fill your life with the positive instead of focusing on what you are not doing. It's about crowding out the bad with the good. *For example,* you don't quit smoking; you live healthily.

- Also, even after you have broken the addiction, there may be times when the temptation is powerful. Here it's essential to view these temptations as tests of your will power rather than a sincere desire of yours. As you overcome each test, you will gain strength and abilities that will allow you to withstand other temptations when they arise.

As individuals and collectively as a species, mastering negative thinking, depression, suicidal thoughts, and addiction is essential to our happiness and development as people. Each of us needs to do our part. Mastering life challenges like these are what makes you mentally stronger and a better person. It's working together to end the negative and control the positive that we take another step down our "True Path," add another critical piece to the puzzle of a "True Life," and help create our "True Society."

CHAPTER 10
CONNECT & MAKE A REAL DIFFERENCE

"To effectively communicate, you must realize that you are all different in the way you perceive the world and use this understanding as a guide to your communication with others."
- Tony Robbins

Next, within "Step 6: Unite," we need to cover another human conditional issue. The fact is your ability to communicate affects all aspects of your life. Your communication can be a positive energy source helping those around you. It can also be a negative drain on your life and society if not handled well. We all need to be open and allow a real discussion to take place for solutions and happiness to be found. We all need to be able to communicate and listen effectively so that we can explain ourselves and take in new information.

Communication is a crucial facet of what allows all of us to unite in a common cause and get things done. To have a great life and society, we need to have good communication skills. Excellent communication is essential for higher levels of competitiveness within cooperation and good governance. The fact is the majority of us need to possess excellent communication abilities if we are to build our "True Society." You will take a significant step in helping achieve unity through understanding these key points. This information can also make a real difference within your daily life.

Can You Understand Me?

Because communication is so necessary and key to our success, we have outlined the basics of better communication below. There is also a short companion "Communication Reference Guide" that you can download from our website: www.7Way.Me/wd. It can be used as a learning tool and during live conversations.

Side Note: Because of our fundamental human need to communicate, it may be good to create a simple universal language that we can all use alongside our native one (or at least provide instant translation).

We Communicate, Generally, in 3 Ways:

1. **Audio Communication:** Includes speaking out loud as well as voice quality, intonation, pitch, stress, emotion, tone, and style of speaking. Audio communication can be face to face or through devices like phones and computers. It also includes music with lyrics.

2. **Visual Communication:** Through books, emails, letters, magazines, newspapers, pictures, video, TV, movies, clips, photos, paintings, emojis, symbols, graphs, signs, typography, drawings, illustration, and colors.

3. **Body Language:** Position, movement, including micro-expressions and movements of the face and body. Expression of the body can take the form of dance that can communicate a story and feelings.

Are You Music To the Ears?

Ok, now that you understand how we communicate, let's talk about how you sound when you communicate. This is very important because if you sound good, people will be more open to listening to you. There are seven facets to how people sound. Let's go through them quickly now.

General Tone

Your goal is to use a pleasing tone, so people are listening to what you are saying. Finding "your voice" can be like working with an instrument that needs to be tuned. Finding your most natural pleasing tone comes through breathing in and out of your diaphragm, and then speaking through your throat and out your mouth. Passing too much air into our nasal passages as you speak often is the source of an unpleasing tone. Modulate the tone until it flows naturally yet sounds pleasing. Ask others for help.

When you find your voice, you then speak in a way that naturally rises and falls in pitch while staying in harmony. This rise and fall using a pleasing tone helps people be more open to what you have to say. Tone and pitch convey a lot of information, in many cases, more than the spoken words. You can say just about anything and mean something entirely different by your changing the tone and rhythm.

For example, if others always hear your tone as condescending, an attack, mocking, sarcastic, or angry, the nice words you use will mean little to nothing.

Volume

How loud you speak conveys a lot of meaning. Be sure to keep it at an appropriate level. Talking more quietly can often be more effective than yelling as others have to focus on hearing what was said.

Passion

You should not let your passion or emotions take over your voice, as this can make it hard for others to listen to and understand. Your passion can also create volume issues.

Composure

Remember, being composed does not mean you are necessarily ok with everything or at ease. It only means you are working to have a meaningful conversation during a stressful situation without losing control.

Cadence

Cadence is the speed at which you talk. Varying your rhythm, along with pitch, can help make you easier to listen to and understand.

Pause

The use of pauses during speaking helps when trying to make points as a break can give significance to what you have said or are about to say. You also pause to check in with your audience, asking them questions, ensuring that they are engaged and understanding. Most of us don't like to be talked at for too long and will fade out.

What is Your Body Saying?

Another critical aspect of effective communication is the proper use of body language. Body language plays a large part in your communication. It also can affect how you think, feel, and behave. Everything from what your arms and legs are doing and from your eyes and facial expressions is part of body language. It's essential to check your body language periodically when in a conversation.

Open or Closed

If open, your face and body are facing the person without your arms crossed most of the time. You glance into their eyes here and there and concentrate on what they are saying. It's also important to keep a pleasant and attentive expression on your face.

Closed body language involves turning away, continually checking your phone, crossing your arms, frowning, and other negative facial expressions.

EYE CONTACT

When speaking with someone, it's good to look them straight in their eyes, at times. When you do, you think strong, fearless, but not challenging or threatening. You are seeking a calm, confident, and self-assured demeanor.

Note that if you stare into someone's eyes too long, it can be seen to mean something. Depending on the situation, this can be good or bad. As a general rule, look at them when they speak, glancing into their eyes as they make points. As you talk, do the same.

BE PRESENT IN THE MOMENT

You show respect and can only really understand all of what is happening if you are engaged in the moment. Being present means that you are not checking your cell phone or other devices or even have them visible. It means you are focusing on the people before and after the event by asking questions, getting to know them, looking at them, touching them appropriately, and building friendships. It's also about refining your abilities to communicate, listen, and learn.

PERSONAL SPACE

Personal space is an area of about 2 feet or so around us with its actual size dependent upon local culture and personal preference. If a person enters this space, it changes the dynamic of the interaction. The more intimate the relationship, the more often we permit this close contact. However, if others we don't know violate this space, it often creates an adverse reaction. Therefore, it's essential to respect the personal space of others.

Touching

Touching others in the right way and at the correct times is one of the best ways to connect and is, in fact, one of the most powerful bonding tools you have. If done inappropriately, it can cause problems. A gentle squeeze saying I'm here for you or a slap on the shoulder saying, "That was great thinking!" are physical expressions that can mean a lot.

You must also be aware that too much touching, particularly touching people you don't know well or in inappropriate and intimate places, can cause discomfort and impede your communication. There is no set rule here as each relationship and circumstance is different. You need to use your judgment and take cues from the other person as well as model your behavior toward people who seem to do this well. Some basic ideas to consider:

- Less intimate places to touch people briefly are on the shoulder or arms.
- Intimate places are hands, face, back, and generally any place on the body other than the shoulder or arm.
- Your acquaintances are generally not touched or, if so, just briefly during a conversation.
- It's important not to touch people too often, especially in the wrong places.
- If doing anything as a group, like playing a sport, team building, or military training, it's important to touch each other as this will help build the bond. Things like a slap on the shoulder, saying, "great job," and high fives are all great bonding tools that will allow all to perform better as a unit.

Handshake

In many cultures shaking hands is the custom. In these cases, we should ensure that a good connection is made by not grasping too quickly. Let the hands settle together, then offer a firm, but non-crushing grip for a few seconds.

Power Positions

Power positions can cause a chemical chain reaction within your body, as does laughing and smiling. Power posing is where you take a few minutes to put yourself into a power pose. You can join this with "Visualization Meditation" (See the "Life Manual: Our Practice: Mental Training: Meditation" for more) for times where you need to be strong, like before a speech or at the start of your day. Power poses will increase your confidence. When visualizing these, think superheroes. You can pick any pose that feels powerful to you.

Positions include poses like:

- o **Hero Pose** arms on hips, legs are a little wide apart, chest out, shoulders back, chin level with an intense facial expression while leaning slightly forward.
- o **Winner's Pose** is the same as the hero, but with arms raised over your head.

Communication Necessities

"The most basic of all human needs is the need to understand and be understood. The best way to understand people is to listen to them." - Ralph Nichols

Within this next section, we cover the basics of listening and speaking with a few tips on text communication at the end. This information is vital if we are to have meaningful conversations, create lasting, mutually beneficial relationships as well as make a real difference in the world.

Note that the information below is intended for general use. Therefore, some ideas might not be appropriate in all situations, such as professionally and militarily.

ARE YOU REALLY LISTENING?

The first step in effective communication is to master listening. Listening is an innate ability that must be trained if you are to use it to its fullest potential. Your listening skills significantly determine how far you can go in life because it dramatically affects your ability to communicate and cooperate with others.

The first key is to "actively listen" and "seek to understand" before working to be understood. To do this, follow the tips below.

- **FOCUS**: Think and focus on what they are saying as if you are looking to repeat what they said back to them.
    - Do not focus on your thoughts or arguments, only waiting for the person to stop talking.
    - Do not say things like, "You talked, now it's my turn," and then say a bunch of things that have nothing to do with what they just said.
- **DO NOT INTERRUPT**
    - If you interrupt people, they will feel disrespected and that you don't understand them.
    - In general, do not interrupt. However, sometimes, in the natural flow of a conversation, it's ok to ask clarifying questions. For more help, if they are not clear, and you don't understand, see "If I Don't Understand" below.

- **FOLLOW** the lead of the person initiating the discussion. Do not highjack the conversation and turn it into something else. Following also means not to bring up sensitive topics at inappropriate times.

    For example, when someone is sharing something exciting and happy that happened to them, don't bring up something negative like their need for money, a medical problem, an old fight, a chore you need them to do, etc. Let the speaker have this moment and stay with them.

- **FACTS & VIRTUES?** Listen to find their fact base and core virtues.

- **DIFFERENCE?** Listen to find the differences between what they know to be true and what you do.

- **FEEDBACK:** Give Feedback on what they said. Feedback can be done with body language, using nods, etc., or verbal acknowledgment. Be sure they understand that you feel and understand their pain or frustration if expressed before anything else.

- **REPEAT** back to them what you think they are saying to be sure you got it. Repeating will ensure that you got it, and they understand that you did. It will also help the other person know you are listening. Only after you understand, and they know that you do, can you move on.

    o *For example:* "I'm trying to understand what you are saying. Can I repeat back to you what I think I understand you are saying? You can correct me where I'm wrong."

THE WAY | STEP 6: UNITE – CONTINUED

LISTENING & SEEKING TO UNDERSTAND HELPS IN MANY WAYS

Through seeking to understand others:

- o You might learn something new or that you can use.
- o Knowing the objections can help you find better ways to communicate your thoughts.
- o You might find a fact that is different, thereby reconciling a misunderstanding.
- o It will help you learn about the person, which can help you bond more deeply.
- o You can learn things about yourself that you could not otherwise. You might be misjudging them.
- o It can help you get clarification and fix any miscommunication and misunderstanding.
- o Their ideas added to yours can make everything better.
- o You might change your mind or find something even better.
- o Remember, it's essential to be open as you can't have a real discussion or generally learn if you are closed-minded. Ask yourself, do you want the other person to agree with you and confirm your thinking, or do you possibly want to learn something and see different perspectives? Do you want a real discussion? Are you open to reason, logic, facts, and to change in the face of newly discovered truths?

IF LISTENING & YOU DON'T UNDERSTAND

If you don't understand what the other person is trying to communicate, it's important to seek clarification to ensure you do. True communication is a shared responsibility between all parties.

It's ok if you don't fully understand right off. It's natural. Often, it's difficult to express something in a linear manner or to everyone's satisfaction without some discussion. At times, some of you might have a hard time expressing yourself for many reasons, including being nervous. The first key is to see this as an opportunity to help refine your communication skills.

If you don't understand, you can wait for them to finish and say things like:

- "Can you explain this point some more. I did not fully get it?"
- "Can you give me an example of how this would work?"
- "How do you know, is it from experience or research, or do you just think it's true?"
- "I think I see part of what you are saying. Can you explain this part about "XYZ" a little more, please?"

TOO MUCH TOO FAST?

If someone is saying a lot and you can't keep up, it's ok. You can always go back and ask questions. Try to follow the general thread to get the best understanding you can. It's better sometimes to let people express themselves as best they can the first time. Letting them go and being attentive lets them know they are being listened to and valued. In the end, the responsibility is on them to remember everything.

- "I want to understand more. Can we start again, and can I ask questions as we go?"
- "I'm sorry I'm not sure I understand what you just said. Can we go over it again?"

Often after going through something a few times, both sides become clearer.

The Way | Step 6: Unite – continued

Appropriate Interruptions

If the flow permits and the other person accepts, it's appropriate to interrupt here and there during a conversation to ask for clarification or to give information at the right times. It's important at these times not to hijack the conversation.

How to Ask Questions to Get Truthful Answers

When we don't understand, we ask questions to get clarification. It's key to ask until you are sure you understand. The basic questions consist of seeking to know: Who, Where, When, Why, What, Which, and How.

- Who: Person
- Where: Place, Position, Location
- When: Time, Event, Moment
- Why: Reason, Explanation
- What: Specific Thing or Object
- Which: Choice, Alternatives
- How: The way or manner or form

Ask direct questions, and you will get the best answers. You can go as far as to directly assert that there is something wrong or a problem. Clarity will allow you to see if the other person will contradict you. As in, "I know we have a problem, what do you think it is?" or "What problems do we have or what problems are showing up in this situation?"

Don't say things like, "We don't have any problems, do we?" or "That situation does not have any issues, does it?" or "What can you tell me about this issue." These are leading or open questions. You will get better results and more honest answers by clearly stating the issue and asking a direct question.

Consider This When Offering Opinions & Presenting Ideas

People can be touchy. When you offer your options and present ideas, you want to do so in a way that is easy for the other person to hear and understand. Doing so will help you get through to them more easily. So, consider these points.

1. **Short:** Keep it as short and concise as possible, as this will allow others to better understand you.

2. **Open:** Openly present your idea, be diplomatic, and have an appropriate pleasing tone. Do not be too firm.

3. **Condescending:** If telling people things that they might already know, we can be seen as condescending (talking down to them). The way to avoid this is to "set the frame" with the person before offering information on something they might already know.

    - "I know you may already know some of what I am about to say, but I'm saying it for context, clarity and to ensure that we are on the same page."

4. **What Not to Say:** Do not say things like "You Should do X" or "You know what you need to find out is X." Instead, say things like, "Have you considered X&Z?"

    The reason you do it this way, especially in the beginning, is that you don't know what they have or have not done, learned, or know, so it's usually too early to offer definitive advice. Also, telling people what they should do is a command. Most of us don't like to be commanded to do things. We do want to consider well-meaning advice, however.

WHEN ASKING FOR HELP CONSIDER

It's important to ask people for help and not command them or demand that they do what you want. Even if it's your child or worker, you should still ask. We ask because it's polite. Those who know they need to do it regardless will follow, or you can go to the command level if they do not. This technique means that when you do offer commands, they are taken more seriously. Also, it means people will feel better about helping you because it's courteous and seems to provide a choice by using a question.

- "Do this for me" vs. "Can you do this for me, please?" Or "You can help me with this" vs. "Can you please help me with this?" Or "I need you to do X" vs. "Can you help me with X, please?"
- "I will let you do this for me" vs. "Can you do this for me, please," Or "Can you help me by taking X to the X? I would appreciate it."
- "When you come this way, take this with you…" vs. "When you come this way, would you mind taking this with you…?"

WHEN ANSWERING QUESTIONS CONSIDER THIS

The key to answering questions is to answer definitively and then give details.

For Example:

- "Yes, and I can tell you why and give you the details if you are interested."
- "The answer is 300 meters, and here is the calculation…"
- "No, I can't do that, and here's why…"
- "No, I can't do that for two reasons, and they are one…"

- "The answer to your question has three parts: the numbers, application, and distribution. On the numbers, they add up to 1500, the application will be finished on March 15th or thereabout, and distribution is worldwide starting in all major cities ten days after the application completion."

It's OK to Follow Up

Often, you have the option to follow up on something instead of dealing with it immediately. Delaying is good to use when you don't know the answer or how you feel, but know you can find out if you just had some time. Delaying gives you time to provide a detailed explanation. You can wait to answer to ensure that you are complete and do not miss anything. The key is to remember that you have the option to follow up with them later.

Here you can say things like: "Let me pull everything together and get back to you on that next week." Or "I don't have the complete answer, but I'll get it to you tomorrow."

After you tell them this, it's your responsibility to get back to that person. Your duty can start by sending a quick email letting them know you are working on it. Then follow up regularly if it takes a while, letting them know you are working on it. When you are done, give them the answer.

Email/Text/Comment Protocol

In today's world, much of our communication is digital. It comes in many forms, including short texts, IMs, DM, emails, attachments, links, emoji's, videos, audio, pictures, etc.

The key here is to remember that it's easy for a misunderstanding to occur through these quick and often impersonal forms of communication.

The Way | Step 6: Unite – continued

They often do not convey intent correctly. Also, since it's not interactive, digital communications can catch people at bad times, which can make it hard for them to see your message in the right light or context. It's also important to realize that a text can seem cold and accusatory.

To help you navigate this area, please consider:

- Remember, people are insecure, don't like confrontation, and generally want any digital communication to be easy and quick.
- Try not to tell someone what they did wrong or criticize and critique them in a text, email, and other quick forms. After you resolve the issue, it's ok to follow up with the main points and what was learned for the record if it's needed.
- If you desire to express your deep feelings and thoughts in written form, you do so as an attachment. Within the email body, say something like "see the attached file. It's a heartfelt letter covering X. Please read it when you have some time alone and can consider my feelings." You can also send it by regular mail.
- It's important to note that the written word does not easily lend itself to expressing emotions as well as using your voice on the phone or in person. Therefore, consideration and extra care of this fact should be given to the words you use, especially if there is a misunderstanding. In this case, you will need to write out explicitly how you feel and how the other person makes you feel.
- Don't offer advice on what you think they should do in a text unless asked or agreed to by the person beforehand.

- It's ok to ask for a meeting in an email to work through an issue. You can confirm agendas and even set rules in this way. Just don't get into discussing the topic.
- If someone is asking you questions in an email, answer all the questions asked. There is nothing more frustrating when trying to do work than having to go back to ask the same questions over and over. If you don't want to answer a question in an email, tell them that and set up a meeting.
- If in a professional relationship, it's good to respond to every communication within 24 to 48 hours, even if it's just to say you received the message and that you are working on it. We respond this way because it allows others to know what's happening, and they don't have to track it down.
- Within email and in general, do not spread disturbing, horrific, or sexual images, especially when pretending it's something benign. Also, do not spread gossip, rumors, lies, conspiracy theories, deep fakes, or fake news.
- Remember to be friendly and use emojis to lighten the mood. Try to make it fun, easy, and ask for help and advice.

COMMUNICATION ISSUES

"You can have brilliant ideas, but if you can't get them across, your ideas won't get you anywhere." - Lee Iacocca

There are a lot of different communication issues you can have. Some of the more common are covered here. Knowing how to handle these issues helps create more understanding and happiness within your life as well as within our society.

TALKING & WE THINK THE OTHER PERSON(S) IS NOT UNDERSTANDING?

If you are talking with people and you are not getting the feedback you expected or feel that they are not understanding, you can stop and ask open questions. Be sure to let them answer. If there is a misunderstanding, you can work to clear it up with them. You can also do this here and there as you go to make sure they are following you.

- "Do you feel you understand me?"
- "Can you repeat back your understanding to me so I can see if you got it?"
- "What do you see as the main point in what I just said?"

IF ATTACKED

It's ok to assert yourself here and there if being attacked. If they are swearing, name-calling, and threatening, you can interrupt. Start by letting them know that they are being negative and then ask a question—something like:

- "Hey, I know you're upset, but let's keep this civil. Can you tell me what is going on calmly?"
- "I'm sorry, but if we are going to continue, you are going to have to step back and stop yelling at me. Please, can you calmly tell me why you are so upset?"

- "Wow! That is an aggressive statement. Why do you feel that way?"
- "Hey, that was not a very nice thing to say. Why did you say it?"

If you are wronged, you can be firm and use volume and emotion, but be sure to do it in a way that leaves the door open for a peaceful resolution.

ARGUMENT – MISCOMMUNICATION OR HAVING PROBLEMS COMMUNICATING?

Sometimes when you are communicating with others, individuals, or groups, something happens, and it turns into an argument. It can be your fault or their fault or both. It does not matter. Often these situations are simple break downs in communication and misunderstandings that can be cleared up with a little work.

First, it takes all people involved to work on this. If only one party is trying, and the others are still irrational, angry, and not listening, then it's better to wait until there can be a rational discussion.

1. **Notice:** The 1st key is to realize it's happening before it goes too far.
2. **Stop & Go Meta:** Next, stop the chain of negativity with a quick statement or by "going meta."

Saying Something Short Like:

- "Hey, this is getting out of hand. We need to stop and work to clear this up." Or "Hey, let's stop for a minute, take a breath and get our emotions and thoughts in line and focus using reason and logic."
- "This is making (me, both of us, all of us) uncomfortable. Can we take a minute and step back to see if we can fix it?"

- "Can we talk about how we are handling this issue? I love (like or value) you and want us to work this out without hurting each other. Can we work together on this?"
- "I feel we just had a miscommunication and would like to clear it up. Can we talk for a minute?"

Go Meta: When "going meta," you <u>do not</u> talk about the actual point of conversation. Instead, you have a conversation focusing on <u>how</u> you are talking, the feelings you have, and volume, tone, and words used. The goal is for all to understand what is happening beyond the words and to set ground rules so that you may have a productive conversation and resolve any issues.

"Before going back into the conversation, let's set some ground rules about how we are communicating. Let's not yell and let the other person finish. Let's write down all the key points and work to understand each other. Writing this together will help us get to the root of our issues and not perpetuate a misunderstanding. Once we fully understand all the issues and each other's perspectives, we can work toward a resolution. How does that sound?"

Everyone needs to agree to what you just said before moving forward. If they do not, you need to clarify and adjust the terms to suit everyone.

3. **Seek Understanding:** Next, seek to understand the other's perspective: arguments, ideas, fact base, etc.

   a. **Actively Listen:** See "Are You Really Listening" above for details.

b. **Respect them** by watching your tone and body language. Stay positive.
c. **Question Them:** Ask them to explain the parts that you are having trouble with and ask questions.
    - Find the crux of difference that is at the heart of the misunderstanding.
    - Seek to clarify & discuss: What are they thinking, and why do they think that way?
    - Why does it make you feel this way?
    - Remember to use "Your Code" as a filter. Would you like it if someone did that to you? Is equality an issue here?
d. **Find the Kernel of Truth and Virtues** at the center and build a shared fact base.
e. **Focus on the facts**, not misconceptions and feelings. Use logic, reason, and science for help.
f. **Missing Piece?** It may be that there is something implied, assumed, and not stated that needs to be brought into the light. It may be what has <u>not</u> been explained or understood that is holding things up.
g. **Body & Tone**: Sometimes, it's not what is said, but the tone and body language that is the issue. Sarcasm, talking down to, and bad body language can lead to feelings of not being heard or understood.
h. **Ever-Listening** might also be an issue. Ever-Listening is when you always hear someone as being negative when they are not. Ever-Listening often happens in families and with long term acquaintances. *For example*, you hear your brother as always talking down to you.

i. **Go Passive:** You don't have to respond or be moved by everything. Be calm. Don't let the other person push your buttons and enrage you. Passivity is needed in all problematic communications at times. See it as a test of your self-control abilities.

j. **Open Mind:** Do not be so set in your opinion that you see all others as not understanding you. Work to follow them to find the crux of the issue, the core of their belief. Be able to explain it back to them to their satisfaction.

Being open often will help you find something you were missing or did not know. Understanding the other can help you find the misunderstanding. Being open can all help you find better solutions, change your mind, as well as help you find a better way to explain your position so they will understand.

k. **Find & Define:** Once the differences are found, clearly define them. State what is happening as you see it, have them do the same.

   1. Each person repeats back the other's position to ensure they understand. Clear up any errors.
   2. What do we agree or don't agree?
   3. What are the differences in our facts?
   4. What do you want?

After knowing what they are saying by asking questions, you can address the differences. However, once you have gone through things in this way, you might find it settled.

Explaining Something Complex or Potential Volatile Communication

Often, you know a difficult conversation is going to happen, and this is especially true when dealing with life problems and issues where you feel the need to defend yourself. The keys in these situations are to:

1. **Do Not be Defensive** – see "Criticisms, Accusations, Etc. – Receiving" below for more detail. Being defensive will only make things worse, even if they are wrong.

2. **Give Background:** Setting "the stage" for a challenging conversation helps every one to get into the right frame of mind.

    - "I would like to talk about X because of Y. Is now a good time, or should we plan something?"
    - "So, it seems you have something you want to talk about, let's set up the rules before going farther (Going Meta – see above)."

3. **Explain WHY** you are going to say what you are going to say.

    o "Experience has shown that…"
    o "Let me take you through our thinking on this…I know you might have heard some of this but bear with me. It's important to set the context."
    o "This has come up before, and here is what we discussed (explain)…how is this is different?"
    o "We have all heard about X. However, let's go over the main points so that we can take this to another level."

- o "While you brought this up before, we are bringing it up now because it still seems to be an issue."
4. **Repeat:** As you go, it's good for each party to repeat back the other party's position to ensure that it's understood.

CRITICISMS, ACCUSATIONS, ETC. – RECEIVING

When accused of something or when receiving criticisms, it's crucial to take a few steps to ensure that you are understood and do not make things worse.

Do Not Be Defensive: It's imperative not to defend yourself immediately, even if you know they misunderstand, misrepresent, are mean, or are wrong. The reason for this is that if you cut the other person off and defend yourself, no matter how right you are, you can be seen as defensive, not listening, uncaring, closed-minded, a bully, or misunderstanding.

The key is to wait until they stop, then ask questions. Seek to understand the real issues. You can say something like:

- "I can see that this is important, and it hurt and upset you. I'm glad you brought this up."
- "To help me understand, can you give me an example?"
- "What exactly do you mean by 'X'?"
- "You say I did X. How do you know that?"
- "You say this is too much, compared to what?"
- "Please tell me why you feel this way about X?"

Only after you have explored the issue with them to the point where they know you got it, it's ok to show them your perspective if it differs. Sometimes offering your view is best done at a later time, even another day if they are upset.

Space is vital, for this gives you time to consider and think about what the other person said and for them to cool down. No matter how much you may disagree, it's real for them. Can you "put yourself in their shoes" for a minute and see their perspective? Is there truth or a fact in here for you to learn?

Can you find a link from where they are to the truth and fact? Think about this situation and how you represent the "10 Laws" and your belief, intention, action, and word within this situation. Is there unity or discord? Are you rationalizing or hiding because it might mean you are wrong or might look bad?

Holding off for a time before responding will allow you to digest what they said and change if need be. It will also help ensure that when you do come back, your facts and approach will be more thought out and comprehensive. When addressing the issue again, you should start by restating their view to their satisfaction, particularly if there is a need to show a difference, and then say things like:

- "During our last conversation, you said X. Is that right?" Get Confirmation – clear up any issues. If major, then wait and come back. If minor, go on.

- If an issue you can say something like: "I have a different experience which is…" *For Example:* "When I said, 'See you later,' I meant it in a genuinely loving way, not the way you took it. I had no idea that someone in your past, who used to say that, betrayed you. We say that in my family in a loving way all the time, because to us, it's much nicer than saying 'Goodbye' because it implies that we are looking forward to seeing them later."

USING THE WORD "I"

When explaining yourself or presenting ideas, it's good not to use "I" too much. If you use the word "I" too much, it will make you seem defensive as well as narcissistic. To be clear, it makes you SEEM this way. Most of you who use "I" a lot are not necessarily narcissistic or defensive; you just had role models who spoke that way.

For example, when trying to explain yourself, you do <u>not</u> want to say things like:

- "I" was trying to…
- What "I" meant was…
- "I" am just trying…
- "I" want…

Instead, ask questions like:

- "Can we talk about X?" "In this situation, my goal was X."
- "In this situation, what do you see as the goal of this meeting?"
- "Why do you say X?"
- "In this situation, my goal was to help you with this, which would make our relationship better. It did not work out that way. What should have happened?"

CRITICISMS, ACCUSATIONS, ADVICE – GIVING

No one likes to be wrong. We especially do not appreciate being reprimanded and talked down to, particularly in public or over typical human error. After all, humans are not machines; we all make mistakes.

Therefore, we all need to take steps to ensure that mistakes don't happen or only happen rarely. In this way, we can consider and make allowances for our human failings. One of the keys is to realize that by treating others with respect (as equals and how you would like to be treated), you are not accepting the mistake. You are merely focusing on your real goal, which is to correct the error and prevent it from happening again. Many times, it's our systems, processes, regulations, and procedures that are at fault rather than the person.

Even if it's a personal fault, if unintentional, your goal is not to beat up on the other person, so they feel bad. Here you are merely looking for a positive way to present the issue that allows the most favorable solution.

Also, if you are truly earnest about treating others as equals and as you would wish to be treated, then you need to handle these situations with care as they can often get out of control or create lasting wounds. Lasting harm happens, especially when you know they were trying and working to do the best they could.

For example, your son is cleaning your car, and in the process, he breaks a mirror. Clearly, he made a mistake. Does he deserve to be yelled at and treated like he did something horrible? He is learning. Maybe he did not know it would come off like that or that he was that strong.

To point out a problem in a positive way, you start with positive and non-confrontational communication, as this helps open the conversation. Next, you ask questions to find out how, why, and when to let them know that you understand. You then go forward following the steps below without the need for conflict. Here you affirm their self-worth before dealing with anything else.

The Way | Step 6: Unite – continued

Example: If someone at work used the wrong email address or copied the wrong people and did not do what you had told them previously, you can say something like:

- "John, thanks for updating the email. BTW, could you use the new email address instead? See my email from 12/11 for more info about this issue (attached)."
- In this example, they can see that you asked them to do it previously.
- The appropriate type of response to something like this should be.
- "Sure, Tom, I will do that from now on. Sorry I missed it the last time!"

Other Examples: Remember, issues handled better in a conversation, and you start by asking for information while directing them to the problem.

- o "Looks like this did not come outright. Remember that email with the changes? Is there an issue?"
- o "Hey, did you know that XYZ had changed?"
- o "Do you know why XYZ happened/did not happen?"
- o "Why was X not moved?"
- o "How did this get broken?"
- o "Why did you send that email after we talked about not sending it?"

You must wait for their response as they might admit the error. If we follow all the best practices and they do not change their behavior, we can be firm. Again, treating them with respect and give them a little time.

- "Did you see the email on the 10th about X?"
- "Do you remember our conversation about X?"

Be sure to get their confirmation before moving on.

"Well, John, this situation has happened again. We need to ensure that it does not keep happening. What do you think will work? How about we go over your process for tracking these types of issues as we might be able to come up with a better solution? We need to do this because if you can't do it, we will have to XYZ."

The "XYZ" is where we outline the consequence of not following through on their word. Like losing your job, not going to the game, concert, or losing internet access. If they do not change, they must know the consequences. You must also follow through with them if it happens again for them to learn.

Therefore, it's essential to make the penalties reasonable. If the penalty is too light, they will not see it as a punishment or a deterrent. If too harsh, you can stifle their growth as well as your own. Keep in mind; the goal is to teach and change the behaviors, not to hurt people unduly.

HATS BLACK, WHITE & RED

Often when you speak, you can do it from different perspectives. The three basics are negative, positive, and emotional. Here you use a black hat for negative, white for positive and red for emotional. When communicating, you can use this in many ways. All must understand what the hats mean before using them.

For Example: You can say, "That was very interesting. You just said "XYZ," and I have a lot of different thoughts on it. Let's start with the "red hat" and how that made me feel; it was great. I was thrilled watching it.

Next, I want to put on my "white hat" and talk to you about why I thought it was good. Not only did it make me happy, but it will also help others in their everyday lives.

Next, let me put on my "black hat." You know there might be some who see this as an indictment or judgment, and it could cause trouble."

By doing it this way, you subtly separate what you are saying from your personal beliefs and offer them three analytical examples of thought. This separation makes them easier to hear, and if done in this order will make the negative easier to take.

TALKING TO OURSELVES

Ok, now that we understand the basics of communication with others, we need to look at how to talk to ourselves. It's natural to talk to yourself. However, in some cultures, there is a negative attitude associated with talking to yourself like you should not do it, and if you do, there is something wrong with you.

We naturally do this because hearing something allows us to gain perspective on what was said. Talking to yourself can be a powerful tool of self-discovery and a way to communicate with and change your subconscious mind. Talking to yourself is simply a communication technique and natural.

YOU TALK TO YOURSELF GENERALLY 4 WAYS:
1. **Command:** Here, you tell and order. Command usually covers things you want or don't want. "I am doing XYZ, and I am doing a great job, or I will not do XYZ, and it stops now." See the "Life Manual: Our Practice: Mental Practice: Focused Meditation: Affirmations" for more on this topic.

2. **Listen for Rightness:** Here, you speak out loud and listen to what you say to see if it rings true. You do this to check yourself to see if what you said is correct or if something might need to change.

3. **To Question:** Using the Socratic method of asking probing questions to find the truth can often help you find the truth.

   You can say things like, "Is this really what you want?" And "If yes, why?" "What bad things might happen if I do this? Does doing XYZ follow my "Code?" "Am I treating them as I would want to be treated?"

4. **Mistakes:** Sometimes, when you make a mistake, you may start to berate yourself by saying negative things like, "Why are you so stupid!" or "Why did I do that, I'm so dumb." The key here is <u>not</u> to beat yourself up or call yourself negative names.

   Instead, when you feel like you made a mistake and are upset at yourself, you should talk to yourself as a friend who is helping you overcome the problem. Here you might say things like, "Ok, wow, that just happened. Now how do I fix this?" or "Yes, I did that, and it was a mistake. How am I going to learn from this, fix it, and not let it happen again?"

I, YOU, ME & WE

When you talk to yourself, you might switch perspectives even more by the pronoun you use. You can say things like, I will, we will, you will, and each time it will change the perspective of who you are. Talking this way helps you as you can see flaws or the rightness of things when tested in different ways.

Note that this is just a technique. Using it does not mean you are multiple people. You are just asking, listening, and answering from different perspectives.

In the end, talking to yourself in productive ways can help you not feel alone, judge things more effectively, and find a better way. It's also an outlet that allows you to express yourself in a safe way where you are the only one to judge. Talking to yourself helps you refine yourself so that when you do things in the world or when speaking with people, you naturally do a better job. Even though this is natural, you may not want to do this in public, unless you wear a phone microphone, or people might look at you strangely (hee-hee).

CHAPTER 11
MENDING THE BROKEN

"Diversity is about all of us, and about us having to figure out how to walk through this world together."
- Jacqueline Woodson

So far, we have learned a lot about how to be a better person and put ourselves out there in a positive way as well as some problems with our society. Within this chapter, we continue to explore "Step 6: Unite" as we learn how to handle negative relationships.

To have a more positive world and relationships, we must all work to change the negative into a positive rather than to only seek the existing positive. Therefore, as you work on your life, and with other positive people, don't abandon people that are having a hard time needlessly.

To have a more positive world and relationships, we must all work to change the negative into a positive rather than to only seek the existing positive. If we are to build the "True Society," it's important to include everyone that is friendless, lonely, abused, disenfranchised, ignored, poor, and forgotten because it's the right thing to do and because they can quickly become desperate. This desperation can manifest itself in many negative and violent ways within our society.

The desperate are also often the easiest to manipulate by those looking to exploit them. It's desperate people who may feel that violence is the only way to draw notice to the injustice and to survive. We help them because we are humane and care.

It's important to realize that if the lonely and desperate are included, there will be less of a need for them to lash out as there will be someone there for them. Often, it's just one person who can make the most significant difference to another person. So, join together and stand up to bullies in groups, invite the lonely and friendless to events, and introduce them to people of like interests. Sometimes this simply means not ignoring people and saying "Hi" or giving a nod as we pass. It can mean looking at someone in the eye who has done a service for us and earnestly thanking them and wishing them a good day.

Those of us who are lonely also need to take responsibility and not blame the world. You need to work on creating a pleasing and attractive personality as best you can. You need to get out there and find friends and positive people you can relate to. The easiest way to do this is to join a positive group that does something you enjoy. Through the internet, you can connect like never before, so finding that group of people that share a positive interest is easier than ever.

To be clear, the goal is <u>not</u> to live and be around only those who see life as you do and who are at your level of intelligence and wisdom. The goal is to live and be around people you like who are good, positive, open-minded, and are looking to better themselves and the world. The level of skill or talent does not matter. Only their positivity, goodness, willingness to learn, and teach are essential. The diversity of positive people will allow you to offer aid and to be aided.

This positive direction will allow you to become better, emulate good behaviors and thinking patterns, learn more, and help others. Ensuring that all people are integrated within our society and that they have positive social groups and friends means there is less loneliness, fear, depression, and violence. The resulting effect is more peace, happiness, and security for us all.

If you are having a hard time with this idea, you might ask yourself this question. Isn't treating people with respect and including them better than working to ruin their lives because they are different, especially when you know that those who end up alone, desperate and enraged are often those who see violence as the only answer?

Remember, everyone has a snapping point if pushed too far, and we can rationalize almost anything if needing to survive. Therefore, we need to construct our society so that it does not create desperate people or place so many at subsistence levels or below. We all also need to learn self-control and how to manage our anger issues and snapping point.

In the end, our shared human conditions force us to work together, on all levels and situations, to create a more positive world. It has been set up this way so that you can be part of something wonderful and not be alone. It's in your positive interactions with all the people around you that you can make a real difference and change the world for the better.

HOW TO FIX NEGATIVE RELATIONSHIPS

"Don't settle for a relationship that prevents you from being yourself." - Oprah Winfrey

A negative relationship is a way to refer to a relationship that covers a wide range of physical abuse, mental abuse, and conflict. These high conflict relationships can damage your health and shorten your life.

The longer they persist, the more damage they do. Negative relationships maybe those with people who physically hurt you, threaten to do so, or come in the form of mental or emotional abuse.

For example, they might always be coming at you with negative comments such as putting you down, making you feel bad, destroying your creations, mocking you, being rude, etc. Also, these abusive people may not listen, are sarcastic, say hurtful things covered by "just joking." They break their word, don't consider you, regularly use communication tactics against you, and rarely do anything nice for you.

A negative relationship might involve people that have bad habits and vices like smoking, drinking, drugs, slander, gossip, mocking, prejudice, hate, and more. If you feel bad when you are around them or start to develop the bad habits they have, it's a sign that you are in a negative relationship. For more information on ways that people can lead us from the truth, see the "Life Manual: Fuel: Information: Tactics Used Against Us."

Note that these negative relationships can also include celebrities, news and talk show hosts, comedians, tv show characters, and other people who are very negative to selective people or groups. You might not personally know them, but because you can hear them all the time, they are considered close to you. Because of this, they can be very damaging to you and your outlook on the world if they are self-righteous, full of hate, and negativity. The key here is to acknowledge which relationships are negative so you can then deal with them correctly.

The six steps on how to deal with a negative relationship include:

Step 1: Safety & Security

The first question is, are you or your loved ones being harmed or in fear of your safety? If yes, get to a safe location, seek help, and work to resolve the situation from there. If you decide to try to fix things, it must be done from a safe location where you and your loved ones are protected and secure.

If you do not have a safe place or people who can help and you are in immediate danger, you can go to or call the police or help agency. If that is not an option, you can also go to a public place where there is security, like an airport or hotel. Security can provide you with witnesses and potential help while you plan your next steps.

Seeking safety is even true for those of you who can handle yourself during a physical confrontation. The bottom line is that you <u>do not want</u> to put yourself in a situation where you get pushed to your breaking point when you would be required to use violence to protect yourself. If you did hurt or kill someone in the process or get hurt or killed, it will do nothing but complicate the situation.

Step 2: The Challenge & Lessons

Understand that there are significant lessons and training opportunities within these destructive relationships. You must look at them before you engage with others as well as throughout the process. Humanity's ability and desire to change a negative situation, relationship, person, and environment into the positive is how we improve as a people and as a society. Fixing the wrongness is one of the constant primary human conditions that challenges and tests our species, for it forces us to choose and act if we are to make a meaningful difference.

The process of creating a better relationship, especially if the other person agrees and is motivated to do so, is an excellent opportunity to learn about yourself and grow in ways that you could not otherwise. You can also help someone else become better and create positive relationships with deep roots that can aid you on the rest of your journey.

Conversely, if you try to fix a relationship where the others are not in agreement or motivated, the relationship will not improve. This process will then be a massive waste of time and energy. It can even lead you away from your "True Path," hurting your health and shortening your life. This is because it's insanity on your part to think someone will suddenly change and do right by you when they do not want or care to do so. Therefore, you must use care when dealing with these situations, finding what can be fixed and leaving the rest.

Regardless of who the issue is with or what is at stake, there are lessons you can learn that have nothing to do with the situation and everything to do with your development as a person. Those who are the hardest to talk with and understand create a situational opportunity where you can grow a lot as a person as well as in your ability to communicate and manage others.

This challenge is especially true for people in permanent positions in your life, such as family. Also, sometimes the closest relationships, as with a family member, are the most difficult yet are the relationships you would like to work the best. Therefore, it's essential to work through the challenge and to develop yourself to be your best while you also work to improve the relationship. If you are successful, you will grow, they will grow, and together you will go farther in life than you could otherwise.

Self-Control Lessons: Some of the main lessons, training, and challenges that center around self-control and development include:

- **Communication**: Use all the good Communication Basics (see above) and avoid being negative and the use of tactics. For more, see the "Life Manual: Fuel: Information: Tactics Used Against Us."

- **Time & Mental Focus:** How much time you spend and your mental focus regarding these people is essential. Remember, you can choose to think and feel anything you want. You do not have to engage them on their level or respond as you have in the past. You can think of ways not to spend time with them. You are working to live a life where your primary mental focus is on your life and the positive, even in the face of the negative.

- **Emotions & Feelings:** You can choose to feel or not feel as you want. You can choose not to let others "push your buttons" and make you have negative feelings like sadness, anger, or frustration. The key to this is to view your situation from a 3rd perspective as someone from the outside looking in, then realize there is no justification for letting them make you feel this way. Through this perspective and realization, you can more easily deflect and transmute negative energy.

- **Transmutation of Negative Energy:** As you know, negative relationships can create negative energy. The key is to use your transmutation ability to change it into positive energy, which you can then use to power your life in positive directions. See the "Life Manual: Our Practice: The Power: Transmutation" for more.

For Example: You can envision all the negative energy flowing through your "transmuter" as you repeat silent positive litanies instead of listening to or engaging with that person when they are negative toward you. You can even work to cultivate feelings of happiness by recalling a special moment of joy while with them to lighten your mood. If things get too intense, you can leave early or come up with excuses not to be around them.

- **Fight or Flight Response:** Often, a negative relationship will trigger a fight or flight reaction either when you are with them or by just thinking of them. This situation is an opportunity to work on controlling this reaction. See the "Life Manual: Our Practice: Mental Practice" for more on how to do this.

Lessons of Wrongness: In this age, there are a lot of positive people that focus and talk about the negative aspects of society and other people. This constant negative focus happens because often people don't know the solution, or if there is a solution, it seems far out of our reach. Therefore, the answer is often left out of the discussion altogether, which can make a positive person seem negative and bring people down. This negativity makes you look like part of the problem, especially if you keep pointing out all that is wrong in others or the world while offering no solutions or hope.

For example, you help your mom go shopping. She buys bottled water, and then you tell her about the toxins in it and how the plastic is destroying the world. Then you go home and help her put her things away and tell her about all the problems with her choices because they are mostly refined and processed food. Also, you say that the cleaning products she chooses are harming the environment.

You don't just do this once, but over and over for years. You do all of this without talking about solutions and how she can help or about your struggles.

Can you see how very negative we can come across in this example? Often, the person saying these things will feel that they are doing a positive thing by sharing what is wrong. However, without the correct delivery, timing, and solutions being the focus, it all sounds negative and judgmental. The person hearing all this can be taking it as an indictment and criticism of their knowledge and choices.

The key here is first to realize that this is something you do. If unsure, ask friends and family. See "Step 7: Perfect: Periodic Life Review" for more. Then stop this behavior, so you are not so off-putting. Instead, if you do see something amiss, you can ask them if they would like to know something.

For example, instead of just telling your mom these things, at a good time, you could say something like, "Hey Mom, I did a lot of research and found an easier, cheaper, and healthier alternative to bottled water. Would you like to talk about it sometime?"

Another key aspect of fixing any problem relationship is to look for the virtues at the heart of your and the other person's perspective. If they exist and are clear, they can help you find common ground. This is because, most often, disagreements between good people have more to do with the shared fact base than a disregard for the other side's virtues than anything else.

STEP 3: THE GROUPS & YOUR CHOICE

In this step, you recognize that there are two kinds of people in your life. The relatively permanent and those who are in your life by choice.

1. **Permanent:** They are a permanent fixture like a family member or co-worker.
2. **Choice:** They are someone that you choose to spend time with, like a friend or acquaintance.

You then put the negative relationships you have into one of these groups. You do this because this will help you find a perspective that will affect your choices later in this process. For now, keep this in mind as you go through the next steps.

STEP 4: THE ALLIANCE

Here your goal is to create an alliance with the other person(s) where all parties work together to improve the relationship. The reason you start with trying to work with them instead of just cutting people out is that, as noted, this is a foundational human challenge created by human conditions we live under. It forces us to change the negative into a positive to truly succeed.

To say it another way here, you have a negative but safe relationship with someone you genuinely care about, and you want to discover if they will join with you in making the relationship better. If they are open to the idea, it's vital to clearly agree and even talk about basic terms at the start and through the process. Agreement of terms combined with your positive work, overtime (at least 90 days), will create better habits within your relationship.

So, you can make lists and include things like agreeing to be open to discovering everyone's issues, adhering to the communication basics, working through issues while focusing on the goal of solving the problems permanently. Everyone is doing everything without seeking blame or making other people feel bad.

It's also essential to agree to immediately let the other person know that they are <u>not</u> doing what was committed to. Be sure to setup how you will notify each other of the breach beforehand. Choosing the exact method and words is essential as this can help prevent future problems. This is because everyone will know what to do and to expect. The expression of the breach can even be one word, that when spoken, lets the others know you feel the terms have been violated. The goal here is to focus on fixing the problems so that everyone can live within a positive relationship. You must know and acknowledge the negative for this to happen.

If the person commits to working with you, be sure to live up to your end and go the extra mile here, especially in the beginning. A little extra positive effort in changing a negative can not only make things easier, but it can also yield long term benefits. The more negative people who change into positive, the easier everything becomes for all of us. The power of mass unity is valid within the circle of your immediate life as well as globally. This is because everyone will have more support, see more positive role models, and be a better role model. This all creates more hope, positive energy, and momentum.

STEP 5: MANAGE THE NON-COOPERATING NEGATIVES

Those people who are negative and not willing to join with you must be either "managed" or "cut off." In either situation, there will be negative energy, which you will need to manage effectively, so it does not damage you.

Again, control is absolutely needed because negative relationships hurt you physically by stimulating a harmful chemical reaction within your body, which will distort your thinking and damage your body. The longer this exists, the higher the damage and the more in danger you are of creating this way of being into a habit.

There are many reasons why you have to or choose to manage a non-cooperating (not vested in positive change) or nonproductive (not improving over time) negative relationship instead of cutting it off entirely. Some might involve family, work, longtime friends who have gone astray and children.

Effective relationship management is critical, for they can either make you stronger and a better person or weaken and even destroy you. Therefore, successful management is the ability to use these negatives as a way to improve yourself. Control is needed because if you can't manage negative relationships properly; they will:

- **Take Time:** Negative relationships take your time, preventing you from doing positive things for yourself and others.

- **Wear Us Down:** Over time, a negative person can wear you down, diminishing your coping abilities even further, leaving you open to even more harm.

- **Twist to Negative:** If you don't handle a negative relationship well, you can fixate on the negative, which can perpetuate negative feelings and thoughts. The longer this goes on, without complete transmutation, the more damage it does to you on many levels. It also takes you away from focusing on your life and the positive.

How to Manage: You manage a non-cooperating negative relationship through the use and development of self-control skills. These include good communication, proper use of time, positive mental focus and attitude, transmutation of negative energy into positive, as well as emotional and "fight or flight" response control. (See The Life Manual: Our Practice" for more.)

You also can limit how much time you spend around them, focusing on them, and responding to them. To be clear, this means limiting the time you spend with them both mentally and physically. You spend your time thinking about positive things regardless if they are around you or not. As you progress along your "True Path" and integrate the skills within *The Way*, your ability to manage negative relationships will increase.

STEP 6: CUT THEM OUT

If you are in a relationship of choice that is high conflict, and they are unwilling to work with you for positive change, it may be useful to separate from that person. Separation is essential when you can't positively compensate for all the negative energy. Also, if they will not work with you and you stay, you are, in a sense accepting and condoning their behavior, which can perpetuate and even exacerbate the problem.

Sometimes, the best thing is to remove yourself or them from your life in a peaceful and positive manner. When you break off a relationship, you do so in a way that you would want it done to you if the circumstances were reversed, ideally in a way where you can grow, and they might learn and also grow. In all but the most extreme cases, you do not just ghost people (just disappear without a word). It's very rude, reflects very poorly on you, and can create a lot more negative energy than there need be. If having a hard time doing this, think of a time when you were clueless about something and needed a bit of a jolt to realize the truth. How would you want to be treated?

In this way, you are working to be a catalyst that inspires the person to use the energy created by the separation in a positive way to help them improve. Your positive action is how you can help fix society, for often people can't see their flaws even when they are in relationships with other people.

By trying to create a positive transition for them, no matter how negative they are, you will help yourself down your "Truth Path," too. *Note* that your only responsibility is to do this in the best way you can. Then leave it alone. You are not responsible for what they do with it. You never know you might help them to the point where they come back someday changed for the good and are the person you hoped they could be.

THE 2 STEPS TO THE SEPARATION

Frist - Care for Self: It's imperative that you first separate yourself in all the ways you need to be safe. Separation might mean removing yourself from a location, not answering text messages and calls. Here you do not engage with the other person and remove yourself from the situation. Separation is especially crucial for battered women and children. Work to fill your life with the positives of your choosing.

As noted, if you manage or cut someone out, there is often a lot of energy generated. In this situation, it's vital to envision this energy as freeing, unbinding, and liberating, and to use it in positive ways to develop yourself. It may be that after such an event, your mind will continuously go back to thinking about them, the situation, how you handled it, and how you might have done things differently or better. Your focusing on the problem can often create negative feelings. When this happens, first look for the lessons. Write them down to ensure that your whole being understands that you got the message. Then let it go.

Letting it go is done by focusing on the positive. If you drift back, be mindful and focus on something positive. Understand that to focus on that negative relationship is a desire we all share, which is to fix a problem. The key is that once you have done what you can, the test becomes moving on, which means breaking the bad habit of focusing on this negative thing you can't fix.

Again, we let go by focusing and filling our life with the positive. You can think of this as replacing an old bad habit with a new positive one as in replacing old negative friends with positive ones. It might take a little persistence and work, but after a while, the transition period will end, and the situation will be changed. In this way, you use the energy in this transitional situation to push you further down your "True Path." Doing your best during these trying times is what makes you a stronger and better person when you come out on the other side.

Second - Write/Tell Person Why: As noted, a key aspect of this process is to do break this off in a way that you would appreciate if the circumstances were reversed, ideally in a way they can learn something positive and become a better person.

To accomplish this, you need to tell the negative person why you ended the relationship and even offer some <u>constructive</u> criticism and advice if you have any. You are doing this because we must all work to change the negatives within society to positives for it to happen.

Again, this should only be done from a place where you are safe, and this should <u>not</u> be done if you feel it would put you in further jeopardy. It's also important not to overly focus on this task. Your goal is to do this in the most direct, clear, and shortest way possible.

For many, this helps us find closure. You are not looking to be mean, vindictive, sarcastic, or mocking.

You start by just collecting themes and notes here and there when it's convenient. Taking only a little time is essential, especially in the beginning, as you primarily don't want to focus on them or negative thoughts and feelings. As the days pass, themes and ideas will become evident, feelings will recede, and logic and reason will reassert itself. You can then look through all the notes you collected into a bulleted list. Your thoughts can then go within a letter you send.

Here is an example email. You can also do this over the phone or in-person if you feel safe and good about it.

Email Body: Hi (Name). I have been out of touch. Attached is a letter explaining why. Please read it when you have a quiet moment to yourself. Best (Your Name Here)

Attached Letter Reads: Dear (Name Here), I'm sorry I had to end our relationship. You would not work on fixing it with me. I do wish you the best. The main issues I had are listed here.

- o Lying: You constantly lied to me, even over small things. Example A, B, and C.
- o Your Word: You always tell me things you will do, then don't. You don't even tell me you can't do them; you forget. When I ask, you get all defensive or say I'm sorry or even get mad at me. It's best to keep your word or do not give it if you can't. Giving your word and saying you're sorry all the time when you break it makes you irresponsible, clueless, uncaring, and a liar.

- Timing: You are always so late. A few minutes here and there is ok, but hours and days without contact are more than rude. It's best not to be late, but if you have to, let those waiting for you know asap.

Anyway, I hope this helps you to find your True Path. I suggest you read *The Way*; it might also help. (You don't have to reference this book; it's listed as one thing that may help them. You can offer any advice you feel might help like joining a recovery group, taking better care of themselves, etc.)

Goodbye, (your first name)

Again, try not to spend too much time on this. There is no set time in which you must get it done. Just collect your thoughts, say what you need, have no regrets, find closure, and let it go. Remember, you are not in this life to be at the mercy of negative people who do not want to change for the positive.

If you care about them and truly want to help them, you can't accept their negativity. Instead, you must work to change the negative into a positive. You do this for your own sake, for the other person, and for everyone they will ever come in contact with. This break could be the catalyst they need to help them on their "True Path."

Note: If you are the one being broken up with in this manner, take time to work on yourself and give the other person a break. You may find it was the best thing that could have happened for clearly, you were not in a mutually beneficial relationship.

Chapter 12
True Power & Being the Solution

"We need to make sure we're all working together to change mindsets, to change attitudes, and to fight against the bad habits that we have as a society." - Justin Trudeau

So far, we have covered a lot of ground concerning aspects of close relationships as part of "Step 6: Unite." These local social connections with people, as well as the societal systems we use daily, are the "Micro" level, as these are the people and institutions you are in direct contact with throughout your daily life.

Now we are going to cover "Macro" level relationships, which include all the people that affect your life without any or much direct contact. This perspective includes all those who lead and work within the foundational systems of society such as government, business, communications, health, justice, religion, media, and entertainment as well as basics like education, water, food, housing, clothing, sanitation, transportation, emergency services, and energy. We are going into a little detail on some key aspects of our "Macro Level Relationships" because they determine much of your life as well as the fate of humanity.

Pyramid vs. Engine

Before going into the "Keys of Power," it's essential to understand its basic structure. Here we are using a metaphor that hopefully most of us can relate to.

The Pyramid: Our human conditions setup a hieratical world view. In this perspective, we have placed a person, most often male, at the top of a pyramid-like structure.

We see this represented in our organizations like a government, religion, or business where there is one person at the top of an organizational chart.

This type of structure is used by authoritarians, kings, militaries, and others. While it might be an appropriate structure at times, especially within specific military systems, this top-down example does not represent actual societies, governments, or businesses to a high degree. This king of the hill view leads to the improper flow of information, stagnation, corruption, and inequality. It leads to a false sense of superiority in some areas as it undervalues critical aspects of the organization and more.

The Engine: Our societal systems are not like a pyramid but more like an engine in which all the components matter and are equal. Regardless of the size or expense, an engine can be brought down by a small, inexpensive part as quickly as it can by a large, expensive one. All parts are equal because if any component fails, the overall performance diminishes, or the whole system fails.

The way this works is true with all our societal systems as well. If key components fail like leadership, sales, accounting, delivery, etc., the whole system can fail. Here the organizational chart would put leadership positions at nexus points rather than on top. We all need to do our part to ensure the "engines" within our society are all running well. For any system to thrive, we need to realize that all the jobs are equally important.

THE KEYS TO POWER

"All the power that we exercise over others depends on the power we exercise over ourselves." - Cotvos

To create the "True Society," we must learn to direct Power effectively. To do this, you must first understand the basics of power. Power is what allows us to create change and get things done. Learning to channel power correctly within our society is critical. Without an understanding and thoughtful direction, we end up with confusion, strife, corruption, destruction, and inequality.

Improper use of power also creates situations where it stagnates and concentrates in the hands of a few. When power is concentrated into the hands of a few, with little or no checks and balances in place, corruption flourishes. This corruption compounds the problems of society. For all these reasons, it's imperative all understand "power" and work together to direct it correctly within our society.

WHAT IS POWER?

Fundamentally, power is the control or influence over people and things. This control and influence are what allows power to get things done.

The 2 types of Power are:

- **Soft Power:** The ability to attract, cooperate, and co-opt as a means of persuasion.
- **Hard Power:** The ability to coerce, use force, or give wealth as a means of persuasion.

WHAT ARE THE TOOLS OF POWER?

There are 4 tools used by the powerful to get things done. The tools of power include violence, media, information, and wealth. To control one tool at a high enough level can give access to the other tools.

1. **Violence** is the use of or threat of physical force to injure a person or damage something. Violence is a tool of power because it forces obedience through physical coercion and intimidation of self or the innocent or loved ones.

2. **Media** covers news, TV, movies, books, the internet, magazines, music, newspapers, etc. The power to create, deliver, or not deliver information has a significant effect on how we, the masses, act and react as a society. What we learn, our ways of doing, thinking, and feeling are influenced by the media we consume.

   There are those in power who use this tool to change public opinion and control collective knowledge. They control and determine what issues are being talked about, as well as what is not.

   It's also the tool used to confuse, distract, divide, manipulate, and mislead us from the truth. Too often, sensationalism, sex, and horror are at the forefront of the media because it plays on our basic instincts. There is usually minimal context or information on how to participate in the solution. The media of our current age is typically designed to manipulate us in some way, not to help us in our lives.

   Mass media can also be used as a force for good, spreading truth, positivity, and solutions. Our media managed correctly can not only make our lives more enjoyable but also lead us to higher levels of success in all areas of life. Let there be no mistake, media exists and will exist; it's up to us to determine <u>how</u> it exists.

3. **Knowledge** is made of gathered facts. These facts brought together and used by an intelligent person is knowledge. Knowledge applied well is wisdom. Knowledge is a tool of power because information creates action and makes things more effective and efficient.

   If knowledge is shared only with a few, the greater the power, generally, this is because they can then charge a premium for the knowledge, or they can do something others cannot.

For example, the knowledge of how to build a house that can withstand a hurricane or a faster microchip or medicine to cure a disease are all forms of knowledge many would like to have. Our knowledgebase has grown so much that we call our current age the "Information Age," which means more wealth is now generated by those who have knowledge than by other means.

4. **Wealth** is made of valuable resources, materials, or possessions. Within our society, it mainly takes the form of money and assets like gold, cars, art, and property. Wealth is a tool of power because it can be used to direct action within our society. To create our "True Society," wealth must be directed and managed well; therefore, it's covered in more detail below.

In the end, the four tools of power must be used wisely, or we will all suffer. Wise use means those at the center of power must do the right things with these tools. As we know, this does not always happen because of the flaw we all share and the fact that our centers of power are not always appropriately managed by those of merit.

What are the Centers of Power?

Ok, now that we know what power is and the tools of power, let's look at how power manifests, concentrates, focuses and centers within four critical areas of human life. These include: Position, Fame, Desirable Traits, and United Power.

1. **Position:** Because of the human condition, we naturally form organizations with hieratical structures. These structures create positions of power which we call a

position of leadership. Many positions of leadership, like parents, priests, teachers, governors, kings, and presidents, automatically give us power over others. Some of the most powerful are either the leaders of, or those who control the leaders of, the major systems of society such as government, business, media, education, and religion.

Remember that all leaders are nothing without followers and that we affect positive change through laws and policy. Since leaders get their power from their followers, we need only unite correctly to put true leaders in positions of power.

The societal systems for creating and choosing leaders are critical to the success of our civilization. The best are equality-based merit systems, where the genuinely qualified are in positions of power and in all other jobs within our society. An "Equality Based Merit System" means all citizens have equal access, and those chosen deserve and are worthy of the position. *For example,* they have high-quality education and training, experience, past results, abilities, and temperament.

Highest Position of Power: Creating great leaders and citizens all starts somewhere. Children become adults and fill the positions within the systems of society. Therefore, if there are many maladjusted adults and leaders, we are not raising our children correctly and/or do not have a conducive society. Since we are all born ignorant and need exceptional care, the solution begins with those who raise us.

Those who raise a child are the number one determining factor in that child's mental, emotional, physical, and spiritual development. Caregivers provide nutrition, exercise, instill habits, affect the child's founding core beliefs, ways of thinking, and perspectives on the world.

This fact means we can create a conducive environment whereby our children can go much further in life. Correctly raising our children ingrains virtues and best practices as their first way of doing things. Having the best practices as core habits will make their entire life more fulfilling. It's more fulfilling because our children don't have to try and change later in life, like many of us need to. Instead, they will simply live positive action every day naturally doing foundational life tasks well because that is how they were trained from the start and is, therefore, all they know.

Ingraining the best practices into our young is by far the most effective way to create people who will make good leaders. Having lots of great leaders naturally crowds out the bad. Therefore, the most influential leadership positions are held by those who raise our children. For more on how to do this effectively, see the *Child & Family Guide*.

- Power Source: Those in positions of power can command people, change law, policies, and the direction of a group. Those in these positions affect current and future generations. Those in these positions get their power from their followers.

2. **Fame:** The famous can be those who are media celebrities such as artists, actors, singers, writers, comedians, sports stars, politicians, and religious leaders, as well as those who have done great good or evil. Fame is different from leadership positions in that those in positions of power may or may not be famous.

Also, you don't need to hold a high-level position of any kind to be famous.

The famous, like leaders in the centers of power, get their power from their followers. However, this power can fade fast. Celebrities often work hard to stay in the eye of the media by acting in a way that is of interest or fascinating by a mass audience.

The more able the famous are at creating fascination and mobilizing their followers, the more famous they become, and the more effective they can be at creating or adding to change. While all celebrities can help you understand and focus on real issues if they choose, it's the gift of some comedians and satirists to point out significant problems within our society in a way that can make you laugh and think. Comedy is a power like no other as it can cut through to the heart of an issue and open minds with an accompanying sense of joy and happiness.

Consequences: Those who achieve fame for any reason are automatically held to a higher standard as they become role models for people. Those who become role models to children are held at an even higher standard. Fame also limits one's ability to interact with the world in a normal way, and over time, this can warp the perceptions of life. In many cases, fame is something most people think they want until achieved.

- Power Source: The famous get their power from the mass attention of people. The greater the attention, the more famous. This attention can give access to tools of wealth and rally their following to get things done.

3. **Desirable Traits** include beauty, strength, intelligence, wisdom, and talent. The importance we assign to desirable traits comes from a biological need to reproduce. This need causes a fascination with beauty and other desirable characteristics. Many of these traits are tied to our body as in how strong, fast, healthy, fit, and beautiful we are. Others are related to our mind, as in how intelligent, wise, and creative we can be. It's because we admire these traits that we want them for our progeny.

    Our species' admiration of these qualities means those of us who possess these traits are often automatically given more deference, acceptance, and power over others. Desirable characteristics can lead to laziness for those possessing them as they just use them to skate by without every applying themselves or making real choices. This is because some who have been negatively programmed, these traits can evoke uncontrollable fascination, envy, jealousy, lust, and hate.

    In the end, those possessing desirable traits can help in positive ways or hurt you if not handled well. Because of our deference and openness to them as a society, they can help to focus our attention on important issues and gather people if used correctly. Therefore, it's incumbent upon all of us who were given these gifts to use them for the greatest good.

    - Power Source: Those having desirable traits derive their power from natural deference. Power comes from followers and those showing deference.

4. **United Power:** Throughout all of human history, it has been proven, over and over, that we, the people, united in a common cause, are the greatest power on the planet.

"Our Greatest Power" has two parts consisting of "Personal Power," which is what you can do as an individual in your everyday life, as well as the power you gain when you "Unite" with other people in common cause.

"Unity to be real must stand the severest strain without breaking." - Mahatma Gandhi

Unity can be used to create significant change. We have united to form and destroy nations throughout time. Together we built all the great wonders of the world, past and present. The unification of people can be coerced or done by choice. However, it's unification by choice in the creation of the positive that is the most fulfilling and leads to our "True Society."

The more resources and people a movement has, the faster we can accomplish what is needed. The fact is we, the human race, can achieve just about anything if enough of us work on a problem for long enough. Real cooperation is needed if we are to thrive and solve large societal issues; this is because they often require large amounts of people, time, and wealth to accomplish.

All of us striving for the good also brings hope and positive energy, which can help us all achieve more. Most often, societies change after one person gathers a small group together, and they all take united action. Their concerted efforts allow more and more people to join in an organized, focused way.

Small groups of likeminded people working together have changed the world throughout history. People can't say "it can't be done" as real positive change is always accomplished this way. Often it just takes those who can't see to get out of the way of those who can. The simple truth is we can create a wonderful world, and we must do it together.

To understand "Our Greatest Power" a little more, let's look at it in terms of time and money.

Time: If you live to 80, you have about 700,800 life hours (24x365=8,760 and 8,760x80=700,800). If 700,800 people spend 1 hour doing something, that's 700,800 hours of work done. That's a whole lifetime of work within one single hour. Time of this nature can be referred to as staff-hours as in our company performs 1 million staff-hours of work every day or all the gamers put in 8 million man-hours on that game within the first weekend.

Money: 1 dollar given by a billion people vs. one person giving 1 billion dollars still equals 1 billion dollars. However, while the money is equal, 1 billion people have much greater power for all can unite in action.

Can you see that the more of us there are, the easier everything becomes? The broader, more inclusive, and focused the group, the more power it has. All the systems of society run because we the people do the work and consume the products and services. If we did not, most organizations would not be able to exist.

The majority of the powerful only have power because we "the masses" allow them to have it. The power level of a group, cause, or movement comes through the number of people who join. Therefore, united, we are the most powerful.

A cause or movement's goal for positive change becomes even easier if, within the group, some are at the "Centers of Power" and have access to the "Tools of Power." The higher the position, fame, and access to the "tools of power" like wealth and media, the more legitimacy the group can gain. Also, the group can have less confrontation and friction when trying to implement the solutions. It does not take many from the "centers of power" to magnify and boost the momentum of the cause if some members are very powerful, famous, and wealthy. In fact, the joining of we, "the masses," with the few in the "centers of power" magnifies the effort and can thereby achieve much greater results in a much faster time.

KNOW YOUR GREATEST POWER

As noted, you as an individual also have great power that you can use in your everyday life. Your power is exercised by being a good role model, caregiver, and through where and how you spend your time and money every day. It's through all the small positive acts you do: the little positive interactions, courtesies & manners, attention to details, doing a good job & going the extra mile, and all the rest that helps make a society run smoothly and get better and better over time

The fact is we can't create our "True Society" without all of us being mindful of all the meaningful little things that we should and should not do every day. Mindfulness is needed because our society reflects us as people. To say it another way, we are our society.

For example, it's when the vast majority of us choose not to pollute, litter, and to clean things up is when it will get done. It's only when we see each other as equals and treat each other as we would want to be treated that we can begin to build a peaceful, happy world.

It's up to us all to be more polite and grateful to everyone around us and to treat others as we would want to be treated. It's up to each of us to work to be a better spouse, friend, child, worker, leader, caregiver, and role model. It's up to us to be good "consumers," spending our money wisely, and a "prosumer" who works to improve, repair, repurpose, reuse, recycle, and give away things we are not using to ensure that we do not waste.

It's up to all of us to vote, take a poll, volunteer, donate, protest, and participate in meaningful positive ways. You can be a positive influence and make a significant difference through everything you do. You can be the one that speaks out against injustice or a follower and supporter of those who do.

Individually, you change the world for the positive by living rational, positive action. Collectively, this positive way of living adds up to a force that naturally changes our world for the positive. In the end, you are either part of the problem or the solution. For humanity to truly use our greatest power of unity effectively, each of us must mindfully use our power as we go through life. We must unite with other people in a positive common cause to get the big things done that need doing.

To say it another way, your "True Power" to create great positive change is found in what you do every day and in what we do and don't do together on a large scale. So, for you to truly make a great positive difference in the world, you must be mindful of your actions and Unite!

THE PROBLEM WITH OUR GREATEST POWER

The problem with "Our Greatest Power" of unity is that it's often diffuse, unused, misguided, corrupted, manipulated, and not unified. The reason for this is because we "the masses" need good leaders to unite and direct us.

The problem is that frequently instead of good leaders, we get fanatics who want to win by any means necessary. Often these corrupt authority figures infect us using communication tactics designed to divide and control us. This prevents us from making good decisions (See the "Life Manual: Fuel: Information" and the "Life Manual: Fuel: Information: Tactics Used Against Us" for more).

POWER & OUR FLAW

"None of us is perfect and have some or the other flaws. But flaws can always be done away with if we just try."
- Anurag Prakash

Because of our nature and the human conditions under which we live, we are the flawed being led by the flawed who are running flawed systems. Our flaws manifest themselves within our lives as corruption, mistakes, oversights, failings, vices, and sin. These flaws were designed within us, at this stage of existence, because it forces us all to make choices, often in the form of a reaction to temptation.

Our actions and reactions regarding temptations are one of the main ways we learn and are tested. To be clear, this primary human flaw allows for corruption and mistakes to be made by <u>any of us</u>, which means that those at the centers of power are flawed just like the rest of us. This human flaw means that those in the "Centers of Power" may not be there by genuine merit nor using the "Tools of Power" correctly.

We can plainly see this human flaw at work within our leaders by the level of discord within our global society today and throughout all of history.

If our society contains ignorant, uninformed, and confused people, we can't blame it all on them, but instead, we must look at the societal systems, caregivers, and those at the centers of power for the cause and way to fix it.

Example: Is it reasonable to expect an ignorant child born of uneducated parents, living in poverty, and little or no education to somehow know how to be the best person they can be from birth without help?

Are all the children in these horrible situations to somehow just know the right way to live, how to overcome the negativity around them, and get out? Isn't it more reasonable for those adults who do know the solution and have access to resources to implement a plan to help them? We all lose if any of us are lost or diminished.

We must all realize that the fault lies with all of us through our actions, inactions, and the societal systems we create and support. If we accept the unacceptable and corruption, we are part of the problem and are corrupt. Those who know the answers and have the resources must join together and fix our broken systems, and the rest of us must help them to do so.

The fact is, for many of us, the society surrounding us is not conducive to becoming our best. In this age and throughout all human history, the vast majority of us have been barely surviving, let alone thriving. So many of us are desperate, hopeless, and hungry. We are weak and sickly from being malnourished. We are not that smart because we have been malnourished since conception and are uneducated or poorly educated.

We are easily manipulated and controlled by others because we don't know any better and need hope. In the end, too many of us live in fear, without any real help, protection, or justice.

These desperate circumstances should be of great concern and eliminated because it's those of us who are left behind, forgotten, abused, and desperate that act out in negative ways. In desperate times, many of us will revert to a savage state where "other people" are either predators or prey. We will rage at the unfairness of it all and at those who don't seem to know or care about the horrors we are living.

Here we either survive by any means or let the world destroy us. Most of us don't want to be the prey, nor do we want just to give up and die. Instead, most of us will go down fighting if pushed to our limit. For this reason, if any of us are diminished, we are all diminished. If any of us are left behind, we are all in jeopardy.

HONORABLE TRAIT

The fact that humanity knows that we are all infected by this flaw, and yet we do not yield, nor accept it, is part of what makes humanity a noble species. We were given these flaws, failings, vices, and sins to help us learn what is truly important. This is because they challenge and test us to see if we can choose correctly and live up to our true potential.

To be clear, it's through free will and real temptation that your choices reveal your character, and you determine your fate/destiny. The reason for this is that your choices would not mean much without temptation, free will, and a real chance of failure. The stronger the temptation, the more opportunity for development or destruction. That is why temptations are built into our human condition.

Your growth can be either positive or negative, depending on your choices.

We can see time and time again that it's the arrogant, misguided, misinformed, corrupt, and inept that bring down our societal systems and lead us to ruin and war. We should not be led by the willfully ignorant, corrupt, power-hungry, or greedy. Nor should we be led by those who can't get over traditional & petty hatreds.

Our human flaw can plainly be seen in the claims of, "It's always been done that way" and "Everyone does it this way" and "It's just business" and "I was just following orders" and "If I (we) don't, someone else will" as rationalizations for perpetuating the wrongness. In cases of societal corruption, we all must work together to remove it.

COMPENSATION FOR OUR FLAW

On the way to our "True Society," we must account for and work to overcome "Our Flaw." Here we are working to create a great life for all where we overcome corruption and those who would win at any cost. Preventing these flaws from infecting our children and societal systems requires real system-level best practice integration as well as diligence.

As a society, we compensate for our flaw by using checks and balances, and by having those of merit at the "Centers of Power" using the "Tools of Power" effectively. To have the right people in these positions, we need to consistently be raising good people. To help with part of this equation, I have created the *Child & Family Guide*, which you can refer to anytime. The rest of what we need is below.

CHECKS & BALANCES

As stated, the reason we need checks and balances within our society is that we all can be ignorant, corrupted, make mistakes, and bad choices. So, let's look at what "Checks and Balances" really mean.

Checks have to do with setting-up systems so we can ensure something is working correctly. We do this generally in 5 ways.

1. **Rules**, laws, best practices, reviews, regulations, and inspections that ensure work is being done at least to an agreed-upon standard. The key here is that the rules need to be as simple and as clear as possible while providing the required quality level. Our goal is to create best practices within our society so we and our world may thrive.

   Enforcement and penalties need to be in place so that violations are prevented and discovered before harming people or our environment. Also, for cases of negligence, malfeasance, disregard, and neglect, the penalties need to be so steep that even the most uncaring will be vigilant. The reason for this is that they know to do otherwise would mean their downfall or destruction of the organization. This level of penalty and real enforcement also serves as a deterrent for all those others looking to break the rules for selfish reasons.

2. **News** consists of entirely factual information presented in context so people can make informed decisions, have a better understanding of our world, and make a difference. We refer to this as investigative journalism, "The Free Press," and as "The 4th Estate." We do this because of its importance to all of society as a significant part of our checks and balances system.

   It's important to note that real "news" is not partisan, biased, opinion, interpretation, or commentary, and the focus is not on the presenter.

Fake news is often made up of stories that confirm the world view they are pushing while leaving out or spinning facts that go against their desired world view. Fake news also comes from those who look to create social problems to divide us, so we are easier to manipulate and conquer.

Any show, network, or platform claiming to be "News" that consistently disregards these values is fake news and propaganda where the intent is to lead people to draw conclusions and make decisions they want. To learn more about how to protect yourself and about real news, see "The Life Manual: Fuel: Information & the Tactics Used Against Us."

3. **Whistleblowers** are those who stand up and show us where there is great corruption, malfeasants, or other significant problems. Real whistleblowing is when great wrongs are exposed because the public needs to know, or because there is no other way to fix the issue from the inside. The key here is to understand that information that exposes corruption, theft, and lies that affect other people is just and right when there is no other way.

However, it can go too far if this release includes other secrets and puts innocent people at risk. For some issues, it might also be enough to disclose this information to the proper authorities instead of making it public. To be clear, whistleblowing is not publicly sharing every embarrassing detail or small transgression. In these cases of a minor issue where a correction is needed, you can try to work directly with the person or organization first.

Whistleblowers who bring great injustice and wrongdoing to light should be able to stay anonymous, hailed as heroes, rewarded, respected, and protected. This is because, without them, these problems would most often go unnoticed.

4. **Public Shaming** is a drastic tactic that should only be used in specific situations. If done reasonably and without violence, this can be an effective way to curtail unwanted behavior in a public person or leader and in all those who would emulate them. Public shaming is most effectively used against corrupted leaders as it can expose them and force change.

    Public shaming must never be used as a tool against children or teenagers as there are better ways to teach them, and they need time to learn without that level of attack. Also, we all need to be sure not to use this tactic against each other in everyday life and on social media for small issues. We do not publicly shame each other because there are better ways to help each other see our issues. The reason is that this tactic can ruin people's lives long after the lesson has been brought to their attention and learned.

5. **Trust & Verify:** If something is truly important, we must verify that the information is, in fact, true. Again, because of our flaw, we can make mistakes. We also must ensure that our sources are good as we can't solely rely on those who have a vested interest in the outcome to be free of corruption. Therefore, it's good to have other people go over crucial information to ensure something is not amiss. This practice is not an insult; it's merely a prudent standard operating procedure that protects everyone.

BALANCES

Within a society, there are organizational configurations that give power to relatively equal groups -- this is called a balance of power. We can see this in many forms of government and business where different parts share power.

For Example: In the USA, there are the Executive, Legislative, and Judicial branches of government. We can see this in business with power split between the CEO, Board of Directors, and through stock if a public company.

Within our society, we use balances this way so that these separate groups need to cooperate to get things done and follow established laws. Ideally, it also means no single person or group can dominate over others. Everyone has a vested interest in the other's wellbeing as all are dependent on one another. When sane and reasonable people are brought together in this way, they can discover all the facts, gain perspective, understanding, and implement real solutions.

This type of balancing of power allows groups to unite to control another if it has gotten out of hand. Ideally, this structure forces cooperation, explanation, conversation, and idea development to take place. If the process is healthy, it allows everything to be scrutinized and made better. If the parties are genuinely looking to solve the problem, it can lead to harmony, synergy, synchronicity, coincidence, and serendipity.

In the end, with sane and reasonable people all working toward real solutions, consensus can be found. Yet, as we know, any of us can be corrupted, and often it's those in the highest positions of power that are the most corruptible without proper checks and balances in place.

All true leaders welcome these types of fair accountability systems as they want to avoid corruption and mistakes as much as the rest of us.

Checks and Balances ensure that people who are in positions of power have others checking on them to ensure that they have not lost their way or made mistakes. Building solid checks and balances into our all our societal systems is the only way to ensure that we are protected from corruption and error now and in the future.

THE CHALLENGES & LESSONS OF POWER

There are significant challenges and lessons found within the lives of those of us who possess power, and for those who do not. The more power one attains, the more significant and more consequential the challenges and lessons for all of us.

These lessons center around four prime areas:

1. How the Power is used?
2. How the Power is not used?
3. How the Power affects your attitude toward self?
4. How the Power affects your attitude toward others?

Also, we should note that as organizations age, there is often a mismatch between followers and the leaders within that organization. The mismatch creates separation, and if the organization is a major one, this division can wreak havoc for all their workers and consumers. Concerning the "Lessons of Power," there are a few main reasons for separation that include:

1. The leadership has fractured over time, becoming more extreme, thus diverging from those they claim to be serving.
2. The leadership is corrupt.

3. The personal experiences and collective understanding and desires of the followers have changed, and the leaders have not kept up with the development and look to force or keep the status quo and stagnation.

The lessons of power are many and often personally and socially significant. We can navigate a positive way through by using "The 10 Commandments" as outlined within "Step 4: Center" as a guide for our beliefs, intentions, words, and actions.

Often, it's those in power who feel that they must control and take everything they can to be respected or to stay in power. However, just because you can does not mean you should. The fact that someone has power does not make their decisions right. A primary challenge of humanity is to realize that "power, money, and might do not make right" nor create a society that reflects true virtue. The fact is that individuals gain more power through caring and sharing than by holding power. Through these acts, they prove their character, spread love, economic growth, and help build a healthier society.

It's not enough to be able to give a moving speech written by an expert. Any actor can do that. In fact, speech giving should not be a primary point on which we judge our leaders as being fit for higher office (unless it's a primary job function like being a press secretary). We genuinely need leaders primarily skilled at the qualifications necessary to do the job effectively. An underlying unity of positive purpose, intention, action, and word among all leaders, workers, citizens, and followers is key to the creation of the "True Society."

Our Actions & How to Control Power

It's how we of great power act and react to these challenges and lessons that determines our personal fate, and to a large degree, the fate of our global civilization. One of our greatest challenges for those of us without much power is that we are often taught to automatically trust a certain group of people in positions of power.

Many of us naturally grow up accepting everything said by our authority figures, like those from our favorite news station, political party, or religion. However, as we know, those in these positions can be corrupt and do not disclose the whole truth nor share information we need and even lie to get their way. This problem means we are infected by negative leaders who lead us to make bad decisions. Because corrupt leaders exist, it's always important to question and check our authority figures to see if they are truly worthy. We can't sacrifice our values for short term gains, for we will lose in the long run. The best practice is to be a healthy skeptic, trusting while also verifying.

In the end, we can see much of human history as a struggle between "the few" trying to <u>impose</u> their will upon "the many" vs. the few in power working to find real solutions for the many. We, the people, joined together are more powerful than any one person or group. Unity is the greatest power; it's up to all of us to join together on critical issues because our lives and our world depend on it. Our need for unity means that you, the one reading or hearing these words, must join with others to create positive change. Being part of the solution is the only rational option; otherwise, you are just part of the problem.

CHAPTER 13
THE KEYS TO LEADERSHIP & WEALTH

"The price of greatness is responsibility." - Winston Churchill

Now that we have covered the basics of Power, we need to go through the keys to government and wealth as part of "Step 6: Unite." We are doing this because these critical systems determine how well all our other societal systems run and because we are all deeply affected by these systems.

- **Government** is defined as a system of supreme authority or rule that decides the direction and level of control for all its members and organizations.

- **Wealth** is defined as money and assets such as gold, cars, art, and property. On a societal level, we speak of the creation and flow of wealth through our societal systems as an economic system or economy.

For clarity, we will go into these topics in more detail, for a collective understanding of how these systems work is critical to everyone's ability to make a real difference and help create our "True Society."

BASIC FORMS OF GOVERNMENT

"When a country is ill governed, riches and honors are something to be ashamed of." - Confucius

The primary forms of government listed below are broken up into two main groups. "Groups over the People" are top-down, where a person or small groups decide everything without direct representation of the citizens. The second are "Governments of the People" and are bottom-up as they are maintained by people running for office and voting. To say it another way, "the few over the many" vs. "the many over the few." For clarity, **Anarchy** is the condition of no government. In this state, all are at the mercy of the powerful.

RULE BY INDIVIDUALS OR GROUPS OVER THE PEOPLE

All the forms of government within this group rule from the top-down, allowing little to no public participation in who rules or what the rules are. These forms of government often do not have any checks and balances on those in power, which leads to high levels of corruption and mismanagement.

REVOLUTIONARY

A revolutionary government is a temporary form of government and formed when a government is overthrown. This new group of leaders can come from within the revolutionary leadership as well as from others chosen by the revolutionary leadership.

A small group such as the military or a very large group such as in a popular uprising can cause a revolution. After some time, a revolutionary government will become another form of government unless there is another coup or revolution.

AUTHORITARIAN, AUTOCRAT, TOTALITARIAN, TYRANT, TYRANNY, DICTATOR & DESPOT

In a dictatorship, all power rests in one person often at the head of the only legal, political party. A tyrant is often a demagogue who is a leader that makes use of popular prejudices, false claims, and promises to gain power.

Once a demagogue gains power, they do what they want, most often using power selfishly, treating people like things and not as they would want to be treated. A tyrant often gains authority over the group by claiming some birthright or a link to the divine.

In this type of government, the dictator chooses the people in leadership positions or a group beholden to the dictator. The people who are under their control are forced to do what the government tells them. Citizens are generally prevented from leaving the country without permission, or if they do leave, they might not be allowed to return legally. This type of government often holds people's loved ones hostage to force compliance as well as imprison or execute anyone they want without due process.

Usually, there is little or no attention to public opinion or individual rights. Often the country falls into civil war after such a leader dies if there is no strong chosen successor. The idea that a person or group of any kind is selected at birth or is divinely appointed and, therefore, should rule without seeking consensus or any checks and balances has allowed for some of the most horrific atrocities and perversions throughout human history.

This type of government sometimes claims to be of the people and even a republic because they have more than one political party and hold elections. However, these other parties are just for show and will never win the election or share any power. We all must be vigilant because when times are desperate, insecure, and disasters happen, those in power positions gain more power. This opens leaders up to corruption and our society to dictatorships.

Theocracy

In a Theocracy, an elite group rules everything in the name of their faith. It's this group that chooses the top leader. This chosen leader may claim they act as direct agents of "their" deity, that they are a divine representative, or claim some linage from some great leader of the past. This leader and all the other elites work to control and force everyone to live and think in a way they feel best reflects their interpretation of the religion.

This form of government often uses these "holy works" to justify the most heinous of crimes and evils while cultivating a sense of superiority and even good feelings when participating in great acts of evil. While Theocracy is listed as a separate form of government, it's a form of dictatorship. Here the difference is that the focus of everything comes from a religious leader or group and is based in that religion.

Communism

Communism is a system of government that is led by the communist party, which selects the top leader from within its ranks. Communism is anti-opposition, often using violent means to stifle any such opposition. This type of government usually takes total control over people's lives, telling them where they will work and live. They do not allow freedom of movement or large gatherings. It's only a few people within the top ranks of the communist party that dictate everything within the society. This type of government sometimes claims to be of the people and even a republic because they have more than one political party and may also hold elections. However, these other parties are just for show and will never gain power over the communist party.

Oligarchy/Plutocracy

An oligarchy or plutocracy is the rule by an elite group. Only those of a certain "standing" within society have a voice in the government. This elitism can come in the form of wealth, education, ethnicity, and ancestry. The elite decides who is considered elite and who is not. Their choice is often arbitrary because they base decisions on personal bias and feelings rather than any merit.

Hegemonies

Hegemony is the rule of a social group over all others. This group controls the government and society. Hegemonies can take many forms when any powerful group takes and uses its control to further its ends often at the expense of everyone and everything else. Sometimes multiple groups may even work together to control a population. There are many more types of hegemonies beyond those listed here.

- Power Groups: These can consist of any group in a power position or has access to the tools of power. Think of racial supremacy groups, wealthy people, and crime lords.

- Corporations Rule: Here, businesses choose who runs and wins and what laws the government passes. The rule by corporations can be overt as leaders of the government are filled by those from the corporate world or done through proxies such as lobbyists and yes men.

- Media Rules: Here, the media provides information to the public in a way that we do what they want (propaganda). This influence is used to get us to do things as well as to do nothing. Media oriented hegemonies are often corporate rule but not necessarily.

MONARCHY/ROYALTY

In a monarchy, a family has power and decides everything regardless of skill or ability. Often the royal family is led by a king or queen as well as others in the "royal class" who feel they are superior in breeding and ability with some even claiming divine right or ancestry. They most often pass rulership down to whoever is the eldest without regard to merit.

Throughout all of human history, we see they most often live in ways that are gluttonous, greedy, wasteful, and so extravagant without a clue to their depravity and failings. They usually live pampered lifestyles giving little care or attention to the systems of society or how "their" people live. Often monarchies force their people or other subjected people to live in extreme poverty or serfdom if not outright slavery to perpetuate their wasteful, extravagant, and undeserved lifestyles.

It also should be noted that this false sense of superiority in the oldest monarchies has led some "royals" to breed only within their ranks, often having children with close relatives. This ordained multi-generational incest has created many detrimental genetic mutations that show up within the oldest "royal" lines all over the world. Often the oldest and most respected "royal lines" are the most genetically inferior because of this.

Countries like the United Kingdom and Japan still allow a monarchy to exist even though they have no power in the government, and the government is one of the people. Countries like this often keep these old monarchies around because of tradition and because it can create fascination by the public, which may add to tourism and the economy.

The harm in mixing a system of "equality rule by the people" with an old-style monarchy of "rule of the few over the people" is that it keeps the idea of inequality alive. The perpetuation of inequality happens because all still track the "bloodlines" of the "royals." People separate themselves into "Commoners" and "Royals" (Prince, Lord, Duke, Baroness, etc.). This attitude of "we of this blood" are better than all the rest of you "lower-class people" persists and infects all such societies to the point where those chosen for positions are often still selected based on old "royal" bloodlines rather than real merit.

Philosopher Kings: Plato, an old-time philosopher, referred to righteous kings as "philosopher kings." This same idea is touted by Confucius, an ancient Chinese philosopher who traveled around trying to help rulers do better by the people. The core idea is that a ruler who is wise and good with ultimate power could create an ideal society. The problem with this idea is that people die, and things change. Therefore, we would need a "philosopher-king" after "philosopher-king" in infinitum for this idea to work, and we can't achieve this within families.

This idea of the "philosopher-king" is also a way for a nation to change quickly by giving a good and wise person or group this level of control for a limited time as in "King for a Day." This power allows this wise person or group to fix what was previously agreed quickly without all the red tape. After a set time limit expires, control of the system would be given back.

As far as I have been able to research, this idea has never been tried on a countrywide governmental level. If it ever is attempted, there would need to be checks and balances in place to guarantee that the prearranged changes are implemented, and that this temporary leader or group is not corrupted.

FASCISM

Any of the groups above can also become fascist. Fascism is a political philosophy, movement, or regime that exalts nation and race or group above the individual. They support the top-down form of government, severe economic and social regimentation, and forcible suppression of opposition as well as other decrees handed down by the leaders.

GOVERNMENTS OF THE PEOPLE

All "Governments of the People" depend on a well-educated and informed populous, checks and balances, control of hegemonies, fair representation as well as easy access to information and a secure voting system. These forms of government are referred to collectively as "socialist" as they are controlled by the society's population. Every adult citizen can cast one vote in elections.

The primary socialistic forms of government currently include:

PARLIAMENTARY

A parliamentary system is an elected group often lead by the leaders of political parties. The size of each party within the parliament gives it relative power within the government, with the largest group often filling the top leadership positions.

REPUBLIC

In a republic, voters choose representatives, and it's these representatives who do the governmental work and choose other leaders, including the President.

DEMOCRACY

Democracy includes the basics of the republic. The difference is that the people also vote directly on some significant issues and for top leadership positions such as President, Governors, etc.

Socialism is the most successful and universally desired <u>political</u> system because it creates more happiness, freedom, and prosperity than any other.

CONSERVATIVE, LIBERAL & CENTRIST

Within governments, some ideas divide many potential voters when it comes down to large issues. The three basic camps are "conservative," "liberal," and "centrist." So why is this important? To find out, let us look at each in more detail.

- **Conservatives** are known as the "right" (as in the right-side of center) and tend or are disposed to maintain existing views, conditions, institutions, traditions, norms of taste, elegance, style, design, and manners. Conservatives are often referred to as traditional or old fashioned.

    Conservatives are cautious, want programs to work, money to be spent without waste, to conserve resources, and respect modesty. They want to maintain things that are working well. They are slow to change, especially if something is working, even if the new is cleaner, better, or faster.

- **Liberals** are also known as the "left" (as in the left-side of center) and are marked by generosity and the desire for positive change as soon as it can be accomplished. The liberal works toward a better future, even if it means going against tradition.

Liberalism is about working toward freedom for all, greater individual participation in government, and the rule of law. It's also a liberal ideal to be free from religious and political persecution and discrimination. Liberals can also be too fast to change, give too much, and go too far.

- **Centrists** advocate a middle ground approach regarding government control of the economy and people's behavior. They work toward practical solutions without regard from where they originated. They see every issue as situational, whereby they work to keep an open mind and oppose extremes.

Who is a liberal and who is a conservative is often subjective because some people from one part of the world can see a group as conservative, while a group from another part of the world will see that same group as liberal.

For Example: The USA is seen as liberal, if not the most liberal country in the world. However, within the USA, some see themselves as the most conservative in the world. Nevertheless, when typical American conservative views are compared with those from some other countries, the USA conservatives are seen as liberals and not conservative at all.

In today's world, the words "liberal" and "conservative" have become labels of hate used to force sides and divide us, so we are more easily exploited by those in the power positions of the liberal and conservative movements.

These groups divide us by calling on our primal need for tribes and teams as well as on our values of tradition, loyalty, and freedom. This separation creates bubbles where we only listen to information that confirms our world view, other facts that do not conform are fake, and where no one truly <u>listens</u> to the "other side." Here we have intransigence as each side sees the other as obfuscating, corrupt, lying, disingenuous, etc. because they are and believe everyone else is too. They say things like, "Hey, we are just doing what you are doing (or did to us in the past)."

The truth is either in the extreme becomes detrimental to people, and our society because conservatism taken too far can lead to dictatorship, and liberalism to communism. Both conservatives and liberals focus on virtues which most of us desire. The difference is that often, they focus on them at the exclusion of all others.

Regarding the whole of human society and the true governance of our world, leaders need to be both liberal and conservative. This balance is necessary because real solutions most often require a mix of all virtues. The critical point here is that just as *The Way* focuses on integrating virtue within your life, we as a society need to incorporate all virtue into our political groups. Embracing all our highest values is the only way to find "True Answers" to our problems.

For Example: Real solutions can be liberal, as in creating programs and regulations designed to bring people out of poverty, but we also need the conservative values of work and fiscal responsibility to ensure that the plans succeed, and the money is not wasted. All these values ensure that we are giving a hand up and not creating systems of waste or perpetuating nonparticipation and dependency.

It's important to note that there are those looking to politicize everything so that they can divide us. These people are doing this because we are more easily controlled when divided, and they can gain more power.

Systems like justice, education, food, science, faith, etc. are not political. We must stop making them so and keep politics where it belongs.

Government is to work to protect and better the lives of the people. This focus can require conservative values of fiscal responsibly, with caution through checks and balances, laws, regulations, protection of our resources, and trusting but verifying. It can also mean embracing the liberal values of freedom, protections from the powerful, equality, sympathy, fairness, true justice, improving, and working toward a better, more inclusive society for all.

To be clear, politics that is about "our side" winning "no matter what" and only doing "something" for "something" in return is corruption. If you accept or defend the corrupt, you are corrupt. Corruption holds up the real work that needs doing. We see these extreme negative ways of ruling at the top levels of broken political systems because the leaders are fanatics and/or not there through merit. True statesman/stateswomen do right because it needs doing.

In the end, most of us are not strictly conservative or liberal because we know real solutions require consideration of all virtues. We need this type of rationality within government if we are ever to find practical solutions.

NATIONALIST & GLOBALIST

As we have learned, no one is an island, and we are all dependent on each other. This idea is true for us as nations. Within political thinking, there is the idea of a nationalist/populist and globalist. A nationalist/populist is for the betterment of their nation above all others, even at the expense of other nations. Populist leaders are often wannabe dictators and/or fascists working to dismantle democratic institutions by suppressing dissenting views, controlling news outlets, and using them as propaganda machines, labeling all opposition as unpatriotic, undermining the justice system, and blaming the opposition party and/or minorities for all the problems.

A globalist is for the betterment of all nations of the world, even if it means some countries might have to change in the ways they exploit the world and its people. The problem here is that if taken too far, it can weaken a nation's economy and cause more issues globally if there are unfair environmental and work practices in place.

The fact is we need to hold both views in balance if we are to succeed in the creation of our "True Society." Balance is required because we want each nation to work to be its best, and we don't want every country to be the same. It's also true that all nations affect each other, and any country can destroy world peace. In this light, we can see all the countries within our world like all the teams in a sport's league. Sure, we want our team to do well and win; however, at the same time, we play by the rules, for we all love this league and want everyone to thrive.

Therefore, we need to combine a globalist view of improving our world as a whole, not leaving anyone out and the nationalist view of improving our nation in our unique artful way. This balance will create many great ways of doing things that we can all learn from and enjoy. Our ability to work together as a world is a high-level test of our ability to cooperate as we compete as a species. A test we must ace if we are to survive and thrive.

POLITICAL PARTIES

Now that the basics of conservatives, liberals, centrists, nationalists, and globalists are covered, we can look at the political organizations they create. A political party is meant to represent a large group of people who have similar views concerning key issues. Political parties can be temporary organizations that only last for a short time or that last for many years. The one true party that most of us already belong to is about making all our societal systems work well, improving the lives of all people, and caring for the world.

Political parties have the same issues of corruption, checks and balances, fracturing, extremism as well as manipulation and control by hegemonies. These problems become even more significant when there are only two dominant parties within a country because it's easy for division and entrenchment to be the norm as there are two sides.

The idea of "Us vs. Them" is built into our primal mind. Like sports, we love our team, even if they are not that good at times. In a two-party system lead by extremists, these divisions destroy any chance of real solutions from being implemented.

To be clear, it's this artificial separation of "us vs. them" as depicted by labels like "liberal and conservative" or "red vs. blue" or "rich vs. poor" or "citizens vs. immigrants" that attracts more extreme views which can be the loudest and take over organizations. If those representing "we the people" have an "us vs. them" perspective, our government will not find real solutions. This is because we find true solutions by examining every side looking for all the virtues at the heart of the issue. Over time, this attitude of entrenchment creates a party that is intransigent and will not listen, accept or compromise on any good idea from the "other side," even if it's one they offered in the past.

This stagnation can lead to revenge, games, and payback politics, which puts party interest above the people, the common good, morality, and the real work that needs doing. Everything is done in an atmosphere of antagonism, obfuscation, hate, and intransigence. All discussion and consideration of the "other side's" point of view are seen as weaknesses. This circumstance can lead to extremes of government where "payback politics" is the standard way of business, where the ruling party takes all they can without regard for any other point of view or desire. True governance and statesmanship are not partisan, a competition, or biased.

Corruption within government is made even worse as more lawyers take over elected positions. This is because lawyers are taught that everything is "win-lose" or "zero-sum." Most are trained to fight for their side, create false or one-sided narratives, and spin facts to their advantage no matter the truth or what is right. Those in the extremes work hard to demonize, mislead, confuse, dominate, obfuscate, and not cooperate nor seek to understand. This programing is why some lawyers also do not make good journalists, as they are not open to the truth.

Note that while we have painted lawyers with a broad-brush, some lawyers may have the capacity to shake off their educational background, one-sided mindset, and work toward real solutions.

Dysfunctional government leads to civil unrest. Civil unrest can be acted out in many ways and even lead to a civil war and a revolution. Therefore, it's essential <u>not</u> to be led by the extremes, to be open-minded, explore alternatives to what your group has embraced as the truth. All political parties need an ever-present core value system where we all agree to embrace virtues of all kinds, to cover all the bases, as we work to solve all problems and implement real solutions that benefit everyone.

BASIC ECONOMIC SYSTEMS

"With wealth comes responsibility." - Jonathan Sacks

Now that we understand the basics of power and our governmental systems, we need to switch gears and look at our wealth systems. We are doing this because wealth is like the blood in the body of our society; it needs to flow properly if we are to truly thrive.

There are three forms of economic systems in which governments and businesses trade money for people performing specific jobs within their organization.

- **COMMUNISM:** The government, and the people they control, supply all products and services.
- **CAPITALISM:** Companies and people supply all products and services.
- **SOCIALISM:** A mix of business, government, and people supply all products and services.

Within the three economic systems listed above (communism, socialism, capitalism), there is a supply and a demand for services and products. This supply and demand come from the government, business, and people.

- **Government** is a system of supreme authority or rule that decides the direction and level of control for all its members."
- **Business:** Covers all companies, corporations no matter the size or if legal or officially recognized. Business includes all non-governmental organizations (NGOs), charities, non-profits, religions as well as organized crime, and other black-market type organizations.

- **People:** All that is not part of a business or governmental obligation that we do as individuals to improve our environment, lives, and the lives of others is called "prosuming" or being a Prosumer. Here you do the work yourself or sell or trade/barter your services or products directly to others or give it away.

    "Prosuming" Means:

    - **Source/Supply:** You can create your own supply. You can grow your food, even in some cases, legally forage for things you need. There are "junkyards," collections centers, and even some "dumps" that can contain many items you can repair, repurpose, reuse, and improve on. Many people and organizations will even give things away if you can pick them up.

    - **Improve**: You can improve upon things in your life. *For example,* you can paint, re-landscape, and fix up your house, car, office, neighborhood, and more. You can even take parts from many different things and create something new.

    - **Repair**: Here, you fix things yourself. You can fix anything like a broken doorknob, blown bike tire, broken window, or leaky faucet. There are great "how-to" videos and manuals and maker labs that can help you fix just about anything.

    - **Repurpose**: Here, you take something designed for one thing and use it for something else. You can use pickle jars to hold screws or buttons or take the wood from a pallet and make a table or corks from wine bottles and create a corkboard, etc.

- **Reuse**: Here, you use something more than one time. *For example,* empty, slightly soiled trash bags and use them until dirty. Save all paper clips, rubber bands, and file folders when you are done using them.
- **Recycle**: Here, we turn things in, so they are made into new things like paper, metal, and glass.
- **Product Creation Note:** To help in this area, it's the best practice for all businesses and governments to make products, so they are non-toxic as well as easily cleaned, maintained, repaired, repurposed, reused, and recycled.

The extremes of pure communism and capitalism have been tried and have failed over and over throughout history. The reasons vary, but most fail because of corruption, ill-treatment, and extreme exploitation of people and our environment. They are unbalanced systems that do not take human nature or our needs into consideration.

The most successful and universally embraced economic system is socialism, whereby a mix of government, business, and people supply all services and products. Socialism has created the most wealth and happiness for more people over a longer time than any other system.

Socialism is the economic system embraced by countries like the USA, Canada, Europe, India, South Korea, China, Russia, and most of the rest of the world. Here the only differences are found in how free and happy the people are, in the rules they play by, and the level of products and services that the people, businesses, and government provide. The key to any socialistic economic system is <u>finding the right balance</u> between government, business, and people within equality, reciprocity, and virtue.

SUPPLY & DEMAND

To ensure that we are all on the same page as to our role within our local and global economy, now we are going a little deeper into some key economic concepts. We start by outlining the primary catalyst behind all human economic systems.

The catalyst is our basic need for things and services that we cannot provide for ourselves if we are to thrive. Our "need" is a basic human conditional fact. The "need" in society is expressed as "supply and demand." Simply put, the demands of society are supplied by governments, businesses, and people.

For Example: People need food and want apples to eat (demand). I can provide apples and get them to their local market (supply). The consumer can pay the price I need to cover the costs and maybe a bit more (profits).

The more people that want/need something, the higher the demand. The higher the demand, the more people are motivated to provide the service or product. The scarcity of a product and degree of difficulty to make or acquire it can also affect the price.

We can only provide and sell products and services if:

- There is a want or need for it.
- It can be made or produced.
- The Consumer can pay for it.
- The Consumer has access to it.

The process of supply and demand is made possible because we trade money for a person's time in the form of a paycheck for jobs. This trade is what gives "the masses" of workers the money to consume the products and services supplied.

This continuous flow of wealth between the people and societal systems is the basis of all socialistic and capitalistic economies. One of the most important keys to fixing our societal systems is found in finetuning this flow of wealth between people and systems.

COMPETITION & A LEVEL PLAYING FELID

For our global socialistic supply and demand economic system to work, we need fair competition and a level playing field. "A level playing field" references all laws and other rules that regulate how we do things.

Here we ensure that we set our playing field at a level where the rules are the same and fair for everyone. It's a level that respects all the "10 Laws" as outlined in "Step 4: Center," which means that people and our environment are cared for properly and respected.

A global level playing field is an example of real species-wide cooperation within competition at its finest. Here we are seeking to push everything to new heights of excellence instead of perpetuating a "win at all costs" or "win/lose" or "lose/lose" attitude. A level playing field is about winning because of open, honest competition and true merit. It's about fair work and pay and about working to provide access to lifestyles and a world that everyone can enjoy.

WHAT IS A TRUE BUSINESS?

To create a continuously improving world, we all must understand a few key aspects about business. We acknowledge that this topic is huge and that we are not covering it fully in every detail. However, within this work, we are simply looking to point out the basics and a few key nuances. This is to ensure that we are on the same page when it comes to discussing significant issues within our economy. This general understanding will help us all avoid a lot of problems as we live our lives. It will also allow us to know what actions to take to fix the businesses around us.

Business Core Focus

Below are the main points of focus for a "True Business." It's important to understand these points obviously as business owners but also as workers and consumers, for this will help all of us make better choices.

- **Cost:** "Net Cost" is defined as the price of the asset such as a computer, wood, contractors, or employees plus any expenses incurred for buying and maintaining the asset. "EBITDA" stands for earnings before interest, taxes, depreciation, and amortization.

    Businesses work hard to account for everything that costs them anything in these numbers, including saving for a rainy day, for future growth, research, and development. In business, we use these kinds of numbers to determine how much a service or product costs. Since using the wealth within the company as wisely as possible is key to its success, a "True Business" ensures that all costs are known and handled well without waste.

- **Customers:** Customers buy products and/or services from a business. Businesses can't exist without customers. To that end, a "True Business" uses honest marketing to reach potential customers.

    We, as the business, work to earn their loyalty through satisfaction in our work. We listen so that we may genuinely provide the solution people need now and in the future.

- **Efficiency:** A "True Company" looks to refine its products, services, processes, procedures, and eliminate bottlenecks, waste, inefficiency, and other issues. The reason we work so hard at being as efficient as possible is that it's through efficiency and the correct division of labor and tasks that we can increase production, sales, revenue, and more.

  To effectively work on efficiency, we must listen carefully to all complaints from our workers and customers as there is often an underlying problem causing these complaints that could be hampering our business. Next, we analyze everything everyone is doing to see if anything they are doing or not doing can be improved.

  Improvements might come in the form of significant changes as in job divisions or small things like moving the mixing bowls closer to those using them. You can find companies that specialize in helping other companies become more efficient in all areas, which can significantly help speed up the process and remove bottlenecks.

- **Product/Service:** Companies exist to solve problems for their customers. A "True Business" primary focus is on its product or service. Successful companies continuously work to offer the best and deliver it in a way their customers need.

- **Workers:** A "True Business" values, respects, and cares for its workers. We do this because we are human and want everyone to live a great life. Also, we do this because happy, satisfied workers who are vested in a company's success allow that company to be more efficient and productive.

Fair treatment includes things like a great working environment where consideration is given to our bodies, minds, and lifestyles. It's when compensation levels are equal for the same work and where compensation is at a level where workers can access the quality societal systems at the "Happiness Level" (more on this below).

- **World:** "True Companies" care about our world. Caring means they do everything with respect for our environment, animals, and people's lives. Good work includes caring for the whole product cycle and working to improve things like how we gather raw materials, how we transport them, how we make things out of them, how they are disposed of, recycled, and more.

    It's about building and making things that are safe and work well for a long time, that can be fixed and recycled easily, that don't pollute and work with our environment instead of against it. We need to care for our world in a way that protects our public commons of air, water, and land from being despoiled. Good companies do this to ensure they are not adding to the destruction of our world and people's lives but instead are improving everything.

A CONSEQUENCE OF CORE FOCUS

For a "True Business," the benefits listed below come as a <u>consequence</u> of doing well with the primary focus that was just covered (cost, customers, efficiency, product/service, workers, and our world).

These include:

- **Market Share** refers to how many customers the business has compared to the competition.

For example, an International cell phone company might have 50% of the total market, and on the local level, a restaurant might have 30% of the local lunch crowd. Saturation occurs when a business cannot serve more customers as in the cell phone store sells all the phones they have in stock, or the restaurant is full. All businesses start with zero market share. A "True Company" looks to expand its market share as long as it can provide quality services and products.

- **Growth** refers to added income and/or how many new customers were added when compared to how many were lost.

- **Profit** refers to money the business makes beyond the NET/EBITDA. Profit is extra money. It is not money earmarked for future projects, rainy days, growth, employee compensation, pensions, research and development, disposal of waste, and care of the environment and all the rest as the business has already made allowances for these expenses under "Cost."

    Profits can be reinvested into the business to improve, upgrade, accelerate growth, gain market share, help the community, and more. Even a "non-profit" company is allowed to make some profit. It's just limited. Governments allow this because nonprofits need to be allowed to use extra money to grow, improve, and save.

    To be clear, profit is <u>extra money</u> made only <u>after</u> businesses "core focus," as outlined above, is cared for properly. Currently, much of "profit" claimed by our most "successful" companies is not all real profit. It's the wealth stolen from the people doing the work by underpaying them, and/or by forcing people to work under inhumane circumstances, and/or by making low-quality products, and/or by improperly caring for our world by carelessly destroying it and through dumping toxic waste into the public commons like our air, rivers, and oceans.

Also, the idea of having tax laws that allow the very wealthy and very wealthy corporations to pay less than the middle class, or zero, and then add incentives as a way to improve a country is flawed and has been proven an incorrect strategy throughout history.

We find the proof in the fact that there is no guarantee that wealthy people or the people behind the business will spend the money in the ways that are needed, raise wages, or even spend the money in the country of your desire. Instead, this giveaway most often leads to further stagnation of wealth, greater unfair exploitation of people and the environment with no real gains in the home country other than maybe more low paying jobs.

Some types of our societal systems that should not focus on profit as an indicator or goal include systems like healthcare/medicine, nursing homes, justice, policing, prisons, anti-fire and emergency services, general education and training, orphanages, news, history, military, daycare, and elections.

In many cases, as with prisons, healthcare, and orphanages, if society is doing well, there will be less of a need for them. To go further, if there is a motive for profit in these systems, those in them have a vested interest in keeping them going. To grow these businesses means they need more prisoners, unhealthy people, and orphans. Therefore, the corporate directive for growth and profit in these systems is contrary to and in direct conflict with the overall societal goal. This contradiction creates many other problems within society.

For Example: If our healthcare system focused on making people healthier, people would not need as many drugs and treatments. If we find homes for the orphans quickly and don't create a lot of new ones, there is less need for orphanages. If we raise our children better, have great educational systems, reform inmates, and create opportunities, there will be less of a need for prisons.

We should not push for extreme profits by exploiting human misery and basic needs. These systems are often better run by the government or as non-profits.

- **Rightful Pride:** Doing a good job is its own reward. Feeling good about your work, your people's lives, and how you care for our world is a wonderful feeling that cannot be understated. Many would say it's the whole point of doing business. This is because it's through the thoughtful care of all who are in positions of power within organizations that will help create our "True Society." This positive energy and being a good role model are not minor things since they make all your hard work worthwhile and inspire people.

Problems within Our Global Economy & Solutions

Now that we have more of the basics covered, let's look at some major problems within our global economy and some of the solutions. History shows us that adding socialist governments (governments of the people) and socialist economic systems (the combination of government, business & people) together brings the most happiness and positive growth to our world. Refinement of this approach and our societal systems is where we will find our "True Society."

The main issue at the heart of most economic problems has to do with the flow of wealth. Wealth flowing correctly within our society is like blood in a healthy body. The problem is that wealth naturally stagnates within the centers of power. It's this stagnation of wealth within "The Power Centers" that stifles the flow of wealth between people and our systems. Wealth stagnation is one of the leading causes of poverty as well as economic and social unrest of all kinds. We can see many rebellions throughout history as a response to the stagnation and concentration of wealth and power in the hands of the few.

The unrest exists because poverty perpetuates ignorance and causes anger, rage, hopelessness, depression, and desperation. As we know, desperation leads to the rationalization of harmful acts and violence. It can make workers care less about their work and even hate the company for which they work. Also, the poor, ignorant, angry, enraged, and desperate are then often easily lead astray by those looking to exploit them for their own ends.

As we know, a "True Business" is successful when it manages the "Core Focus" (costs, customers, efficiency, products or services, workers, and our world) well. The effect of all this good work is growth, a fair profit, and pride in a job well done. While most of us know this to be accurate, many countries have laws and business rating systems focused primarily on profit and growth as indicators of health for public companies (a public company is one that sells stock that can be purchased by the public through stock exchanges). These unfair rating systems force publicly owned businesses into a position where they must continually make more and more profit and keep on growing if they are to get a "healthy" rating.

Public companies have to continue making more and more profit irrespective of their: market share, customer loyalty, and satisfaction, their cost to profit ratios, savings, number of good jobs created, their efficiency levels, how many they sold last month, or how well they treat our world. Even if the company is doing well in all the core areas, they are considered failing if not creating higher levels of profit or if they stop growing at "expected" rates. This unfair method of ratings and the laws that support them have forced the creation of inhumane organizations that look to grow and make more profit through extreme exploitation of people and our environment.

A Simple Example: There is a privately-owned bagel shop in a large city that supplies an excellent lifestyle for the owners and their ten employees who all take pride in their work. They work hard to improve the core of their business and can serve hundreds of happy customers every day.

They have a perfect location, customer loyalty, and enough of the local market share to sustain them indefinitely. By most definitions, this is a successful business. However, if this were a public company, it would be a failure because it's not growing nor producing more and more profit. Its stock could plummet, forcing it into bankruptcy, closure, and sale.

Solving Poverty

Poverty also severely and negatively impacts business and our government, because the poor are not able to buy products and services nor pay much in taxes. Poverty leaves companies without their correct level of customers and the government without needed taxes. Poverty weakens our local and global economy and all other societal systems. It also weakens our government as it's often required to provide even more assistance to the poor with fewer resources. We can't solve these kinds of problems using force or even law.

Example: The law can't prevent the desperate from committing violence, theft, or other "desperate" acts to survive. The law punishes those that get caught and maybe serve as a deterrent for a few on the edge. The real effect of the law is that desperate people work to hide these "desperate illegal" activities rather than stop them because to stop often means an end of survival.

To eliminate desperate acts, we must end the desperation within our society. Only through the proper care of our societal systems, all people, and our laws can we make a real difference in the world, ensuring a positive future for all.

Mini-Money-Tangent: If we are to have lotteries and to help wealth flow in society, they should only give rewards that can make a difference. *For example,* only amounts above $500 should be awarded. There should be many more mid and high-level rewards as in thousands of $10,000 winners. The top prize can be capped at $1 to $5 million, with hundreds of people winning this level instead of one.

The Way Out of Homelessness

Another huge factor in the health of a society and economy comes from who has a place to live and who does not. One way to help eliminate desperation within our society is to help those who are homeless.

The reasons for being homeless vary yet usually fall into one of three categories.

- **Lost:** Here, the person has problems that stop them from normally participating in society. These include things like mental issues and addiction to alcohol, drugs, and gambling.

- **Broken:** Here, tragedy has befallen them. *For example,* you had to flee because of war or violence. Or you lost everything in a fire or flood. Or you were kicked out of your parent's home or ran away because of abuse. Or you lost your job or had extra medical expenses, or you got hurt, sick or too old and could not pay the rent. There are many others.

- **By Choice:** There are those of us who have a nomadic soul and want to wander the world, making friends, working here and there while living a carefree lifestyle.

In all cases, those who fall into these circumstances need a hand up and our help. We can fix the problem of homelessness by working with them and sorting them out.

- o **The Lost** need different types of help. Here we can provide transport to care and rehabilitation centers that can help them recover, learn skills, and find a place to live and work. Or for the incapable, they can be moved to a location where we can respectfully and humanely care for them.

- o **The Broken:** We need to find those who are broken out of tragedy and have skills. We can find them a new job somewhere and move them there so they can start over. We need to find all the people who need help and provide them a safe place that they can stay, train, learn, and become self-sufficient.

If incapable because of age or another issue, we need to create places where these people are respectfully and humanely cared for.

- **By Choice:** Those who are good and choose to be nomads can be given badges/ID, so when in an area they can swipe them into a computer to find small jobs, cheap/free healthy food, safe lodging, and other help, so they don't become desperate. Those of us who live this lifestyle must also be responsible and not fall to the dark side when desperate; instead, we must seek help. We may also consider a network of communes where people can live simple lifestyles caring for themselves and the others in their community.

Creating systems that prevent homelessness from happening in the first place is the best solution. This strategy means we need a society that does not create so much desperation with no place to get help. Prevention means excellent educational systems, job access, just pay, training with safety nets in place that help people get back up when they fall. In the end, properly handling homelessness means more happy, self-sufficient, productive people adding to the collective good. It also means a safer, cleaner, and nicer place to live for everyone.

TRUE JUSTICE

Fixing our justice system will also help fix our global economy as the law determines how everything runs and how we are treated. It's also crucial as there can be no lasting peace without true justice for all. While we can't cover all that is needed to reform our justice system within the scope of this book, I have provided the keys to get us on the right path so the rest can fall into place.

First, it's critical to understand that justice is a virtue and tied to our conscience, empathy, sympathy, wanting to live rationally, best practices, and doing the good/positive. This means justice is blind, based on equality, nonpartisan, and apolitical (Note that most other systems, i.e., education, science, news, health, etc. are too). Justice is also more than just about following a law; it's about fairness and what is truly right. It's about fixing the wrongness permanently. At its heart, justice is about treating others as you would want to be treated if the situation were reversed.

Ok, now let's go into some specifics. The basics for citizens, when confronted by police, to prevent yourself from being killed include: obeying the officer's instructions immediately, to stop moving and to not make any quick movements. In most cases, it's a good idea to drop what you are holding and to slowly move your open hands, palms facing the officer so that they can be seen. Do not yell at them or make any aggressive fast movements. Speak to them with respect, and if you have to move, ask them before you do anything and do it slowly.

To fix our Justice system, which includes the police, we first must realize it is not a catch-all; it can't deal with everything nor fill the gaps in other malformed societal systems. For example, our Justice system should not be dealing with homelessness, mental health, addiction, social disputes, dog catching, and other issues. So this means our police organizations need to be the right size and properly funded so they can do THEIR job. We do not want an overfunded justice system that is so bloated that we use it for things for which it's not qualified. We need other social systems to have qualified workers and funding to do those jobs.

To be clear, the best person for handling most issues in society is rarely the person trained to use violence with a gun. Fixing our justice system is about proper standards, rules, ensuring policing best practices, training, oversight, checks & balances, and accountability. Also, all police actions should be recorded and publicly available, so we all know what happened exactly, and there is no hiding anything.

In most cases, no force or the least amount of force should be used, and care taken not to hurt and injure people. Here non-lethal weapons and control methods are used in most cases with lethal options only used as a last resort in extreme circumstances. Here it's about training police to be guardians and not warriors. Nor should the main police force be militarized (special units like SWAT are ok). Citizens should not be stopped, searched, harassed or ticketed for minor infractions when a warning would serve as well. We must eliminate paid bail for minor violations and other predatory practices. Nor should we have a system where money and property confiscated goes directly to the police, as this will incentivize harassment, illegal seizure, and shakedowns.

Our police and justice workers must show all citizens respect and be good role models. At all times, they must treat others as they would want to be treated and speak to people as they want to be spoken to, no matter how the others are behaving and speaking. This is critically important for treating people with respect, and being courteous shows strength and is being a good role model that they can then emulate. To help with this issue, often, the best practice is for the police to live within the communities they are policing, even if it's part-time.

This strategy helps them to become a part of the community and not an invader.

Next, we must realize that over 90% of people in prison are poor, illiterate, and/or have no high school diploma and are minorities. Many, if not most of them, have been abused as children. The fact is, it's the poor, neglected, uneducated, desperate, and lost that are the majority of those who end up within our justice system.

Because of these societal failures, most prisons should be reform centers where we don't mix the first time and the nonviolent with the repeat and violent; where we don't lock up the mentally ill and addicted - instead we get them help. Most prisons should be concentrating on education, skill and job training. We should be teaching all the basics to life management as covered within *The Way* as well as using therapy and therapeutic techniques to create positive changes for as many of our citizens in these circumstances as possible.

We can even provide jobs while in prison. Work helps them atone for what they did, contribute to their care as well as learn skills that will help them after they are released. As a society, we do this so that when they get out of prison, they are better able to assimilate into society in positive ways.

After someone has served their time and is released, a support system, work, and temporary or even long-term relocation and housing should be provided whenever needed to prevent recidivism (becoming a repeat offender and going back to jail). We need to end for-profit prisons because their goal is to have more and more prisoners - not to help anyone. We should give back voting rights to those who have paid their debt and served their time. We also need to end the death penalty because killing is wrong, the practice teaches violence is a solution, and too many have been killed unjustly for this to continue.

We, as citizens, all must understand that policing and working within the justice system is very challenging and that they need our help, respect, and support. We cannot label all policing as bad or treat them all poorly. Good police are doing a vital job in our broken society - we need them. All good justice workers should have our thanks and respect - not our scorn.

If those of us in positions of power, like law enforcement, who do not treat other people well, the lacking will build up resentment, mistrust, and even hatred. This negativity builds up because the disrespect conveys contempt, distrust, dislike, and even hate. Few if any of us respect those who hate and treat us inhumanely. To be respected, you must be respectable. As law enforcement, we must realize we are working to protect and serve ALL the citizens, even those of us who have gone astray.

The rest of what is needed to fix our justice systems is complicated, but much of it boils down to justice workers and citizens treating each other as equals and as they would want to be treated if the situation were reversed. It's about fairness and treating all people humanely, with dignity and respect. We want everyone to be working toward the common good and to be productive members of society. Therefore, we must not become jaded; instead, we must create a conducive, mutually beneficial system - a justice system that reflects the best of us. A justice system of equality, transparency, and fairness that is working to protect and serve, reform and educate, so we create a better society for everyone.

In the end, the true strategy is to prevent the need for the justice system to get involved in the first place.

We do this through the proper formation of society. Here we work to build a society where everyone sees each other as equals, and there are few to none who are poor, illiterate, uneducated, abused, and desperate.

UNFAIR WORK

Many of the other significant problems that we face today, on a global economic level as well as on a societal level, come from the past legacy systems and old ways of thinking that include an underdeveloped sense of morality.

Our current economic systems are a byproduct created from humanity fighting its way up from slavery, serfdom, and other forms of forced labor without regard or respect for people or our environment. We can see this old way of thinking when we look at how people are typically educated and work. We see that people are told to act like machines where they are not allowed to move much and can only do what they are told for long hours. They work with little consideration given to them as human beings or their life beyond the job. The consequence of this twisted humane system is that a very select few overly benefit at the expense of the many and our natural world.

The current structure of work creates many angry, enraged, and desperate people who need not be. We can clearly see the dysfunction within our economic systems for many poor people work full time (35+ hours a week) for highly "profitable" companies. Some even working 70+ hours a week. These hard-working people are most often on the front lines doing demanding jobs, often in hellish conditions.

Yet these full-time workers live in poverty where they have little security or access to quality societal systems. For many of us, our income, after full-time work, is still at such a low level that we can't even afford to buy healthy food to feed ourselves and those under our care. For those who are poor yet can afford to buy healthy food, it is often not sold anywhere near poor neighborhoods making their actual costs much higher. Instead, their local stores only carry low-quality, unhealthy, and high-calorie junk food.

In the end, we must create fair systems of work and compensation if we are ever to create our "True Society." These fair systems of work will only happen if we the masses band together to force it to happen, and/or those in power choose to help us make it happen. So do your part and encourage others to do theirs.

Dinosaurs Must Evolve or Go Extinct

"It is no measure of health to be well adjusted to a profoundly sick society." - Jiddu Krishnamurti

Another major issue that our economies and societies have to deal with is our legacy systems (those systems that are very old yet are very dominant like farming, oil, and gas). Most often, those who run legacy systems work hard to perpetuate the status quo so that they can benefit from their creation for as long as possible. This outlook is natural as they have a lot invested in the system, and change is difficult. This tendency to hold on to the past, outdated systems, and poor ways of managing our economy hurts our society and growth as a species in many ways.

For example, horse breeders and carriage makers fought hard to outlaw the automobile. Then the gas automobile makers worked hard to prevent other types of cars like steam and alternative forms of transportation like trollies and subways from being used or legal. We can see this issue today with the fight between toxic energy, packaging, and farming vs. clean energy, packaging, and farming.

These forms of lower economic thinking, which have plagued us for thousands of years, are based on the extreme exploitation of people and our natural world. These ideals are often perpetuated today by those in the centers of power because of a twisted sense superiority that is programmed into them. Often, those of us in these positions have a malformed sense of empathy, sympathy, and appreciation for all people and the environment, which prevents us from seeing problems and finding real solutions.

Also, many people in leadership positions are frequently in their jobs not through merit, and therefore, do not have the skills needed to make things run well. They are often corrupt, only looking out for themselves and others within their group. Those of us in these positions who would like to do the right thing are often constrained and prevented by jury-rigged laws and systems as well as by the corrupt, those fighting for the status quo and against positive change.

These negative types of people and organizations fighting against positive change are called "dinosaurs." A "dinosaur" is often a big organization or company with a significant market share and an investment in technology or way of doing something which they do not want to change, refine, or replace. Instead, they want to keep it going as long as possible even though it should be replaced by something better and cleaner.

We can see the human race is still mostly ruled by the dinosaurs who look to impose their will upon us for so many of us are still gravely mistreated, abused, underpaid, enslaved, indentured, and disrespected. Our environment is also being despoiled at a pace and to a level that we may never be able to recover from if we don't do something very soon.

We, the people, are very tired of getting so little while a few people take the vast majority of the wealth that we help create. We don't want a handout. We want a fair share, what is right and just. We all want to live wonderful lives. Societal Systems that are not fair, moral, equal, or just and that do not work for the vast majority of people create unrest. Such malformed and sick societies are primed for revolt and revolution. Therefore, we must fix all our societal systems and global relationships, or else we are doomed to a future of self-destruction.

"Those who can't change their minds can't change anything."
- George Bernard Shaw

BALANCE VS. BOOM & BUST

Our economic issues mount as we add poverty, homelessness, injustice, unfair work, and dinosaurs to the false way public companies are judged. The construction of our global financial system (stock markets, banks, investment groups, etc.) is one that cycles from boom to bust. Boom to bust means that our economy is designed to rise to unjustifiable heights and then burst, so it then falls to destructive levels. This "boom to bust" economic structure makes it possible for a few, as if playing a game or gambling, to make extreme amounts of money at the expense of large groups of people as well as our companies and world governments.

The harm is compounded when "dinosaurs" stall our natural growth toward our "True Society" by holding onto things that are no longer needed or desired. The keyword here is stalls, not prevents, for we can see from history that no matter how long it takes, humanity will rebel, often violently, to overthrow those oppressing our advancement toward a better world. In the end, ONLY the "dinosaurs" that adapt, evolve, and change survive.

If a company can't provide what we need safely and respectfully without destroying people's lives and our world, then it should not exist in that form. If this is a vital component, we need to find a better way to get it done. This whole idea of continuous improvement through renewal, and finding the better way, is at the heart of capitalism. Here we naturally allow those who can do it right, and better, to take the place of the old who cannot. In fact, the founding principle of competition within capitalism states that if a business can't give us what we want in the way we want it, it should change, cease to exist or change hands. It's a founding principle because the bad companies' destruction opens the door for others who can do it right and give us what we truly need and want.

We who are looking to change the world in positive ways are not here to kill the "dinosaurs." They will kill themselves by not adapting. We can help expedite this process by encouraging "dinosaurs" to evolve and by stopping to work with those who don't. We all need to help and support those who are willing to change, working to improve and to do things right

Our transition toward the "True Society" need not be an "us vs. them," "zero-sum," "win-lose," "all or nothing" or "violent" situation. We can create positive, peaceful change through being our best, cooperation within fair competition, and through the journey of seeking consensus. *Note*, you will learn exactly how to force peaceful, positive change within "Chapter 15."

CHAPTER 14
ACHIEVING GLOBAL HARMONY

"To be wealthy and honored in an unjust society is a disgrace."
– Confucius

To continue our journey into "Step: 6 Unite," we need to examine a few more keys to achieving peace and a positive global trajectory. To survive, thrive, and be happy, our shared human condition forces us to need and want a certain level of security, convenient access to the systems of society, their products or services, and the free time to live a good lifestyle.

Achieving economic harmony and global stability is not only possible; it's necessary if we are to thrive as a species. We need our economic systems working for us and to ensure that we are all participating in the economy correctly. There is no end to the work that we can do now, and that will need doing, for this is an ever-present human conditional task where we must consistently seek to improve if we are to get anywhere.

In fact, the vast majority of us will spend most if not all our money and time to attain what is needed to survive, thrive, and achieve lasting happiness. The level of societal access and income that brings the highest degree of satisfaction is called the "Happiness Level."

Societal system access involves things provided by the government like roads, voting, disaster help, and more. It includes all the stuff we buy from businesses and people like food, phones, housing, and more.

This access includes being able to go to places like libraries, schools, shops, parks, museums, amusement parks, clubs, movie theaters, and more.

The security aspects of the "happiness level" include the fact that you and your loved ones must be relatively safe as you go about your daily lives if you are to be happy. Long term happiness comes from knowing that our loved ones, and we will be well cared for during emergencies and in old age. Happiness is knowing that there is a fair, equal, transparent, responsible, and respectful form of justice, policing, and emergency services in place to protect and help every citizen. We reach the "happiness level" when we are happy with our lifestyle, our access to quality societal systems, and prospects for the future.

SOCIETAL SYSTEMS ACCESS

Our human conditional needs are the foundation of our global economic system. Again, the primary systems of society include government, economics, business, communications, health, justice, religion, media, and entertainment as well as the basics such as education, water, food, housing, clothing, sanitation, transportation, emergency services (fire, paramedics, shelters, etc.) and energy.

These systems must exist, work well, and be easily accessible if we are to be happy with them. If any or all of these systems do not exist or are underdeveloped or do not run well, no matter how high the income levels, there is unhappiness and even unrest. Proper access is especially needed when we talk about the basics such as good education, water, food, housing, clothing, sanitation, transportation, emergency services (fire, paramedics, shelters, etc.) and energy.

All of our societal systems must work together to provide a conducive environment for people to grow so everyone can become their best and live a wonderful life. We gain access to these systems and their products and services in three ways.

- **Provided:** These goods and services can come in the form of free use of roadways, libraries, and emergency services as part of a government program paid for through taxes and other revenues as well as by the wealthy as a gift. It can come from other organizations that provide emergency services, charity, and other aid. It can come in the form of gifts from companies to their workers and the society in the form of vacations, free tickets, transportation, and even in the form of building parks, cleaning up a problem area, and more. Provided goods and services increase access to amenities without increasing people's income or ownership.

- **Purchased:** These are all the products and services where money is used to pay for them.

- **Traded:** We may also trade something we have or even trade time for products and services. *For example,* I have a table I don't want, and you have a lamp you don't want. So, we trade the table for the lamp. It may be that we can work on a task in trade for an object instead of money too.

In today's world, we mainly gain access to what we need through purchase and by having them provided.

Fair Compensation

Within a well-run organization, all work is of value. There are no unneeded jobs or useless work, for it all adds up to the whole. The output is what's important.

Therefore, all jobs that are needed are worthy of fair and just compensation. To say it another way, all of us who work full time should be compensated so we can live within the "happiness level."

For Example: If you have enough money, you can buy good food and choose to live in a place where you have access to highly developed societal systems. If there are enough of us with higher levels of wealth in an underdeveloped area, the systems can be improved around us.

Investing in underdeveloped areas is an essential point, as this is one way that we improve these areas. Just because a place is very inexpensive to live in, and underdeveloped, we must still compensate all workers in this area as if those systems existed. Fair compensation is needed because the added wealth in an underdeveloped area will act as an energy and catalyst attracting business, government, and other organizational development.

Money is a social construct and has no value other than what we agree on. The part of the "Happiness Level" involving income is a range of compensation that allows the highest degree of happiness one can derive from money. The range of the "Happiness Level" is dependent on the costs of living in that location and which societal systems are provided and which need to be purchased.

Within the USA at the time of this research in 2018, the "Happiness Level" compensation range is approximately between $55,000 and $250,000 a year. The happiness level is a range with a cap on both ends because it depends on where you live, and happiness from income can be an issue if too low or too high. In either case, it can mean extra stress, worry, and fear as well as housing and security issues. It can also lead to isolation and many problems with socialization, education, and assimilation into the greater society for our children. That being said, and to be clear, it's poverty that is one of the most significant problems for people and our society.

To arrive at the "right levels" of compensation, we must first consider the "10 Laws," which direct us to treat others with respect, equality, and in a way that helps them on their journey to becoming their 'True Self." After all, we are all working and giving away the most valuable hours of life to fulfill personal goals. These goals include being able to survive and create a good lifestyle where we and those in our care can thrive.

The fact is that we are all equal and deserve fair pay for work. This means that all who work full time deserve to be compensated in a way that allows access to the "happiness level." This level of compensation includes all workers, even those considered salaried or part-time. Their wages are calculated based on comparable full-time work. At the very least, if we compensate people correctly, it will eliminate much of the desperation in the world, have a tremendously positive effect on our global economy, on our overall societal attitude, and give us the ability to change in a positive direction globally.

If we cannot pay some people (police, teachers, startup workers, volunteers, etc.) to the "happiness level," we can make up for this by providing it and/or by allowing them to pay less for some things and/or to pay no tax. We can distribute special negotiated or donated discounts, passes, or deals on corporate products, transportation, healthy food, education, entertainment, healthcare, retirement communities, and more. The reason alternative compensation works is because people want the benefit and don't often care about ownership. Alternative compensation works for companies and society at large.

For example, if we gain a season pass for our family to the local amusement parks or for free public transportation, we don't care that they were given to us through our work or government instead of purchased with our money. To some people, these things being provided is like receiving a great gift that can bring added happiness.

HEALTHY GLOBAL ECONOMY

"Capitalism – which in its purest form is entrepreneurism even among the poorest of the poor – does work; but those who make money from it should put it back into society, not just sit on it as if they are hatching eggs." - Richard Branson

We must seek unity between humanity and our economic systems. A humane global economic system is necessary if we are to truly master our society and world. To create harmony and balance, we need to make sure that all our societal systems reflect our human values/virtues and morality. We do this through a grounding in the "10 Laws" and by ensuring that we have proper laws and checks and balances in place. These precautions ensure our systems are on the right path while allowing this fact to be verified and fixed if needed.

Proper compensation would mean less of a need for government programs that cover the gaps left by the missing compensation companies steal from their workers. It would mean more money would flow to the government, businesses, and other systems. This proper flow of wealth strengthens all our societal systems, which means more economic stability and improved lifestyles for all. "All" includes the wealthy because, in such a fair and just world, they would not be demonized and would not have to live in fear and be so isolated. Currently, many people feel wrongly justified being rude and threatening them, their families, and businesses with violence because of the injustice in which so many wealthy people take part in and condone.

If people are secure and can access the systems of society to a high enough level so that they have a reasonable certainty that this will continue, then people are happy. This happiness and access help us find our "True Path" in life. One of the primary goals of our 'True Society" is to create lasting happiness for all of us. We do this by creating a pleasing conducive environment and by ensuring that we are all, at least, living within the "happiness level."

We would all benefit on many levels if the majority of us were free from living desperate lives focused on survival. Over time this freedom and happiness will have a positive synergistic effect within all of society that will lift us even higher. This positive effect becomes magnified because our positive attitude will be reflected and magnified by everyone. This positive energy can create tremendous momentum that can carry us all to heights unimaginable from our current location. The better we, "the masses," do, the more positive economic growth there will be adding to the collective happiness of all people.

"If you're in the luckiest 1% of humanity, you owe it to the rest of humanity to think about the other 99%." - Warren Buffet

Practically, this means that we need: fair global economic competition on a level playing field set at a fair level, a correct rating system for companies, fair compensation for work as well as a well-formed economic system with banks, stock markets, and investment brokers working together for the common good.

No country or people can be left behind or exploited by the rest. We must "lift all boats," so all people can rise if we want our future to be secure and prosperous.

Fundamentally, for an economy to get and stay healthy, it needs to keep the money and wealth flowing in this circular fashion from the people to the systems and from the systems to the people at a high enough level and speed. We most often accomplish this by providing "good-paying jobs" within the various societal systems. Good paying here means to the "Happiness Level." The circular flow of wealth is what can support and perpetuate high-level societal systems, growth, and a healthy lifestyle for all.

If these societal systems, especially the basics, do not exist or are underdeveloped, raising the money flow to the people in that area can provide the needed catalyst/stimulus for the systems to be created. Investment is the basic process by which we continually create better societal systems, economic growth, wonderful lifestyles, and prosperity for all.

Solely from an economic viewpoint, paying people more and developing underdeveloped areas means more customers for business, more paid in taxes, and fewer needed government assistance programs. It's through the process of our systems working to meet the evolving positive demands of the people that we drive our society to greater and greater heights of excellence. If our society is working well, we all have access to highly developed societal systems. This high level of access for all creates happiness at a level where the energy becomes synergistic and provides even more positive energy for us to use.

Therefore, our goal individually, collectively, and organizationally is to wisely choose how we use our wealth, as well as how we participate in society.

Our ultimate societal goal is to create a system whereby most everyone is providing for themselves to a level that allows them to live happy lives and have time to meaningfully participate in society.

Important Key to Global Stability & Lasting Happiness

Basic economics and the foundations of supply and demand show us very clearly a critical step in solving our local, country, and global economic problems. We find the answer in the fact that companies need customers, governments need taxpayers, and people have needs. There are billions of potential customers and taxpayers not in the system.

To get them contributing, all we need do is first compensate all those who are currently working to the "happiness level." In many cases, this can be done all at once on large scales as many industries with large exploited workforces are reaping huge undeserved profits.

Since there are so many hard-working poor, this money will bring in billions of new customers and taxpayers when done. This added customer base and money flow will help everyone and spur demand for more workers, businesses, organizations, etc. as well as less government assistance programs. It's this added wealth and demand that will allow us to bring the rest of humanity up to the happiness level.

Healthy Personal Economy

Now that we have covered many of the macro aspects of our global economy, we need to shift into a micro-level and talk about your personal responsibility. A healthy global economy is dependent on everyone's personal financial health. So, let's take a quick look into ways you can manage your economic affairs and help our world.

Proper care of your wealth, no matter how small, not only allows you to have a better life, but if you spend well, it will build a better society in the process.

Being fiscally responsible allows you to more easily stay on your "True Path" as you are more able to provide for your needs. It's essential to understand how to manage and care for your financial life as early as possible, hopefully before you are old enough for it to begin. This early knowledge helps all young people avoid the many problems that come with poor buying habits, debt, bad credit, and overextended credit.

BE FRUGAL & PROSPER

Being frugal, economical, prudent, thrifty, careful, and pennywise are ways we refer to people who know how best to care for their wealth and things as well as how to use everything to the fullest. Put another way, being frugal means that we do not waste. Those who take this idea too far get twisted into being stingy, ungenerous, and miserly. In the end, being frugal means that we care for our money, things, and have good spending habits.

GOOD SPENDING HABITS

- **Needs First:** Good spending habits mean that you focus on providing for your "needs" to the correct level that allows you to develop properly.

  For Example: You spend more on food to ensure that you get the proper nutrition rather than buying more and more shoes. You might stop buying store-bought coffee every day and replace it with green tea from home and healthier snacks you take with you.

- **Planning:** You should only buy when you have plans to do so. You do this by creating shopping lists as well as wish lists. You can then prioritize the lists to ensure that you get what you need without wasting money impulsively. Planning also involves saving for big things like education or training, going on trips, retirement, emergencies, future kids, and rainy days.

If you have extra money after your needs are covered that does not need to be saved, look to fill the gaps in the things that you <u>do not</u> have that you need or that need to be replaced. These are things that add to your health, happiness, education, and security. Things like a better air & water purification system, expanding a hobby, learning a new skill, or by installing a security system and taking a self-defense class.

Planning means you do not buy on the spur of the moment unless you have pre-planned such an action as when you are on a trip and allow yourself to buy things you like or if you see something that is on your list. The key in these situations is to set a limit on what can be spent and stick to it.

In the end, it's always much more satisfying and prudent to buy something that is at the top of your list than to buy something in the spur of the moment that you don't need or already have.

- o **Live Within Means:** Living within your means does not mean that you have to be satisfied with this state as it might not be conducive. It just means that you are not going into debt and ruining your credit while you work to improve your situation. Living within your means gives you time to plan how to grow and get what you want.

- **No Debt:** Debt is not acceptable other than in rare situations. In general, you do not want anything that causes you to have to pay interest over time, as this makes everything more expensive and wastes your money. The exceptions to this rule are things that will make you more money later, like a business, or something that you need but can't pay for all at once, like a house or car.

- **Care for Things:** Do not replace things that you already have that work well. Instead, look to repair current items and acquire new things that you do not have but would improve your life. Getting the most out of what you have and not needing new things helps you save not only your resources but also our society's resources. If you don't want it, give it to someone who does. This best practice will also build a critical habit so that when you have what you want, you will care for it.

- **Deals:** You can also seek out discounts, last year's models, and refurbished items to help cut costs. Using coupons, buying older models, and waiting until sales can help save a lot of money over time.

- **Saving:** Spending money after you save for what you want is the best way to acquire things. This strategy might mean taking on extra work to get it faster. Savings are also crucial for unexpected problems, old age, and retirement.

In the end, living frugally means there is no bad debt and that you are caring for your wealth properly. Planning and executing your strategy correctly will give you a sense of accomplishment. Following this strategy is an excellent way to build self-reliance, strong decision-making skills, and more.

PERSONAL BUDGET

So, as we have learned, the goal is to live frugally and to prosper. To do this, you need to know exactly where the money is and where it goes. A personal budget is how you track your finances. To develop your budget, you create a simple balance sheet. This is where you list all income and expenses and calculate totals. In the end, the idea is to wisely spend less than you earn. Or to put it another way, you need to have a larger income than expenses.

For Example: If income-expense=profit, you have extra money and can work on developing your life. However, if the equation ends in the negative as in income-expense=a negative, or close to negative, there is a problem.

The level of the problem depends on how much savings you have. Often this means you are going into debt and paying interest (money for the loan). These added costs mean the price of everything you bought increases. Also, if the level of debt continues to grow, at some point, there will not be enough income to cover the debt, interest, your needs, and extras. Therefore, a positive balance sheet is a must if you are to have security.

TO CREATE A BALANCE SHEET

1. **Total Income:** Write down how much income you earn or receive every month. List all sources separately and add them all together for the Total Income.

2. **Total Expenses:** You need to put the expenses into 2 general categories of <u>Needs</u> and <u>Extras</u>. Needs are things you need to survive and live like food, water, clothes, and housing. Extras are things or services that you like but don't need to survive, like buying coffee creations, going to the movies, and buying alcohol.

They can also include luxury versions of things, as in, you can make green tea vs. buying it from a store.

You are also going to group them into <u>Fixed</u> and <u>Variable</u> Expenses. A fixed expense totals the amount needed for that month as in $300 for food. Needed variable expenses are things you need, but don't happen monthly like an insurance payment due once a year. List all expenses as outlined, then add all the totals together for one <u>Total Expense</u>.

Needs, <u>Fixed</u> Monthly Expenses:

    a. Housing and Utilities
    b. Food
    c. Water
    d. Clothing
    e. Transportation
    f. Energy
    g. Tax
    h. Insurance: Another key to your security and happiness is preparation for a disaster. One of the ways you do this is through insurance. There are a lot of different kinds you can get like health, dental, property, car, work, disability, life, flood, and earthquake.

        Understanding your coverage is essential. So, be sure you know the per-incident and lifetime limits for the worst-case scenario. This is because when it comes to insurance, you often need it because the worst-case scenario has just happened to you. Therefore, the key is to be able to afford the deductible and to have enough coverage so you can recover from the issue. Your ability to cover the deductible is crucial because if you cannot pay the deductible, you often don't get anything.

    i. Etc. (Keep adding all your needs)

Needs, <u>Variable</u> Expenses: These can be a set number or a range as in $150 to $300 if needed.

a. Tuition or Room and Board for Child at School
b. Insurance if it fluctuates or is paid yearly
c. Medical costs and medicines
d. Interest & Tax
e. Etc. (Keep adding all your variable expenses)

Extras <u>Fixed</u> Expenses: These are things you don't need but enjoy.

a. Store-bought coffee
b. Maid / Gardner
c. Streaming service / Cable
d. Etc. (Add in others)

Extras <u>Variable</u> Expenses:

a. Trips
b. Unplanned shopping
c. Movies
d. Alcohol
e. Gambling (note that gambling is not a wise use of money. If you gamble, it should only be done with genuinely extra money and only with a minimal amount. Gambling is also dangerous as it can become addicting, ruin your life, and support organizations who do the same to other people. There are many other great ways to have fun and better uses for your money.
f. Etc. (Add in others)

THE WAY | STEP 6: UNITE – CONTINUED

PROFIT OR LOSS?

Now that you have your total income and expense, you subtract to get the final total, as in Income-Expense=X.

If Loss or Low: If you are spending more money than you earn or the profit is very low, you have a problem that needs to be fixed. This negative level of income often means you are going into debt and are likely paying interest (payments made for borrowing the money). Here you can try different strategies to fix the problem.

1. Lower "Needs" Fixed and Variable Costs.
    - Look for deals on everything. It might mean refinancing your home to a lower rate without fees, or it might mean you get a better deal on your cable because it could be combined with other costs or because you have been a long-time customer.
    - It's much less expensive to make your own food. You can cook healthy meals as outlined within the *Life Manual* vs. dining out as it's much cheaper. Also, this type of change can be much healthier.
        - *For Example:* "The Soup" (cost per bowl about $3 to $4) is all organic and loaded with so much of what your body needs vs. that $20 deep-fried, pesticide-laden meal at a restaurant or even that $5 fast-food deal that is hurting your health and longevity. (Find the recipe for "The Soup" in the "Life Manual: Fuel: Food: Recipes: The Soup" and www.7Way.Me)
    - Consider moving to another location that fits within your means. Some places have lower costs of living that allow for a much healthier lifestyle.
    - Lower other expenses: See what you can use less of that can save money. Think about utilities such as

water, electricity, gas, and all the other things on which you spend money.

2. Lower Extras Fixed and Variable Costs by cutting out, changing, or lowering your consumption of things you do not need. Look at all the habitual little things you do as they can add up to be a lot.

   For Example: Buying a $3 coffee every day will cost $1095 a year.

   - Some can be replaced with less expensive versions, like making your coffee/tea at home vs. buying it from a shop. Or simply take natural caffeine pills.
   - Look to repair vs. replace as this can be much less expensive than buying new ones, like resoling your shoes vs. purchasing new ones.
   - You might have to cut out some activities for a while, like eating out or going on trips on weekends. Instead, make your food and do free things locally.

3. Earn More: This might mean getting another job, a new higher paying job, or adding another revenue stream. You can receive more training or education to move on or move up. You might also add other revenue streams through your passions like gardening where you sell food to local markets or riding bikes to save on car costs or by offering lessons or repair services.

IF PROFIT

Having a profit means that you have enough extra money to plan and provide for your security.

1. **Debt:** Pay off high debt interest first (bad debt) and all others next. Ideally, you should not have any debt other than for large purchases with low levels of interest and

fees. The best reason to have debt is for an investment that will pay off the original debt and make you even more money. It's also reasonable to cover an expensive long-term need like when you open a business, buy a home or car, and can't pay for it all at once.

Bad debt is anything that you pay interest on other than these needed large purchases or something that will make you more money later. Good Debt is 0 percent or very low interest (3% or less).

The key to getting out of debt is to pay off all your debt ASAP. If you can't pay it all, move it to another creditor so you can pay a lower interest rate during the repayment process. Then pay as much as possible above the minimum until it's paid off.

2. **Savings:** We will all experience "a rainy day" at some point. At the very minimum, it's good to have at least three months of total budget coverage in a form that can be turned into money very quickly. Having enough savings to walk away from bad situations and follow your passions has a value many times greater than the size of the bank account.

There are also many things in life that you might need to save over time to afford, like education for your children and big trips. The earlier you start saving for retirement, the earlier you can achieve your goals. Saving your money in a way that you earn the highest interest possible will also help things along. In the end, properly saving your wealth allows for more personal freedom and security.

3. **Investing:** The idea of investing is to make more than you put in and/or to create positive change. Ideally, you want your investments to grow to the point where

they could care for you without you having to work (passive revenue streams or residual income).

You can invest in things like real estate and other businesses where you make money and build equity. You can create something to sell over and over like a book, music, an invention, or art. One of the best strategies is to create your own business and to use a trust. Investing is also about looking for safe investments such as annuities, government bonds, and other stable sources of income, so you are diversified and safe.

Be careful of stocks and combined funds, like mutual funds, for example, as this type of mass groupings of companies often will mean that you are investing in businesses that are not treating this world or people well. Not knowing means that through your investment, you may be participating in destroying our world and people's lives. Therefore, it's essential to know the company's practices toward their workers and our environment before investing in any company and only continue investing in those that honor the correct code.

It's important to realize that the stock market is not totally based on science or fact and should be treated more like gambling. It's more of a gamble because your investment is only worth anything when you take it out. Also, the stock market can collapse on emotion at any moment. It has also been proven over and over that the largest and seemingly most stable companies can be corrupt, lie, and also collapse without warning. This corporate unreliability, along with the fact that many financial institutions which push investments have proven to be more interested in playing money games than fulfilling their proper role within society. This all means that we cannot truly rely on our financial system in its current form and that it needs to be upgraded.

So, before the system is fixed, when investing in stocks, be careful, do research, diversify, and choose companies that have proven to be a positive influence on society, that have a good track record and leadership. Also, don't be afraid to sell some stocks when they are at a high level and use the principle and gains in another investment. Sell high and buy low as the saying goes.

Stock Tip: If investing in stocks, it's good to look for stocks that pay a dividend. Dividends allow you to make money while you hold the stock. Stocks without dividends only let you make money when you sell, and the sale price is determined by the market value at that time. So, if holding a stock for the longer term, dividends can help you expand your portfolio without having to sell your stock or add more money. A good financial advisor can help here.

BASIC ACCOUNTS

There are five basic-financial "Account Types" to consider. They include:

1. **Checking:** While physical checks are rarely used anymore, checking accounts serve as the primary bill payment account.
2. **Savings** accounts are used to store extra money where you make a little money every month from a very low-interest rate.
3. **Money Market** accounts are a type of savings account. These are often used instead of

savings accounts because they have higher interest rates than a bank's savings account and because you can transfer money between accounts so fast.

4. **Investment:** This is the account that holds your investments like stocks, bonds, etc.
5. **Credit** most often comes in the form of cards like MasterCard, Visa, American Express, or store cards. It can also include credit lines, loans, and more.

CREDIT

For those of us in countries who use a credit system, we are going into how to use credit effectively as this is often misused.

A credit rating is a judgment on your financial trustworthiness. Used credit is a loan that you must payback. Typically, if you pay it back within an allotted amount of time, you do not pay any interest. However, if you carry a balance beyond the free period, you will pay interest. Interest is the fee you pay for the loan. If you do an excellent job paying your bills, your credit rating goes up; if not, it goes down. If you have a low credit rating, you may not be able to get credit, and if you do, you will pay higher interest. Conversely, if you have a high credit score, you get more credit at better interest rates.

Ok, now that we have the basics, let's look at how you can effectively use Credit Cards to your advantage.

STARTING OUT

Get any credit card, no matter how high the interest. Use the card to buy everything you usually buy and can afford to pay for that month. Then pay off the credit card entirely by or before the due date every month. Over time, this builds your creditworthiness.

Correctly paying your bills means that your current credit company may offer you more credit at better rates and benefits. As you build a better credit score, you will be offered even better credit cards from many companies.

Zero Interest

When you have a decent credit score, you can often qualify for a zero-interest card. These cards still require you to make the minimum monthly payment during a set time, like for 15 months, but will not charge any interest during this period.

Most will only start charging interest the month after this zero-interest period ends. Other credit cards can be "deferring the interest," meaning that all 15 months' worth of interest will be charged during the 16th month period if the credit card is not paid off or the balance transferred to another creditor. Using zero-interest cards is a great way to build up your credit while you also make money.

For Example: If you get a 21-month zero-interest credit card with an expense limit of $20,000, you then charge everything to this card over the next 21 months up to that level. Be sure that you pay the monthly minimum.

Only charge items on this card for which you have the money. The key is to take all the actual money that covers these bills and invest it. Investing can mean moving your monthly check to a money market account and letting it build up and accrue interest. You can also take out all $20,000 at once and invest it for 20 months in a safe investment that pays relatively high interest and more. Whatever you do, ensure that the investment has no risk and that the money is available to pay off the zero-interest credit card at the end of the term.

As the credit balance rises, your credit rating may go down, and your monthly minimum payment will go up. When you pay off these high balance cards and get more credit, your credit score will go back up to an even higher level. So, when the zero-interest card is up and paid off, and your credit score rises, get another zero-interest card and do this, again and again, building your credit. Along with all the protections the cards offer on purchases/travel, you also earn money back and/or miles, which all helps you save money.

After finished with a zero-interest card, do not close it because having a large amount of unused credit is one indicator that helps you gain a good credit rating. Keep it open and ensure that you use it at least once a year to keep it active. Also, be sure to use earned cash back and/or miles. An excellent way to keep cards active is to set up a bill autopay on that card, so it's used at least once a year. This way, you don't have to worry about remembering to use it.

Note: If you have a lot of credit cards from one bank, you can often consolidate all or most of your available credit onto one card, thus allowing you to close the other cards yet keep your overall credit limit. Also, be sure to get cards from different banks. Try for at least one card at the top three banks.

In the end, this strategy of using zero interest and diversification can help bring more peace of mind as it's nice having all that cash in the bank earning interest and a good amount of non-used credit in case of an emergency.

High-Interest Transfer to Low Interest

Banks often offer to transfer a high-interest balance to a lower-interest account. Most offers come with fees. If the cost is less than you will be paying in interest on your debt, it's worth it. The key to all balance transfer offers is to check the fees. Not all terms are the same. Look for the lowest fee and longest term. There should be no penalty for paying early nor any accruing interest that will be charged if not paid in full at the end. The fee should be a onetime fee with a minimum of about $3 and a percentage of about 3% or less of the amount transferred.

CREDIT USE BENEFITS

There are excellent benefits when using credit cards correctly. They raise your credit rating, which means you will pay less interest for your big purchases that need a loan. Credit card companies also offer a wide range of benefits for using their cards, such as fraud protection, best price guarantee, return guarantee, travel insurance, return help, and other benefits. Be sure to familiarize yourself with these benefits as they can be of great aid, especially when there is a problem with anything purchased. They can even give you access to events and travel.

In the end, understanding, controlling, and monitoring your finances is an essential ability that must be mastered, for it greatly determines the quality of your life and the development of our society.

CHAPTER 15
CREATING LASTING PEACE & HAPPINESS

"We must become the change we wish to see in the world."
- Mahatma Gandhi

We wrap up "Step 6: Unite" in this chapter by outlining the steps needed to create, and if need be, force peaceful, positive change. Fundamentally, we create the world we want through all of us sharing foundational knowledge in key areas of life and then acting on it together.

This shared knowledge base allows us to unite in a common cause with a clear goal. In this age, because of modern communication systems, we have the ability and opportunity to learn, connect, cooperate, and coordinate on a global level like never before. Our connectedness makes our "Greatest Power" of unity even greater.

The keys to changing any societal structure are to work for positive change in people, systems, and laws. We, the people, change ourselves and societal systems through development. We change laws and future generations through voting, putting good people of merit in power positions, raising our children correctly, and following the other best practices outlined within *The Way*.

Creating better people, societal systems, and laws allow us to implement solutions, not just mask the symptoms. This overall clarity and focus by a vast majority of us is how everything can change fast and peacefully. So far, you have come a long way in understanding yourself and key societal structures. Now let's go deeper into exactly how you can help improve our societal systems every day.

Your Participation

"You are either part of the solution or part of the problem."
- Eldridge Cleaver

You are already participating in the creation of the future and are either helping or hurting our progress toward our "True Society." To be clear, you are a crucial player in this great game and are either part of the solution or the problem.

No choice is a choice, and ignorance does not change this fact. Even if you claim not to be participating and do not want to, your "non-participation" is a choice and affects the outcome negatively. This means that when fact and science do not align with your political or spiritual views and desires for what you wish or want to be true, you need to be open to change and make choices with what is real and not what you wish or think should be.

To put it another way, we are all like a great team fighting for our lives. It should be obvious that we need all our players in the game, cooperating, not sitting on the sidelines and/or fighting each other. Evil wins if the good do nothing, the wrong thing, or when we are divided. Therefore, you must do your part and unite correctly to make a real difference in the world.

You should naturally want to help improve all our societal systems as they affect you as we are all citizens and consumers. It's to your advantage that all our systems work well as this harmony will help you and yours live a better life. Therefore, you should see your participation as a duty as well as part of what makes your life worthwhile and meaningful.

BEING MINDFUL OF THE 8 KEYS BELOW IS HOW YOU PARTICIPATE IN THE SOLUTION THROUGH YOUR DAILY LIFE.

1. YOUR PATRONAGE & MONEY

The places you frequent (virtual and real-life), and the money you spend matters, for this is how we support societal structures, businesses, and organizations. Therefore, you can make a real difference in the world through your everyday choices. It's where we all invest, shop, the products we all buy, who we watch and listen to, and all the rest we consume that matters. All of us correctly choosing is one way we force positive change and advance our society.

For Example: If you invest in or spend your money at a place that underpays its workers, exploits animals, and destroys the environment, you are actively participating in this destruction and negativity. Conversely, investing in, going to locations, and spending money on a good business helps everyone and our society improve.

2. YOU MUST VOTE

If you are blessed to live in a country that allows you to vote, you are <u>obligated</u> to do so. To be clear, we in these voting societies can literally vote our way to a better world and our "True Society." As the "Nations of the People" rise and do better and better, they will serve as an example for other countries as well as be there to offer a hand up. This is because, as noted earlier, the "One True Party" that most of us already belong to is all about making our societal systems work well, improving the lives of all people, and caring for the world.

So, do some research on the issues and about those running for office and make informed decisions that help further the common good. Look for those who are reasonable and who genuinely want to work to make all our societal systems work as effectively and efficiently as possible. We must find the best people and vote because positive change is only complete if supported by laws, and our laws can only be made and changed by those in the government.

Since the government sets the tone for how everything runs within a society, if our government is to run well, we need to have the right people in place who are seeking to unite us and implement real solutions. Therefore, if we are to create a great system, it's paramount that you do your part and vote.

While I can't include a complete voting system guide in this book, there are a few keys that are worth mentioning here. First, having "None of the Above" as an option on some ballots so we can show when we are not happy with any of the choices given. Here we can still select the "lesser of the evils" given. While this will not stop undesirables from being elected, it will allow us to gauge how many of us are unsatisfied with the choices.

It's also incumbent upon all the members of a voting society to maintain and improve our voting systems. Caring means ending voter suppression, gerrymandering, and systems like the electoral college and the laws like "Citizens United," which allow oligarchy rule as found in America.

Instead, we need to ensure that every person of voting age can vote. We do this by encouraging free voting by mail, extending the days and time we can vote. Election day should be a national holiday and seen as a day of service to our society. The holiday can include all kinds of voting support and festivities. If there is a need for IDs to vote, then <u>every</u> citizen must be given the ID <u>before</u> it's required to vote.

We must also create standardized ballots that are <u>clear</u> to everyone and easy to count. All our voting machines need to meet the same high-level security and accountability standards. All voting machines must be made in the country and pass federal tests before use, and all must be inspected regularly to ensure they have not been compromised.

For example, all electronic voting must create a paper document that the voter can then verify and then submit. A backup paper copy allows us to confirm that the electronic records are accurate.

Other safeguards include things like ensuring that our voting machines are independent and never hooked up to LANs, Wi-Fi, or the internet, nor have external connection ports. These safeguards also include ensuring that all elections remain the responsibility of the state and local government with federal oversight.

We must be vigilant against all kinds of voter fraud like ballot stuffing and/or the destroying or hiding of ballots. We must also ensure that foreign governments are not influencing us through our media and that all our news is factual. We must be ever vigilant to ensure we are not manipulated into voting one way rather than the right way.

Ensuring the security and integrity of our voting systems is a primary duty to all nations run by the people. Those of you living in countries without the right to vote can work to respect the rights of the nations who do and work to change your system if you are unhappy.

3. GIVE HOPE: HELP CHARITIES & CAUSES

There are many worthwhile organizations, charities, causes, and aid organizations that are doing positive things in our world. These groups have champions who are working to solve the problems for all of us. However, these groups need our money and help as volunteers if they are to succeed. The key is to ensure that the group is reputable and makes a real difference. Our universal desire to help those who can't help themselves and give a hand up to those who have fallen is one of our most noble traits.

Your efforts to help these groups might mean just taking a few seconds to click a button, sign a petition, offer suggestions, give a few dollars, or take a poll. You can do this easily by joining a website that will send you petitions and polls according to your interests.

While taking a few seconds to click and giving a little money might seem trivial, it is NOT, for as you know, your vote and money joined in common cause with <u>many</u> other people is "Our Greatest Power." Never doubt that $1, a few clicks, or a signature on a petition from <u>lots of us</u> can make a big difference. Our collective actions and money are the <u>proof</u> that is needed for change to happen. Also, everyone participating creates a lot of positive energy, which helps attract more followers. All of which can mean the difference between success or failure for that cause.

You can help solve many of the world's most vexing problems by merely supporting the champions fighting for the cause and by fighting on the frontlines. If no organization or champion is fighting for a cause you believe in, you can start something or encourage the right people to do so. You can also get more involved and volunteer.

Volunteers assist on a task, project, or donate materials without compensation. Many groups who are looking to create positive change accept volunteers. Here you can get more involved, spending more time and effort. Participation might mean helping to build a house, deliver food, protest, stuff envelopes, make calls, pick up supplies, and more.

Charity Warning: It's not enough to give and "try" to help. Charities must work and work well if their role in society and what we intend is to mean anything. If a charity is ineffective, it's better off joining with a like organization to help create a larger organization that can make a real difference or to disband so that the money and people can flow to an organization that does work. Disbanding the charity is needed because an ineffective charity is nothing but a waste of money and time that could be better used.

For example, as in Haiti, in 2010, after the earthquake, they built soccer stadiums instead of water, sanitation, and food systems.

The problem today is that many "charities" are run by the wealthy as a tax dodge and a way to funnel money to friends and family. There are also so many charities and causes because our societal systems are not working correctly, and the ones that do exist are not working in harmony. As our systems improve and we compensate for all that our human conditions throw at us, this need for so much charity will diminish.

However, there will always be a need for us to join to help, especially in times of unpreventable disaster. To get us to a higher level of societal development, we must remember that it's not enough to assist in the immediate crisis, we must also mitigate the aftermath. If we do not, our lack of action can create even more significant problems down the road.

For Example: In a natural disaster like a flood, storm, or earthquake, it's about helping people at the time of the disaster but also after it's all over. We need to give a "hand up" so they can get "back on their feet" and care for themselves again.

To end the corruption within charities, we need a public record of who works for the charity, their pay, as well as open accounting, so we know who is benefiting from the charity and how effective it is. We all have the right to see how they spend the money and how effective they are in the mission. If we have proper oversight and checks and balances in place, we can root out the scams and ineffectual charities, which will allow us to focus on genuine charities that really help.

4. BE THE LEADER

As we have learned, our societal systems are dependent on people doing the work. However, some positions have more potential to cause harm as well as solve problems. The reason these nexus points exist is that we create hierarchical structures in which people are in leadership positions where their decisions and actions affect the whole.

Because of our need for leaders, we must have the right people in these critical positions within our societal systems. It's also incumbent upon all of us who are leaders to be worthy and earn the responsibility, trust, and faith people are placing in us. Doing well in these power positions will allow everything to run more efficiently and effectively.

To make this happen, we need to raise good leaders and get them into position. To do this, we need to raise our children correctly, so there is a plethora of great leaders available (See the *Child & Family Guide* for how). We also need to have dependable, uncorrupted, equal, and just merit-based societal systems with proper checks and balances in place. Here the primary focus of all organizations is to find the right leaders to direct the organization so that it efficiently produces the best products and services while respecting and caring for our world and people.

So, if you are a true leader, you need to strive to attain top positions. If you are not, you need to back those who are. If you know someone who would be good, encourage and help them become a leader. You also need to be sure that you do not take a critical job that you are not qualified for, even if offered by a friend and/or leader. Instead, it's better to back someone of real merit or to decline.

5. Take a Government Job

Regardless if elected or hired, all the jobs within our government need to be filled by those of the highest merit and skill. Working for the government is a service to our nation and world. We all benefit from our governments working well and together. Therefore, it's incumbent upon all of us who are qualified and have great skill to:

- **Serve:** If you have top skills, you should look to work within your government. You can see this as a form of duty or service where you take the job for a short time. All nonelected government jobs should be performed as nonpartisan activities where you are looking to do the best job possible regardless of party membership. Even elected officials and affiliated party work must, at times, be nonpartisan, so that we can root out corruption within our ranks and honor the high oaths we swore to uphold. We all work together in a nonpartisan manner so that our government may truly serve all the people.

    The better the people are who work for our government, the more smoothly and efficiently all other systems will run. Many of us working within the government and the private sector at different times can also help create a general understanding of both systems allowing us to find ways to integrate more effectively and for harmony to emerge.

- **Recruit:** We all need to be on the lookout and encourage others of great talent to take a job within the government. We might nominate them to a position or even bring them to the attention of a group looking for good leaders or workers. The more of us looking for qualified people, the better our government will become.

- **Be Nice:** It's nice to show a little extra respect and to give thanks to all those who serve in our government like our teachers, police, firefighters, soldiers, office workers, and all the rest. Showing a little extra respect is good because most, if not all, of those people working there are doing so because they care, and they could get jobs that pay more and live better lifestyles.

6. Fix the Wrongness

Most of you can see the wrong, unjust, ugly, and twisted around you. If you are looking for someplace to start helping, this is a good place. You can't go astray working to peacefully fix the wrongness and corruption within your workplace, religions, government, and local communities.

Dissenting, protesting, and whistleblowing on corruption is not evil, unpatriotic, or unjust. In fact, it's one of the most righteous, noble, and just things you can do when faced with a great "Wrongness" for we can't fix anything without its exposure. Exposure is especially needed when the rest of us, or those who need to know, do not know about the wrongness, and it can't be fixed otherwise.

You can be significant, influential, and make a real difference in the world. You can join a protest, strike, boycott, or blockade.

You can walk out, sit in, and march to help fix the wrongness in our world. You can run for office and join special events for a cause. The key is to get involved.

Those who try to label unified, peaceful dissent and protest as something wrong, evil, clueless, and unpatriotic are usually doing so with the intent of discrediting and minimizing those protesting. The tactic of labeling and dismissing is used so that false leaders can manipulate mass perception, stay in control, or gain power over a group.

To evolve into our "True Society," the injustice and misunderstandings at the core of most protests must be understood and addressed. The fact that people are protesting is enough of a reason to look for the crux of the issue. Often, it's through adding all the issues together that a clear picture emerges. This clear picture often involves virtues and the desire for a better life and society. We all want real, positive, lasting solutions to be implemented.

Therefore, it's critically important that we all honor and protect real investigative journalism, real news, free speech, justice workers, whistleblowers, and peaceful dissent because these are vital parts of the checks and balances system that help prevent corruption. Learn more about what real news and free speech really mean within the "Life Manual: Fuel: Information: Tactics…"

In fact, those who step forward first and show us the way of truth and of the wrongness are heroes. Yet, these people are often demonized and hated by those who do not want to face the truth or who have another agenda. We must ensure that our systems protect those of us who are willing to stand up to the wrongness as they are often victimized, threatened, and even killed.

7. Join Us

The Way is the first step and the cornerstone of a much grander mission. The mission is to be a catalyst that spurs meaningful, positive change within people's lives and our society to create a world of lasting peace and happiness that everyone can enjoy. We have a lot more planned.

So if you are serious about becoming your best, being significant, influential, and making a real positive difference in our world, then explore our website and sign up. Our site is the hub for everything. There you will find great resources as well as training and coaching programs that will accelerate you down your "True Path." You can also join a growing community and participate in online and offline events that can help you and our world. www.7Way.Me

8. Find Your Way

There are endless ways you can participate in furthering the common good. The key is to start now and do something positive. If you don't know what to do, find a good organization, join a cause you believe in, and follow the direction of the leaders. Joining does not have to be a big deal. Your commitment can range from doing all the little things like signing a petition and voting to going the extra mile "once in a while" or for a "short time" on important issues. Again, a little from the many means less work for everyone.

HELP CREATE A MIRACLE

There are no small, meaningless or trivial positive actions. Everything you do matters!
Small positive efforts multiplied by everyone add up to something miraculous!

"It is not necessary to do extraordinary things to get extraordinary results." - Warren Buffet

HOW TO FORCE PEACEFUL POSITIVE CHANGE

"One individual can begin a movement that turns the tide of history." - Jack Canfield

Sometimes our societal systems don't change fast enough and need an extra push. Below I have outlined how we can "Unite" to <u>peacefully force</u> positive change within any organization or society. When we force change, our overall goal is to create peaceful, stable, enduring, and healthy societal systems that encourage and aid us all. The right balance of sympathy and empathy is needed to solve significant societal issues.

For Example: If those running a government have an underdeveloped sense of empathy and sympathy, it leads to the creation of unfair and inhumane laws. On the other extreme, programs that promote sloth, laziness, waste, dependence, and self-entitlement also force people into negative positions in society, which lowers self-esteem and perpetuates many other problems.

Because we need the right balance on a large scale to get the change we are after, we all need to take the correct steps if we want the most favorable outcome.

WHY VIOLENCE IS NOT THE SOLUTION

The very first step is to understand why violence is not the solution leading to lasting peace. Good people always lose when we use violence, even when we "win" the battle or war because this level of negativity changes us in negative ways and creates many other problems. The reason violence has not achieved lasting global peace over all these thousands of years and never will is because when we use violence, we hurt ourselves, others, and our society.

For example, when we use violence, belittle, and yell at children, especially when things get difficult, we teach them to use violence, belittle, and yell to solve problems. The same is true for society. If our government and we all treat each other with violence, mocking, and yelling, we teach everyone to do the same. These negative ways of being twist our lives and leads us away from our "True Path" and "True Society."

The killing, destruction, derogatory language, pain, suffering, loneliness, trauma, and all the rest lead to confusion, loss, desperation, hate, anger, rage, frustration, revenge, and other negatives on both sides. This collective negative focus allows those in power to divide us further into "us vs. them." Being ununified, negative, hateful, mean, unjust, and using violence makes us easy to manipulate and lasting peace impossible to achieve.

Violence as a tool of power is most powerful when never used, or if used, it's only as a last resort and only to the level needed to achieve the goal. Also, to live the virtues found in Law 4 and 5 of equality and treating others as we want to be treated, we must strive for and take the nonviolent path and only use violence as a last resort.

For clarity, as noted earlier, following *The Way* and the path of nonviolence does not mean that we are pacifists who will never fight or go to war. It just means that we see it as a last resort and a failure of our higher values and goals.

For example, there may be situations when we must fight to protect and defend ourselves, our loved ones, and help those who cannot help themselves. We may even need to rise up in great numbers to take down tyrants, hate groups, bad companies, and other twisted, unthinking people and organizations who have fallen to the dark side. The "bully beat down technique" can also help those who can't see why treating others as you want to be treated in all situations is so basic to life. For more on the "bully beat down technique," see the "Child & Family Guide: What Children Really Need: Bully Correction & Support for Their Victims." For a good breakdown of most of the ways to take nonviolent action, see: www.7Way.Me/NonViolentAction.

Our goal as we move toward the "True Society" is to fix and improve, upgrade, refine, and change our systems, minds, and hearts peaceably. The goal is NOT to shut it all down, cause chaos, seek revenge, hurt people, or to blame and point fingers so you can feel superior and self-righteous. Working for peace means as we work to implement the plan, we need to prevent those looking to commit violence by calling them out and stopping them, even turn in those who are committing violence in the name of our cause, group, organization, business, or religion.

"We the People" are all a part of this great mission to create our "True Society," including "those" who are not currently working with us. Consequently, we work to facilitate change in a way that we would appreciate if we were on the "other side" and did not understand. We can only really win by making our enemies into our friends.

We do this because we are treating others as equals and as we would wish to be treated. They may still join us if we make sense and treat them fairly. It might be that "we" and/or "they" are just being human and in error, or are missing something, or don't understand, or are even just clueless. We must be open to the idea it may be our side that is missing something that, once understood, could change everything.

The human race wastes vast amounts of wealth, time, and energy in the production of our destruction and war.

We need to spend more on the creation of our salvation and peace. Often the production and abundance of weapons lead to their use. Ending this waste and the use of violence is very important and achievable.

To truly heal, the first step is to realize as a species, that there is no "us versus them," there is only "we the people" of this earth all working to survive and thrive. Therefore, it's only through unity and cooperation that we can create a better global society and world. All good people would like everyone to have a wonderful life, for our systems to all work well and for our environment to be healthy and thriving.

The goal is to understand all sides so we can be one and get this done. It should be obvious that it's more difficult to achieve understanding, peace, and unity when one side is desperate, devastated, hurt and angry because of the violence being done to them and/or their loved ones. Put yourself in their place. How would you feel and what would you think if someone called you horrible names, then hurt you, those you love, and destroyed the things you cared about? How would you feel about them, and how open would you be to listening to and liking them?

Consequently, if we are really after peace and positive change, we must work to do so without the use of violence. To do anything else will only perpetuate a never-ending cycle of hate, rage, revenge, violence, and war. This is because violence begets violence and hate begets hate. Revenging every atrocity with another leads to horror for everyone. "True Peace" is won and maintained through love, equality, reciprocity, embracing virtue, understanding, and universal goals.

The fact is, we, the people, united in common cause can create lasting global peace. The only question is, will you be part of the solution or be part of the problem?

THE PHASES TO PEACEFULLY FORCE POSITIVE CHANGE

The strategy for peaceful societal change is broken down into 3 Phases: Clarify, Action, and Codify. To attain a peaceful result, we need to be sure to follow the "Nonviolent Tactics" outlined below correctly and to be as open and inclusive as possible.

WARNING: Careful application of this strategy is needed because the use of this method is truly powerful, yet if not handled correctly, it can cause division, mass destruction, and chaos.

PHASE 1: CLARIFY

The phase of clarification has 4 steps, which include doing the research, creating clear demands, building a tribe, and submitting your demands.

STEP 1: DO THE RESEARCH

Research the issue entirely and be sure to consider all sides. *For example,* for all parties involved, what's at the crux of the issue, and what virtues are involved? Knowing all sides will allow you to end up with clear, complete, and truthful documentation that will help make your case and articulate your demands. As they say, "know thy enemy" for it will allow you to refute and have knowledge of everything in advance. Preparation is often the key to success.

STEP 2: MAKE CLEAR DEMANDS

In this step, you outline clear, rational, and reasonable demands. If your demands are not simple, be sure to include steps and timelines where possible. Think of the issue from the other side's perspective and all involved. What if you were on their side? What would you want to be considered? How would you want to be spoken to? If what you want is a big deal and complex or might hurt them in any way, then consider what it would take to implement this from the other side.

Think about all the players. Do you include enough to make a lasting positive difference? Take as much as you can into account before moving on. It makes everything more manageable later.

Work with a diversity of people to see if the demands you have codified are transparent, doable, fair, and will achieve the desired result. As you go through this process, you must look for ways to refine everything. It's important not to play games or ask for things that are not possible, reasonable, or fair. We also don't want to stop systems that need fixing.

For example, we don't want to demand that they close a needed but failing water treatment plant, school, or police department where there is no other. Instead, we demand they fix the problems, even if it means replacing people and renovating.

The exception here is if an organization is doing something inhumane. In these cases, we can demand immediate termination and temporary replacement for those types of heinous acts.

For example, a restart team can be sent into a water treatment plant to get everything operating as well as possible while they work to transition the broken system into the desired form, and they are able to train people.

STEP 3: BUILD A TRIBE

Now that you understand everything and have clear demands, you can join a similar cause that will include your demands or create an organization with a clear message built on what you have just learned and codified. Here you need to place people of merit in leadership positions and add as many people as possible to the group. The exact number required to affect the desired reaction is dependent on the situation. (See "Our Greatest Power" above for more.)

The key is to keep building through the process until enough have joined where the change happens. Adding in those at the "Centers of Power" with access to the "Tools of Power" will significantly accelerate everything you are trying to do. Messaging and marketing are critical. Remember, all is relative, we don't know what we don't know, and people know people, which means that you don't always need a superstar to get the message out. A local celeb and a small group with some money can help a local cause as well as know people who can help with larger ones. They may also know even more people who can help.

One of the best ways to speed up the process is to get all organizations and groups already working on the same or a similar issue to join forces. The reason cooperation works so well is it saves costs, is more productive, and all groups have lists of people that would most likely be willing to help.

Petitions/Polls/Etc.: All causes need social proof. Social proof shows that there are a lot of people on your side. An effective way to do this is by collecting signatures on petitions and by conducting polls that show the size of your following or interest in the issue(s).

Gathering social proof is relatively easy with the use of websites that help facilitate sending petitions and polls to interested people. The reason this works so well is that leaders know that for every person who voices a complaint and who signs a petition, there are many, many more that feel the same way: the higher the number, the more significant.

All petitions and polls should be written so that they are as short and clear as possible. Here we stick to the point and focus on specifics. On the polls and petitions, it's a best practice to ask for a yes and no vote and to know <u>why</u> they voted as they did. The reason why asking "why" is so important is that most often, the answer will shed light on something we did not consider when making our demands. It can help us see a different perspective, which could lead to better solutions or ways to explain our side more clearly.

STEP 4: SUBMIT

Now that you understand the issue, have clear demands, and a tribe to back you up, it's time to give the demands, petitions, or documentation to the other party. The submission should be the shortest and clearest form possible.

The only goal here is to give them the basics and to get them to negotiate with you. You don't want to hurt them; you want them to listen, learn, and change. You don't want a fight; you want to turn a negative into a positive. To create positive change, we peaceably unite, make our objections known with logic, reason, and love. If they are doing the same, we will find a solution.

For example, we may respectfully deliver a 1-page list of demands, a booklet of supporting documentation along with 100,000 signatures on a petition. After that, you wait to see if they will work with you within the reasonable timeline you provided.

If appropriate, you can also make these demands public. Public notice means creating materials and distributing them, so they appear in books, newspapers, journals, on radio, television, and more.

After submission, you must be willing and ready to further explain your position and respectfully negotiate. Participation means being willing to listen and seeking to understand the other side because we need to be sure we did not miss anything that might affect our demands or reasoning. Everyone must be open and willing to adjust based on new information.

PHASE 2: ACTION

The next step you take is dependent upon how the other party reacts to your demands. Are they willing to negotiate with you? Yes or No?

IF YES, THEY ARE WILLING TO NEGOTIATE

A willingness to negotiate in good faith means all parties are open and willing to discuss the demands, understand them, and work toward a solution based on consensus or, if that is not possible, at the very least, a fair compromise. Each party must go into these meetings looking to work for real, positive, meaningful, and doable solutions.

Remember, people can only find real solutions if everyone is sharing the same fact base, looking for the root causes, the virtues at the heart of the issues, and be willing to be reasonable, work hard, and even change.

If you reach an agreement, skip down to "Phase 3" where you ensure everything is codified and legal. After that, the movement can disband, or the leaders can direct the members to a similar or new cause.

However, if the negotiation yields a multi-stepped solution and/or one that is implemented over an extended period, the cause does not end, it just goes into a type of hibernation. Here all parties agree and set up an extended watch and verification system in which the leaders of the cause are in control. The verification system serves as "checks and balances," which allows the leaders of the cause to inform the tribe of progress and problems.

Important Note: Be sure the cause does not take on a life of its own, working to perpetuating itself or its leadership. A cause needs to stay focused on the implementation of real solutions within society. Once it has served its purpose, it needs to be disbanded or melded into a new cause.

IF NO, THEY ARE NOT WILLING TO NEGOTIATE

If you have submitted the demands respectfully and the other party is not willing to negotiate or is not being reasonable or is not negotiating in good faith, you can apply pressure in the ways described below.

HOW TO FORCE NEGOTIATION & PEACEFUL POSITIVE CHANGE

The easiest way to force negotiation within any organization (business, government, NGO, etc.) is to have those on the outside (consumers/citizens) and inside (workers/elected officials) working together. If that is not possible, the goal can still be achieved by one side or the other separately. In either case, the more people that participate, the easier and faster change will happen.

CITIZEN & CONSUMER POWER

For clarity, citizens are legally recognized subjects of a state or commonwealth and are subject to its jurisdiction. Consumers are all people who use that organization (services/products) or may use it.

As citizens and consumers, we have great power. As citizens through our actions with our government. As consumers, this power is wielded by consuming or by stopping the consumption of their product or service. If we don't buy, they don't make money. Over time without enough money, they will cease to exist.

Our cause becomes more influential when we encourage others to do as we are because "Word of Mouth" is often the most powerful tool we can wield as consumers. Our growth and influence are magnified when influencers, those at the "Centers of Power" and those using the "Tools of Power," join our cause. This is because our true power is shown when people's positive or negative opinions are spread around (word of mouth) and are shared by "the masses." It's this power of unity that creates a fad, brings companies to the top, and destroys brands.

If there are enough of us in the beginning, we only use this power of non-use for short periods to show how many people are with us so that we do not hurt the company. The first time is more of a "shot over the bow" to provide a warning than something that is to cause harm. Again, our goal is to get them to negotiate, and this might be enough to get them to the table.

In some cases, a boycott like this might create a personal inconvenience if, *for example,* we are trying to pressure positive change from our cell phone company. In these cases, in the beginning, the key is to find ways to show dissatisfaction without creating too much hardship in everyone's life. If you can find ways that are relatively convenient for people, especially in the beginning, the more success you will have.

Here we look for alternatives like having everyone sign a petition, text, or call a specific number at the company with the complaint, indicating they will cut off use if the company does not negotiate and come up with a solution. The key is to show our displeasure in high numbers relative to the situation to get them to take you seriously and negotiate.

If they do not, as consumers, our ultimate power comes from abandoning the company altogether. The abandonment of dinosaurs unwilling to change allows us to support organizations that are willing to negotiate and work to do things correctly.

WORKER POWER

Workers are those who have jobs and do the "work" within the organization that is of issue. Note that government and critical system worker strategies are covered separately.

Frequently, the workers within an organization will agree with the consumer complaints and will have complaints of their own. Worker complaints often cover issues the consumers can't see that are tied to a poor working environment, corruption, wrongful and illegal acts.

As "Workers," we have great power in creating positive change as we know and can do things no one else can. One way is to join a reasonable and fair workers union that covers all people in an industry. Unionizing is an excellent way to find and coordinate with a group of likeminded and highly invested people.

If there is no union, you can start one or ask another similar union for help. The key is to make sure the Union is after mutually beneficial solutions and not out to take as much as possible without regard to the overall goal.

Workers can also coordinate with other workers and do a bad job, work slowly, cause bottlenecks, delays, or even make mistakes. The key is not to do such a lousy job that you get fired. If asked why you are not doing your usual, you can say that you feel bad or distracted by what is going on. If it's taking too long, you might even look for a job at a better company, thereby depriving them of your talent. If they start losing enough good people, this will also help create more pressure.

If workers are backed up by consumers, the idea is for the workers to do enough to keep their jobs as they support a cause wherever possible. Think about it like this, if all workers show up to work, and there are no customers, it will increase the pressure on the organization to negotiate as they still need to pay the workers or start downsizing drastically. It's essential that those protesting do not show these workers any disrespect or impede the workers in any way. Ideally, we want everyone collecting their checks and caring for their lives throughout this process.

Important Note for Government & Critical Societal System Works

If we need to change a government system, our ability to change it will depend a lot on the form of government. If you have a "Government of the People," then change will be easier. If one of tyranny or top-down control, positive change will be more difficult and may even involve a personal risk. In this case, the form of government may need to change before other positive reforms can be implemented, especially over the long haul.

If we work for a "Government of the People" or critical societal system (water, food, energy, etc.), it's important when we seek positive change to still go to work and do an excellent job. You do not cause problems, bottlenecks, make intentional mistakes, and all the rest.

We continue to do an excellent job to ensure we do not mess anything up, as we need our government and critical systems to run as well as possible, no matter what is happening. The exception here is if you are asked to do things that are inhumane and wrong, then you don't want to be the "I was just following orders" type. Instead, stand up and do what's right for you are being tested. In all cases, when dealing with critical systems, it's best to help create positive change in the other ways listed so as not to harm our critical systems.

For example, if these systems allow us to get our food and water, it's best to work for positive change in other ways instead of stopping them from working. The same is true for any government; there is no acceptable reason for leaders to shut it all down over a political issue.

How We All Can Make a Difference

Now let's go over the things we can all do together and separately to help.

- **As people**, we can join a march and protest where we hold signs, chant slogans, set up blockades, sit-ins, and publicly shame officials who are on the wrong side. Along with that, we can sign petitions, donate money, and take polls. We can wear things like a designated color, pin, bracelet, shirt, scarf, or armband. We can also stop buying services and products from bad organizations and support the good.

- **As workers**, we can go on strike, walkout, stop work, slow work, sickout, testify, blow the whistle, and even leak evidence of corruption and illegal acts. We can also give a list of worker complaints to the leadership of the movement, so they are included with all the rest of the issues. Competitors of the organization under fire, who are doing things correctly, can help the protesters take down the bad players. If working to change a public company, all shareholders can join the effort and vote to fix the company or sell off all the stock to destroy it.

The goal of using these tactics is to stop the company, organization, or its leaders from going on with business as usual. We are forcing people within these organizations as well as the public to consider the cause we are bringing to light. Here we are intentionally drawing attention and making things inconvenient. This strategy is useful when there is little to no media attention or support. If both customers and workers are fighting together, then good coordination between the groups will amplify the effort considerably.

How to Apply More & More Pressure

Ok, now that we covered the basics of the "Nonviolent Tactics," let's go through how to use these abilities to apply more and more pressure and force positive change. As stated, the key is to flex our power for short periods, especially in the beginning, because in most cases, we don't want to destroy the organization outright, we want it to evolve in a positive direction more quickly.

So, as we go through the process, we must be ready to lower the pressure and turn it off when we achieve the goal. In other words, don't start something you can't stop or do things that will not allow for fair and timely negotiations and change to take place.

Simply stated basic strategy, is to apply more and more pressure by increasing the level of <u>intensity</u> and <u>duration</u> of the "Nonviolent Tactics" outlined above.

- **Intensity** covers the level of power and passion we apply. Power and passion come in the form of how many tactics we use simultaneously and how much emotion we show.

    For example, we can create a large peaceful, yet highly charged and emotional public disturbances as we coordinate many other actions to happen in separate locations at the same time. These additional actions can include things like stopping the use of the service/product, a strike, sit-in, sickout, blockade, protests, media blitz, and more.

    Intensity can build and build. *For example*, we can blockade that company starting on one street, then an area of town, then a city to even a country and beyond. We can begin a protest at the headquarters, then move to some stores, then to all stores for a total shut down of business.

- **Duration** indicates how long we do or don't do things. Duration means using the "Nonviolent Tactics" for longer and longer periods. It can also mean we do it more and more frequently.

    For example, we can start by doing this, say every week, then two times a week, to every day. The length of time we spend can go from a few hours, days, weeks to months, years, and even forever. *For example*, we can all stop buying gas from a company for a few hours, a day, a week, a few months, or switch to another company permanently.

WHY THIS WORKS

When there are enough of us combining the level of intensity over longer and longer periods, this will create more and more problems for the organization and its leadership. Most organizations, especially businesses, cannot stay in operation without customers and/or good workers and/or favorable publicity.

When the cause has control of their money and public opinion to a large enough degree, the organization will have no choice but to negotiate with us and evolve, or else they will go extinct like all the "dinosaurs" who do not adapt. The bigger the organization, the faster they will shrink or go out of business without customers and competent workers. As outlined above, this whole process becomes easier when we, as consumers and workers, cooperate to force positive change.

If the organization chooses not to change and is destroyed, shrinks, or is taken over, we have won and made room for better-run organizations to rise and fill the need. Attrition is a crucial facet of capitalism, a fair and free market, and healthy economic systems.

Using all the tactics described above is how we force organizations to improve when they will not do so on their own. We, as consumers, citizens, and workers, must demand that all our organizations strive to be their best on all levels. Uniting and use of these practices is how we become the catalyst that will spur humanity into action and end unconstructive opposition.

All real capitalists believe in good unions and consumer advocacy groups, etc. and work hard to find, fix, and mitigate all issues. "True Businesses" work in this manner because it's through these issues that they see what will make their company and product/service even better. As leaders, we need to work proactively so that things never get so far out of hand that people need to rebel or protest. We want happy consumers and workers, after all.

In the end, it should be clear that it's in everyone's best interest and the best practice to understand all the issues and work to fix and mitigate them. Therefore, as leaders, to truly serve your organization and your greater purpose, you must listen and work with everyone. As consumers, citizens, and workers, we must band together to ensure all organizations provide for what we need on all levels.

COMPLETE SYSTEM OVERHAUL

In some cases, corruption and negative ways of doing things are so pervasive that small changes or a few voicing a need for change will not accomplish anything. Significant changes are needed in companies and organizations who feel harmful ways of doing things are ok because "it's just business," "everyone does it this way," "it's always been done this way," and "if I (we) don't someone else will." In many of these cases, those of us who work within such organizations wish for positive change but are prevented by this "everyone does it this way" mentality that is pervasive within every company in the industry.

In these situations, for something to change, all must change. For often, it's a lot easier to do something that changes an industry all at once rather than hope the many will follow the few, and eventually, things will change. The reason a full renovation is needed is that in these types of situations, those who step out first are alone and get crushed by all the rest that are still doing it the old corrupt way.

Here all agree to the new rules and then all change at the same time. The rulemaking processes can start by allowing everyone to remain anonymous. Then, after a broad agreement from enough of the players is reached, all can be made public and the fix implemented.

Following this strategy means there is no unfair advantage for anyone. Anyone who breaks the rules from this point forward will be crushed out of business by the rest. This strategy gives us the ability to effectively reset a whole system without all the legal shenanigans, incriminations, games, and posturing that will stall everything. In very corrupt industries, this process can mean bringing in an outside group to take over the entire operation or sections while they hire, train, and retrain people of merit to do the jobs properly.

PHASE 3: CODIFY

At the end of a successful campaign, where there is agreement, we must <u>always</u> take a final step and get everything in writing and to make sure it's legal. There can be a lot to this, including things like writing contracts and changing or creating laws. It might mean having to develop or allowing for the creation of new organizations or departments within organizations.

Do NOT take this step lightly. If everything agreed to is not in writing, formalized, signed, sealed, and legal, all the work done is meaningless. I cannot give legal advice other than to say you need to consult with an attorney on these matters.

After your contacts are complete, it's imperative to have attorneys from a competing firm review everything before submitting them. This competitor's check is needed because attorneys are paid to find loopholes and alternative ways to achieve a goal. Fresh eyes from a competitor who is not part of the group can often see things others have not. The key is to be safe, precise, and to be ready to trust but always verify. Also, make sure that if they do break the agreement, the "teeth" within the contract are large enough to allow you to make things right.

Again, be sure to make it binding and legal, for if you do not master this phase, everything else you have done will be for nothing.

STEP 6: UNITE - CONCLUSION

"The ones who are crazy enough to think they can change the world are the ones that do." - Steve Jobs

We have covered a lot of ground within "Step 6: Unite." You learned how to put your best foot forward, deal with relationships, and how to manage key elements and systems of society. The main theme running through everything is that for you to be truly successful, your best, happy, and to have a positive effect on significant issues, you must unite with other people. Unification allows us all to offer and receive happiness, help, motivation, inspiration, as well as participate in solutions. To say it another way, to create real, lasting, positive change in our world, everyone needs to be working to become their best as we unite to help each other and do big things.

A cautionary note. As we go about correcting our society is important not to overcorrect. This is because overcorrecting will send our society out of balance in another way. Bouncing from extreme to extreme is not the way to the "True Society." The way is to find true solutions, not temporary coverups.

In the end, it is up to every one of us, for each of us is part of the key that unlocks "Our Greatest Power." Honestly, if we, as a species, are to fix and maintain our societal systems to the highest degree, you need to do your part as well as cooperate with others on larger projects in a meaningful way. As you become a better person and join with other good people, you will not only make friends and find happiness; you will help make a real positive lasting difference in our world.

To expedite positive change within our society, all of you who are very wealthy and/or in high-level power positions can choose to do right and take the actions that allow us to realize virtue within all our societal systems. This will save a lot of money, time, and limit the trauma and drama we have to go through. Know that we, the masses, will back you up at every turn and that you gain more than you can ever imagine. Remember, just because you can't do everything to solve a problem, does not mean you can't do anything. Getting started as soon as possible and working toward solutions is how big issues get solved the fastest.

For example, you can pay and care for all people humanely. You can form governments of the people and create solid democratic institutions with checks and balances to back them up. You can create equality and merit-based systems and organizations. You can build and sustainably make things that don't pollute, last, and that can be reused/reprocessed. You can clean up and care for our environment and all life correctly. You can ensure every person has proper nutrition, education, and training throughout their entire life. You create media that is truthful, inspirational, teaching positive qualities, and that helps unite us all in positive ways.

You can strive to continuously improve your organizations, products, services, and the working environment.

You can do all the rest to truly be good role models as individuals and as organizations so that others can emulate and follow. You can join together and destroy harmful organizations. With great power and wealth comes great responsibility. Understand that you are in your position because you are being tested. If this challenge is passed successfully, you will gain more than you could ever imagine.

World peace and prosperity are achievable once we realize that we are all basically the same and that for any of us to truly prosper, we all must prosper. All nations will do better when all people around the world are prosperous, happy, well-educated, and leading productive, meaningful lives.

It's through the unity of purpose as individuals and society that allows us all to achieve more than we could otherwise. To be clear, its unity within diversity that leads to our "True Society." This is because it's each of us living a positive, unique life within your local society, mixed with other positive cultures that transform our global human community into a beautiful living art form.

Our unity of definite positive purpose over time will transform our world into an ever-evolving wonder. As we improve and refine our societal systems generation by generation, we can create a world where virtue rules, and deep harmony, synergy, serendipity, joy, health, happiness, and peace are the norm.

Chapter 16
Living Perfection

"When you aim for perfection, you discover it's a moving target." - George Fisher

Step 7: Perfect

Now that you are on your "True Path" and united with others, you need to be sure to maintain all that is good as you continue to grow, develop and refine everything as you move forward. Within "Step 7: Perfect," we embrace both meanings of "perfect."

- "It is Perfect" as in its already its best (adjective),
- "To Perfect" as in to refine and improve (verb).

We find true perfection and peace when we balance these seemingly contradictory ideas. Can you see the imperfect as perfect and perfect as imperfect? Let's go a little deeper into each of these concepts.

Perfect as in The Best

"Being perfect is being flawed, accepting it, and never letting it make you feel less than your best." - Jessica Alba

The ideal, highest state of perfection within our universe is a journey, not a destination or point. To say it another way, for humanity, the journey is the destination. We find the main reason for this within the universal human conditions with specific regard to spacetime (the requirement of time passing as movement happens) as well as entropy (the second law of thermodynamics where all systems naturally fall into a state of disorder).

The universal constant of entropy is undeniable, only managed. Because of entropy, things change, degrade, fall apart, break, wear out, and get old. Therefore, if anything is considered "perfect" like a moment, work of art, or societal system, maintenance is needed to preserve it.

For Example: We can see the perfect needing maintenance plainly when regarding our care for great works of art. Here we must go to great lengths in their care to ensure they last. We control everything from their handling to their exposure to air, light, and moisture. Even with all our efforts, everything is still degrading and will someday be gone because of entropy.

Therefore, it's essential to enjoy the "perfect" when it's here as well as account for this impermanent aspect of our human condition within our life and systems of society. In fact, we can see the whole human race as Anti-Entropy beings creating and maintaining order in a universe that is moving toward disorder.

Perfect is a human mental construction and not something that can genuinely manifest within our universe. Therefore, embracing perfection means we must embrace imperfection. Our instinctual desire and all that we do to manifest the "perfect," ingrains fundamental ways of being into our spirit.

Our need for the perfect can also go too far and cause great problems with our self-image, view of others, and our societal systems. So, if you fail, make a mistake, have something out of place, slightly dented, a little damaged, not quite working right, or askew, it is ok. It's just a life test. If we find it extremely bothersome to have something askew, leave some things out of place or line on purpose. Then work on letting go of the negative feelings of dissatisfaction and compulsion rather than focusing on fixing the thing that is "out of place." It's just a self-control challenge and an opportunity to learn and better yourself after all.

The actual test is to accept and manage these human conditional variables and imperfections to the best of our ability without letting the small imperfections get to us. Therefore, a real understanding of perfect means we can find balance within imbalance and perfection within imperfection.

PERFECT AS IN TO REFINE

"If everything was perfect, you would never learn, and you would never grow." – Beyoncé Knowles

"To Perfect" as in to refine and improve must be incorporated into life if we are to be "Truly Successful" as individuals and as a society. This idea is reflective of the Japanese word "kaizen," which is a philosophy of continuous improvement or to say it another way, "kaizen" means "good change." In this state of mind, everything is perfect because it's improving.

PERFECTION AS MOVING TARGET

Because of our human nature, something may seem perfect for a time. However, once experienced for a while, our feelings can change. Often when we arrive at a place once conceived as "the best," something even better can be envisioned. So "perfect" in our human world is often a target which is ever moving. With this understanding going forward, if we do reach perfection, we enjoy it while it lasts as we look for the next level.

Looking for the next level is essential for those of us in power positions within our societal systems. This is because if we, as leaders, become complacent, we are in jeopardy of becoming a "dinosaur" holding other people back from growing into their "True Self" as well as inhibiting the growth of our society into our "True Society."

PERFECT LOSES ITS LUSTER

After a while, all the sameness that surrounds us can become unappreciated, unnoticed, and even boring, no matter how wonderful and perfect it is. Taking things for granted can hurt us in many ways. If you focus on things you do not have, it creates feelings of loss and scarcity, which creates unhappiness. By focusing on being grateful for all the little things, even if it's simply the fact that you are alive or that at this moment you don't have pain in your little toe, etc., you can find satisfaction and a path to peace.

For Example: After a very traumatic event, many of us gain a perspective of deep gratitude and appreciation for all the unappreciated good around us, down to the smallest details. Here everything can even take on a magical glow and vibrancy not seen before. This event can put everything into perceptive, where we realize what is trivial versus what is truly important. These moments create a lot of energy that can be used to heal and become better. With this understanding, we can gain this clear perspective by looking at life with "fresh eyes" and appreciation even though tragedy did not befall us. Within this perspective, we appreciate and feel deep gratitude for all that is good in our life at this moment, while leaving out everything else.

You can also gain perspective on how wonderful something or someone is by taking a little time away, for as they say, "absence makes the heart grow fonder." It's also a good practice to periodically go over lists of everyday things we are grateful for that often go unnoticed and unappreciated. Understanding these best practices on a fundamental level helps us gain perspective and find peace.

LIFE ASSESSMENTS

"It only takes one person to change your life: You."
- Ruth Casey

To further embrace the idea of refinement within our life and systems of society, we must look for ways to gain perspectives we can't readily see. We need to do this because, in most cases, it's difficult to see all the ways we can improve without outside help.

Groupthink (everyone in a group believing the same thing even if obviously incorrect) can happen within any organization or system. This is why test groups and third-party coaching works so well in all aspects of life and society. A good coach helps you see things you could not as well as enables you to do things in better ways. It's this "outsider's view" that can help you gain perspective, understanding, and abilities faster than you would otherwise.

You can find a coach by hiring a person or firm. You can ask a friend who knows for help. You can look online and find a lot of free materials and videos from great coaches on specific challenges you are facing. You can also perform different types of "reviews" from different perspectives. Reviewing all aspects of ourselves and our society is an excellent way for us to use checks and balances and verification within real-life to confirm and maintain all that is good as well as make everything better and better.

Within a review, you look to see if there is unity within yourself (purpose, beliefs, attitude, intentions, thoughts, judgments, choices, words, actions, reactions, emotions, and feelings). During a review, you are also looking for corruption, your failings/sins, missed information, mistakes, lessons, signs, better ways of doing things, and other refinements. You do all of this without judgment, in a peaceful way and with the end goal in mind.

Periodic Life Review

If you are to live rational, positive action, you must periodically review all of who you are. You do this because you most often don't know what you don't know and can't see what is hidden from you. This is because it's imperative to review different areas of life periodically.

The time between reviews will depend on your lifestyle and needs. In the end, it's better to investigate and not find anything than not to look and have unseen issues negatively affecting you. A quick way to find these answers is to get help from those who know you best.

A good time to do a self-review can be around the New Year, springtime, or around your birthday, yet it can be done anytime you feel the time is right. This review can be rigorous and accompany a whole life cleanse where you clean your living space as well as your body inside and out. It can be something small where you only involve a couple of close loved ones or anywhere in-between. The key is to find a perspective where you can see things that you could not otherwise.

The answers you find can come in many forms. There can be profound lessons that improve your relationships. You might learn of unknown character traits that put others off and ways to compensate for them. Receiving constructive criticism is an excellent way to find unknowns.

In the end, remember all the data you collect is about helping you learn the lessons and make improvements that will allow you to go further in life. It's not to make you feel bad. If you hear things you think are not true, you need to find out why others see you that way. It's valid on some level because they see it. The question is, is there something you did or are doing to create that perspective?

It's in this <u>mismatch</u> that you find the thing you did not know or could not see. The hidden is what you are seeking, as this is a wrong thing that needs fixing. Recognizing your mistakes, failings, missed opportunities, and hurtful ways of being is a great gift, for you can only repair and improve the things you know are damaged or broken.

THE STEPS OF A SELF-REVIEW

STEP 1: CREATE THE LIST

Make a list of all the issues you think you have. Next, to each one, write out the solution. If you don't know the answer, leave it blank for now. Knowing your strengths and weaknesses can help you use your talents to their fullest while you develop your other skills.

For Example:

- I talk too fast, so I need to slow down.
- I don't workout enough, so I need to stick to my practice schedule and do mini-workouts throughout the day.

Ask yourself things like:

- What are my life goals?
- What are the things I want to accomplish in the next 30, 60, 90 days, or 1, 5, 10, 20+ years?
- What do I want to change now?
- What are my worst qualities?
- What is a flaw that I wish I could improve?
- What are my biggest problems?
- What is holding me back?

- What are my best qualities?
- What am I passionate about doing?
- What makes me feel wholesomely joyous, happy, laugh, smile, and feel good?

STEP 2: ADD TO THE LIST

"We all need people who will give us feedback. That's how we improve." - Bill Gates

Ask loved ones to give you a list. Asking can be done in a letter or in person. Asking for help in the form of constructive criticism from loved ones is an excellent way to discover issues that you can't see as well as improve your relationship with them.

Say something simple like, "Hey, I'm doing a life review, and I need your help. This is because, as you know, we don't know what we don't know and can't see what is hidden from us. Can you help find the negative things hidden from me so I can become better? Please tell me everything that you think I'm not doing well, could do better at, and have done wrong? Is there anything I do that is bothersome, or that makes it hard for you to understand or respect me?" Again, make this yours, ask them in a way using the words that you feel would work best in that situation.

Add everything everyone gives you to a list. Be sure to tag who said what. If there are things that overlap, indicate that all three felt that was an issue, etc. Your goal is to get their impressions. Regardless of how it was given, it's <u>imperative</u> to follow the rules of communication concerning receiving criticisms. See "Chapter 10" for more. Following this strategy is critical because the review process can cause <u>a lot of emotions</u> to come to the surface on both sides, so you need to take extra care to handle the situation well.

There are big tests to be found in this process, and handling this calmly and gracefully is the goal. Achieving this goal is easier when you stay focused on collecting information and asking questions to really understand rather than focusing on what is being said.

Warning: As you undertake this process, it's crucial to do this without blame, prejudice, or judgment. You need to be only the observer, a vigilant student who is open to lessons and refinements, an investigator or scientist seeking to collect the facts and then later when alone look for answers.

You are trying to understand and find what is hidden without judgment. You must be open and <u>nonconfrontational</u> to accomplish the goal. You are NOT seeking to be understood before understanding, nor defending, justifying, explaining yourself, creating arguments, or pointing fingers. If explanations are needed, you can offer it in a later step, do not offer any now.

This <u>warning</u> should be taken <u>very seriously</u> because these situations can become very heated, very quickly, if not handled well. What they say has nothing to do with if they are right or wrong or how it's making you feel. They might seem to be rude and mocking. It might hurt to hear what they say. They might say a lot of things that bother you.

During this process, you are to be kind to everyone helping you, which should come naturally because those helping you are doing what you asked. If it gets difficult, remember that you asked for help and that in the end, it will all be so much better. Look at it as a test of your self-control.

So, to be perfectly clear, while doing a review you:

- Do not get defensive or disagree.
- Do not try to explain or justify.
- Do not prime or lead them by asking about anything on your list. You want to see what they come up with on their own without any prompting from you. You can ask about your stuff in a later step.
- Keep open body language and a neutral pleasing tone.
- Only ask questions to seek clarity about what they said in a non-confrontational matter.
- It's important to ask them what they feel the solution might be.
- Thank them for sharing at the end.

The key is to stay open and neutral. You are simply a collector of information, leaving the emotion out of it for now. You asked for this, after all. You can take breaks if things get too heated. It's also important to be gracious and kind during the process, as this will help you get more truthful and complete answers. It will also help your loved one feel much better about you when the process has concluded.

STEP 3: SORT & COMPARE

Now that you have your list and a list from others, you need to spend time going over each issue. The areas of particular concern are: corruption, failings, oath-breaking, lying, meanness, not being true to "Your Code," compliancy, procrastination, miscommunication and communication breakdowns, misunderstanding, irritating personality traits, and other issues. You are looking for mismatches in how you think you are and how they see you. To get started, you need to sort and compare all the items you have gathered.

To do this, we:

- **Match:** Group all the issues you and others had in common, along with all solutions discovered so far. Look carefully at all the answers and write down anything else you can think of that will help you.

- **Sort Only On Your List:** You create a group that only covers things <u>you</u> found, but others did <u>not</u>. You need to take this list and share it with those who were the most helpful to get their opinion. You do this because sometimes these issues might be blown out of proportion in your mind and are not an issue. Knowing this can be a relief and help you focus on other critical problems instead. It might also be something they did not think of at the time but is an issue, which also can help.

- **Sort Only On Their List:** If there are items on the list which you did not pick up on, it's vital to take some time and contemplate them because something is missing or a contradiction or incongruency exists that you must resolve if you are to improve your life.

    Also, these insights will help you gain a clearer perspective of yourself, the other person, and your relationship with them. See each issue existing from the other person's perspective. It's essential you "see" how they feel or why they said what they did. Seeing the perspective is a human ability we all share. It's ok to go back and ask questions for <u>clarification</u> if need be.

    Sometimes your issues can be hard to see, and it might take time to gain perspective and understanding. If you find yourself denying them and having strong feelings about it, there is something here for you to learn, so be patient. At the very least, you have found a test of self-control as well as an issue that could help you, the other person, and your relationship grow.

Allowing yourself to see that negative perspective of yourself does not make it accurate. It's more of a mental exercise. Can you take your mind there? These are your loved ones, after all, and they truly feel this way, so you should be able to see it, no matter how painful or wrong the feeling.

Understand that sometimes, while you might have the right intentions and beliefs, your deeds and words are not seen by others as reflecting these positive qualities. If others say you sound pushy and are dominating, but inside you don't feel that way, there is a mismatch.

This incongruency or mismatch is the valuable information you have been seeking and the primary point of this exercise. Your goal is not to convince the other people that they are wrong but instead to look at your actions and tone to see their perspective (why they are saying XYZ).

Remember, you are seeking to know what others see. It might be buried and take time to see and fix. It might be something simple, that once known, is easily fixed. Regardless, the key is to first see this issue from their perspective.

STEP 4: CREATE THE MASTER LIST

Now that you have all the lists basically sorted and you understand each point, you need to go a step farther. Next, you create a master list with all the problems and solutions, as well as any lessons, perspectives, and understandings you have gained. Group the master list in ways that are logical and meaningful to you as it will help you create action items later on.

For example, if several of the issues have to do with your body or manners or communication, you can group those similar things.

No Solutions: Be sure to separate all the issues you <u>do not</u> have solutions for into one group. The "no solutions list" is the most important group. Having them all together may allow you to see relationships between them you could not otherwise. Grouping them also allows you to better work on them and find solutions. The key to the "no solution list" is to keep it in mind and to seek help. This is because it's more than likely you are not alone, and there are answers and solutions just waiting for you to find them.

STEP 5: ACTION ITEMS

Now that you have your lists and solutions, you need to integrate them within your life. Here you take the solutions and add them into your "Daily Way" and "Habit Building Focus" sheets and apps. Adding them will help ensure that you don't backslide or forget anything. You can also go over the list of problems and solutions periodically. Be sure to keep working on the problems without solutions. These newly discovered issues, when solved, can significantly improve and deepen the bond in your relationships and improve the overall quality of life.

STEP 6: SAY THANK YOU

In the end, after you have made peace with what you have learned, it's a good practice to write a letter to those who helped you, thanking them and even explaining what you have learned. You can also ask for further assistance for problems still without solutions if appropriate.

If you feel that addressing a discovered problem or issue will help the relationship, you can nicely ask the person if they would like to meet and talk about what you found. Only do so if they are open. If done correctly, this practice can help fix issues, straighten out misunderstandings, and create a better relationship. The relationship can improve because you asked for something from them, and now you have given something back, which provides more opportunities.

EXAMPLE SELF REVIEW

During one of my reviews, I found that my beliefs and intentions, while admirable, did not match my words and actions as perceived by other people. I was told that I harped on and nagged those I loved on health issues when I thought I was helping by pointing problems out. What was so amazing to me about this experience was how fast I gained this new perspective after I was able to see it. That new perspective instantly changed my view completely (paradigm shift). After I understood their perspectives, it seemed so obvious to me. It's hard to see how I could have missed it.

Below is an excerpt from a letter I wrote to my family after such a review about this issue.

On Harping: This issue has to do with how I respond to what I perceive as destructive behaviors within people I care for. The issue usually comes up when dealing with unhealthy food, tainted water, etc. I was told I tend not to let things go and bring things up repeatedly and consistently.

Just a little background so you can see how my perspective changed. The disconnect came from my being very into health, my father smoking, and my family not as concerned with health issues as I was. *For example,* when we were kids, we were told to accept Dad's smoking to some degree as he knew that it was harmful. We banned him from smoking in our presence, yet he did not stop when not around us and died from lung cancer.

Part of me felt that by our acceptance, we allowed him to continue, and this lack of action contributed to his death, as though we were all partly to blame because of our semi-silent acceptance. I always wondered if we, and I, had really fought to help him more, could we have helped and saved him? What if we threw the cigarettes out in the trash, worked to do other things with him when he wanted to smoke like going for a walk and talking about his interests? If we continuously worked with him, then could we have made a difference?

What I learned, and again seems so obvious to me now, is that bringing negative things up that others are aware of yet choose to do, is seen as "harping" or "nagging" and can have negative consequences. With Dad, I see now if we all did this, we would have, more likely, pushed him away. Even though out of love and wanting the best, he would not feel comfortable around us.

If we all did it, we would not have had a father to hang out with as much as we did. Now I see we helped him more by what we did. We gave him a place where he could be in a positive environment without smoking and without being nagged.

Thank you for helping me to see this, and I'm sorry to all of those who have experienced this form of negative communication from me! I will do better going forward. If not, please feel free to remind me if I fall back so that I can break this tendency.

Lesson: This was very interesting to me because while my intent and beliefs were positive, the expression came out as negative. My words and actions pushed people away instead of helping them.

In situations like this where you feel people are hurting themselves, it's important to ensure that they know the issue and that you are standing by to help. If they know the problem and that you are here to help, you must then let it go. It's ok to occasionally bring up the issue if it fits into the flow of a conversation or if the other person brings it up. Still, you must realize that if you bring it up too much or in the wrong way, you will push people away.

DAILY REVIEW

Another best practice is to realize the ideal of refinement in your daily life through 2 types of daily reviews. Here you take a moment to reflect on what you are doing and saying. You do this to see if your actions and words are reflecting "Your Code" and your goals for the day as in "am I treating others as equals and as I would want to be treated?" "Am I doing my best today and meeting my goals?"

You can also go even deeper, looking at your other core beliefs, dogma, baselines, and axioms. You do this because as you grow and learn, your perspective may have changed, and your dogma, baselines, axioms, and other core beliefs might be holding you back and need an upgrade. For more on these terms, see the "Life Manual: Fuel: Information."

DURING THE DAY

A "flash review" of how you are doing throughout the day is key to keeping you on track as you integrate virtues into your base programming. It's especially helpful during your daily "Practice" sessions (see the "Life Manual: Our

Practice" for more) and after interactions with people. You reflect quickly right after a communication because it's fresh in your mind. This situation often requires you to react, thereby revealing your beliefs, intentions, words, and actions.

You can easily see how you are doing by analyzing these situations. Did you treat them as you would want to be treated, as an equal and with respect using good communication skills? Checking yourself is something you frequently do in the beginning to ensure that you are on the right track. Think about your "Habit Building" sheet and what you learned from your self-reviews; does anything apply in the situation? Can you see ways you did well and can improve?

NIGHTLY REVIEW

As part of your evening or nighttime ritual (practice session), it's good to include a daily review as it will help you find things you can improve on tomorrow and feel good. It's important not to beat yourself up or feel bad when you see issues. It's a time to feel good as you did your best, found ways to improve, and can now do better tomorrow.

At the end of this practice, it's good to also go through a list of all you are working to improve, as well as the things you are grateful for. This includes the fact that you can and will do better. Finding issues and refining yourself is part of the human condition.

Some questions that you might ask include:

- Did I work toward my goals and follow my "Daily Way?"
- Are the "10 Laws" at the center of "My Code" reflected within my beliefs, intentions, words, and actions at all times?

- Did I treat people as equals and with respect?
- Did I do a good job and go the extra mile?
- Did I get better in any way today?
- Did I participate in society in a positive, meaningful way today?
- What did I accomplish?
- What are the lessons, and what improvements can I make?
- For what am I grateful?

You ask these questions, review your interactions with people, how you spent your time and what you focused on, to see if there is unity between what you think you should be saying and doing vs. what you are saying and doing.

Is there an incongruency? If so, these are tests of self-control and determination. As you go forward, this comparison helps you build unity between your life's primary purpose and your beliefs, intentions, words, and actions. As you gain control and unity of self, you will feel more satisfied with your life as well as be more prepared to choose your future.

PERIODIC REVIEW OF THE WAY

Reviewing *The Way* in its entirety or specific sections here and there is a good practice as this will help you find things you may have missed, see refinements, or gain a more in-depth insight and perspective because you have grown.

PERIODIC SOCIETAL SYSTEM REVIEW

Just as you review yourself and look for problems that need fixing, we can all join to do the same at the social level in several ways. With the development of the internet and new tools, you can participate as part of the world, country, community, interest group, or on an organizational level like a business, government, club, or religion.

We can ask similar basic questions as we did under our self-review. *For example,* are our systems treating everyone with respect and as equals as well as caring for our world? Are the leaders of real merit and doing a great job? Are systems efficient, cost-effective, and working well?

Here we undergo the same rigorous process of discovery as outlined above, so we find all the problems. First, we outline all the issues and solutions we all can see. We then ask all the other people involved for their input. Next, we compare the results and ask questions to seek to understand while creating a master list. From there, we implement all the solutions found and work to find the missing as we go forward.

PERFECTION IN EVERY MOMENT

If you are on your "True Path," you can find a flowing state of perfection within every moment. We find the idea that everything is happening as it should within many philosophies, religions, and spiritual paths around the world. At the core, this means that there is always a perspective of perfection to be found. The key is that both sides of perfection, as in to maintain and to refine, are at play here. This is because it may be perfect now, but it will need to be maintained if it's to endure, and we may always need to refine things.

For Example, if you are on your "True Path," and no matter how arduous from day to day, it's perfect for you are doing what you need and can do in your situation.

This perspective is good as it can bring you solace even when the world around you is very negative or when you are struggling with your life. This perspective allows you to find happiness and enjoyment at any time in almost any situation. This positive outlook from within these problematic moments can help us feel and do better.

Our positive outlook does not mean the wrongness of the world is acceptable; it just means you are doing what you can to move things in a positive direction. To be clear, the horrors that are happening to "other people" in "other places" in our world are not acceptable. Bad things don't just happen to bad people. Think of any of those horrible things as happening to you or your loved ones and know the truth of this fact. Many of us are in awful situations where we can't overcome the overwhelming forces that oppress us. Here we are like lighthouses calling to good people to help and save us from this horror.

To realize perfection in our world, we must all be working to rescue everyone. It's clear that if any of us are diminished, we are all diminished. Evil wins when the good do nothing or the wrong things. Evil wins in this way not only because it twists our societal systems against us, but it also hardens and twists the hearts of good people. Evil wins when good people lose their compassion, empathy, and sympathy and become complacent and hateful. This negative way of existence leads to guilt, regret, sadness, hopelessness, and feelings of wrongness, which can, in turn, open the doors to corruption and self-destruction.

STEP 7: PERFECT - CONCLUSION

Be happy where you are right now, maintain all that is good, find and fix the wrongness as you improve everything going forward. If we all keep fixing and perfecting our lives and systems generation by generation, those who come down the road will <u>start</u> from a place we had to spend a long time working to reach. As we all become better people and create better societal systems, we create greater contentment and happiness. It's through humanity's positive purpose, beliefs, attitude, intentions, thoughts, judgments, choices, words, actions, reactions, emotions, and feelings within all levels of life and society that we create everlasting global peace and happiness.

The Way as a philosophy is designed to help us perfect everything in both senses of the word. In this light, "The 7 Steps" of *The Way* can be seen as a circle, infinity symbol, or möbius strip. Here every time you go through *The Way*, you renew and reinforce key insights ingraining them more deeply as you find new insights.

In the end, perfection is a state of mind that we are working on manifesting in a universe tending toward disorder. If we can manage these seemingly contradictory states of perfection (It's the best vs. It needs refinement) well, we can go farther than we can otherwise. This is because it's through embracing both meanings of "Perfect" that we find guidance on what actions to take as individuals and as a society. A proper implementation will not only create a better life for you and your loved ones; it will also help other people and our society.

The proper application helps so much because it's the adding together of all of our individual positive efforts focused on maintaining what is good and refining everything that creates a better world now, in the future, and is how our "True Society" is built.

CHAPTER 17
YOUR NEXT STEPS

"The first step towards getting somewhere is to decide that you are not going to stay where you are." - Chauncey Depew

Let's briefly sum up the steps we have taken so far. Each of you is walking an untraveled path and is special, unique, and has great positive gifts to offer. If nurtured correctly, these gifts can be realized within your life. *The Way* is a complete system based on our shared human condition designed to help you achieve your ultimate goals.

The Way - Chapter **2**
Step 1: Know - Chapter **3**
Step 2: Want - Chapter **3**
Step 3: Choose - Chapter **3**
Step 4: Center - Chapter **3 to 7**
Step 5: Be - Chapter **8**
Step 6: Unite - Chapter **9 to 15**
Step 7: Perfect - Chapter **16**

The first three steps start you down your "True Path" as to know the positive and good is to want it, and if you are to attain your desire, you must choose. Your choice for good allows you to center yourself in a positive core belief system that covers all of life because this center determines who you are and aligns you with the ultimate goal of being your best.

To become your best, you then follow your "Daily Way" so that your fundamental life habits are virtues and best practices. Now that you are on your "True Path," you put your best foot forward and unite with other positive people to give and receive as well as to participate in societal solutions. It's then through constant vigilance that you find happiness with what is, fix the wrongness, maintain all that is good as well as continue to grow, develop, and refine everything as you move forward.

In the end, the reason *The Way* and your "Daily Way" places so much emphasis on keeping your focus on the positive and the integration of desirable human traits (such as all virtue, a positive core value system, mastery of the foundations of life, uniting with other people in meaningful ways, and perfecting everything) is to ingrain these concepts into who you are as an individual as well into society. The more of us who are on the same page participating in positive action, individually and on the societal level, the easier it becomes for all of us on all levels.

The Way will work for you because it's through this foundational knowledge in all these key aspects of life combined with a customizable implementation strategy that allows you to be "Truly Successful" and living rational, positive action every day. Living this way is what allows everything else you need to fall in to place naturally.

The longer you follow *The Way*, and move down your "True Path," the more key best practices will become second nature, thus increasing the overall positive effect and benefits. As you go, you will likewise gain deeper insights and find new solutions that will aid you even more.

Your progression goes faster because, over every 90-day cycle, you are integrating more and more virtues and best practices, with many of them becoming habits. As you move forward, adding even more positive habits as well as working on refining the existing, you will feel better and better. The positive feeling you get from caring for yourself, and life properly brings opportunities that were previously unattainable or thought impossible. This is one of those effects that you must experience before it can be truly understood.

To be clear, it's through this chosen, persistent, positive self-development over time that you find and stay on your "True Path," become your "True Self," live a "True Life," help create a wonderful world and for the rest of what you need to fall into place naturally.

Even if you don't become fully realized within this life, you win by not stopping, surrendering, or giving up. You win by getting back on your "True Path" if you fall off. You only lose if you give up and stop working at it. Also, since life never ends, you are making progress if you simply persist no matter what happens in this life.

The "True Power" of *The Way* is found within all "7 Steps" working together. This is because it's this combination of all "7 Steps" that makes *The Way* greater than the sum of its parts and a truly transformational individual and collective experience that can work as the catalyst to change your life and society for good. So, if you found value here, please help spread the word.

THE WAY METAPHORS

To aid in the understanding of the "7 Steps" of *The Way* and how they build on each other, we can use metaphors and affirmations. Here we can get in touch with the flow and the deeper meaning.

Light Metaphor: This light metaphor is useful as it outlines the idea of the "7 Steps" of *The Way*.

Note: For some people, "the light" can carry positive or negative religious overtones. However, within this book, "the light" and other like references are archetypes that are primal to our human spirit and are used to help clarify understanding. The light here represents the most primal form of good and positive.

Now envision you are alone on a ship, lost at sea at night under thick clouds and far from any land with deadly reefs all around. All is darkness. You will die if you cannot find the way. Then far off in the distance, you see the light, and a little spark of hope dawns. You know this light, and it's good. It's the lighthouse you have been seeking. Now you make a choice and center your ship on the light. Next, you act, knowing precisely what to do and where to go. The light allows navigating these treacherous waters so you can reach your destination. Once there, you can unite with your people and work to maintain all that is good and grow as a person.

The Way in Light
I **Know** the Light
I **Want** the Light
I **Choose** the Light
I **Center** in the Light
I **Am** the Light
I **Unite** with Light
I **Perfect** my Light (or I grow in the Light.
Or I Brighten)

You can also use each of the "7 Steps" as a positive statement or affirmation. Here you can use the word positive, meaning all that is good. You can use these to confirm your commitment to following your "True Path." See "Step 3: Choose" for more.

I **Know** the Positive	I **Know** The Way
I **Want** the Positive	I **Want** The Way
I **Choose** the Positive	I **Choose** The Way
I **Center** in the Positive	I **Center** in The Way
I **Am** Positive	I **Am** The Way
I **Unite** with the Positive	I **Share** The Way
I **Perfect** the Positive	I **Perfect** The Way

There is one statement that embodies all the above. As an affirmation, it can stand for your true intention to be and become the best you can be in all areas of life. You can say things like: I Am, or I am One, I Am the Positive, or I Am the Light, or I Am *The Way*, or I Live *The Way*, or I Follow *The Way*, I'm on My Way, or I Live Rational Positive Action and more.

As stated, these types of statements can be used as an affirmation or a declaration of your positive intent and path. Using them within "Your Practice" sessions (see the "Life Manual: Our Practice") and throughout the day, helps you align and center, which keeps you on your "True Path."

You can even wear the number 7 or an Icon created by the community that represents *The Way* on a neckless, pin, or bracelet to symbolize your dedication. You can find more affirmations within the "Life Manual: Our Practice: Mental Practice: Meditation."

NEXT STEPS

"A journey of a thousand miles begins with one step."
- Lao Tzu

Now that you have finished reading the "7 steps" of *The Way*, your next step is to put all the knowledge into action within your life. If you are working to be your best and create a positive society, you are on your "True Path" and found this opportunity for a reason.

Now is when it all comes down to you and your true desire. While the knowledge is here, it's when and how you use it that matters for it's your choices and actions that create a life worth living and one that is meaningful.

Below is a little information that can help reinforce what you have learned as well as help you take the next steps down your "True Path."

GET THE RESOURCES

Go to www.7Way.Me/wd (wd stands for way downloads), and you will find all the downloads mentioned within *The Way*, apps, and more. We are working to create more and better resources. Here you can make *The Way* part of your life by doing things like printing out the "10 Laws," Daily Way, Habit Focus, Mental Focus, and placing them in key locations (clipboards, phones, etc.) so you can check yourself throughout your day as well as using the app.

Resources To Download

- o **Your Daily Way:** You can find downloads that allow you to customize and create your own "Daily Way."
- o **Mental Focus & Meditation Sheets:** As outlined within the "Life Manual: Our Practice: Mental Practice," these sheets will help guide you through the different forms of meditation. They also contain lists of positive affirmations, virtues, and more that you can use throughout the day.
- o **Habit Focus:** This sheet and apps are used as part of our 90-day habit-building plan to help keep you on target. Get your customizable version here.

Your Next Steps

- **Yoga Cards:** Get free yoga cards so you can create your perfect routines.
- **Mini-Workouts:** Find lists of short workouts you can do throughout the day. Share yours and see what others have created.
- **Communication Quick Reference Guide:** This guide is a short version of what is within this book under "Chapter 10." It's a guide and learning tool that can be used to navigate live conversations and meetings.
- **Fuel Consumption Guide** outlines how and when to consume all the fuels (light, air, water, food, and information) that were covered within the *Life Manual* and is provided as a separate download for ease of use.
- **Recipes:** The recipes that are included in the food section within the *Life Manual* are also available for download. You can share yours, and we will be posting more as we go forward.
- **Knowledge & Education Resources:** Gain access to the world's best educational materials and learn how to get a free university degree.
- **More!** We are developing more great resources all the time to aid you down your True Path! So, go to our website and signup to get a free membership and stay informed. www.7Way.Me.

You Earned It – Now Get Your Certification!

You have just completed something truly significant and meaningful! Now go to our website, www.7Way.Me/cert. Here you can take a short quiz, earn your "Level 1 Ranking Certificate," and learn how you can attain Level 2.

CREATE YOUR DAILY WAY & READ THE LIFE MANUAL

If you have not already started, now is the time to create your "Daily Way" (see "Step 5: Be"). The key to your "Daily Way" is to use the *Life Manual* to get the in-depth knowledge you need to master the "Foundations of Life."

You can only be your best by mastering these foundations. There is detailed knowledge within each section of the *Life Manual* that can make or break you. Missing any key piece is a weak link, and it can take you down.

To be clear, there is information in the *Life Manual* that is not optional if you want to be your best physically, mentally, emotionally, spiritually, financially, in relationships, as a family, and in society. The manual is separated into the different "Foundations of Life" so you can get all the information on each foundation when you need it. You do not need to read them in order. The main goal is to get a general understanding so you can make refinements to all these areas and then go deeper to get the rest.

CREATE & USE YOUR HABIT FOCUS LIST

See "Step 5: Be" for details. Using the "Habit Focus List" as a printed document and in apps that you see all the time is important. This is because it will help you stay focused on the habits you are building.

Remember, if you do a good job, your constant mental focus habit building turns into actual habits. When that happens, you are living that new positive habit without having to try. You now maintain it as you build more positive ways of being in every 90-day cycle going forward.

Your Next Steps

READ THE CHILD & FAMILY GUIDE

The *Child & Family Guide* contains essential information everyone needs to know. It's NOT optional if you want to be your best and help create a better world. The reason this knowledge is so necessary is that we all need to help raise the children of this world in a way that allows them to become their best. Doing well will eliminate many problems within our society generation by generation.

It's much easier to raise a child correctly than to deal with the destructive aftermath caused by those who are not. To create lasting peace, we must master raising our children as species. Mastery means that parents, caregivers, and all of us in the society need to have a common understanding of the vital information necessary to create a nurturing and loving family and on how to raise positive, productive, and happy children.

Within this guide, you learn all the basics on how to raise your kids so that they are ingrained with the best way of doing things as their first way of doing. A child who builds best practice habits as their primary way of doing means they will go farther in life and won't have to waste time retraining themselves.

CREATE YOUR ESCAPE PLANS & EMERGENCY PACKS

Within the "Life Manual: Self-Care: Health Fundamentals: Disaster Preparedness," you find an outline of the necessary plans and packs that will help you survive disasters. Read it and make your plans and packs today!

AFFIRM YOUR CODE

The "10 Laws or Commandments" covered within "Step 4: Center" are key to becoming your best. This is because, as you know, your core value system forms, affects and determines your attitude, intentions, thoughts, judgments, choices, words, actions, reactions, emotions, feelings, and other beliefs. These "10 Laws" cover all aspects of life and therefore work as a guide showing you the right way in all situations. Reaffirming your code throughout your day and life is how you make it a part of you.

Do this by repeating each commandment and by reading and reflecting on the deeper meanings within "Step 4: Center." You can also do quick run-throughs here and there during your daily life (to make that easier the "10 Commandments" are included in the "Meditation Focus Sheet" as outlined within the "Life Manual: Our Practice: Mental Practice" and for download on our site).

Regardless of how you reaffirm your commitment, the critical part is to "know" what each "Law" truly means as this is the only way to have them genuinely reflected within your life in the form of your belief, intention, words, and actions. In your interactions with other people, ask yourself if you are treating everyone as equals and as you would want to be treated?

THE 10 LAWS

Laws of Purpose
1. The Primary Purpose of Life is to Be Your True Self, Live a True Life, and Go to Heaven.
2. The Primary Purpose of Society is to Create Our True Society.

Universal Laws
3. Respect Life.
4. All People are Equal.
5. Treat People as You Want to be Treated.

God Laws
6. There is No God Other than God.
7. We are All Directly Connected with God, and this Connection Cannot Be Broken.
8. God is Our Sole and Final Judge, and We are Judged by Our True Beliefs, Intentions, Words, and Actions.
9. Respect God.
10. Worship Only God; God Does Not Require Worship; God Can Only be Freely Worshiped.

THE 10 LAWS AS POSITIVE STATEMENTS

1. I Know My Primary Purpose is to Be My True Self, Live a True Life, and Go to Heaven.
2. I Know the Purpose of Society is to Create the True Society.
3. I Respect Life.
4. I Know We are All Equal.
5. I Treat Others as I Want to Be Treated.
6. I Know God is the Only God.
7. I Know I Have a Direct and Unbreakable Connection with God.
8. I Know God is My Final Judge, and I Am Judged by my True Beliefs, Intentions, Words, and Actions.
9. I Respect God.
10. I Worship Only God Freely.

COMMIT TO THE WAY

While you are not alone, you are the only one who can walk your path. Do you see *The Way* is good? Do you feel any desire to live some or all of what it contains?

The Way

If your answer is yes to any extent, then make your choice real by saying something like, "I Follow *The Way,* or I Live *The Way,* or I Am *The Way,* or I'm On My Way" (or something else that makes sense to you – See "Step 3: Choose" for more.)

> I **Know** the Positive
> I **Want** the Positive
> I **Choose** the Positive
> I **Center** in the Positive
> I **Am** Positive
> I **Unite** with the Positive
> I **Perfect** the Positive

> I **Know** the Light
> I **Want** the Light
> I **Choose** the Light
> I **Center in the** Light
> I **Am** the Light
> I **Unite** with Light
> I **Grow** in the Light

> I **Know** The Way
> I **Want** The Way
> I **Choose** The Way
> I **Center** in The Way
> I **Am** The Way
> I **Share** The Way
> I **Perfect** The Way

Affirming and reaffirming this commitment to following *The Way* here and there is a good practice. Reaffirmation can quickly be done through the use of *The Way* in "Light" metaphor or the others. The reason these affirmations help is because it's a metaphorical logic chain that uses basic archetypes to unify your subconscious and conscious mind on your path.

Reread The Way

As we have noted at the beginning of this book, not all the information within *The Way* could be conveyed linearly. So, there are early topics discussed that cannot be fully understood without reading later parts of the book.

Therefore, rereading the book will allow those earlier items to make more sense, which can then bring an even greater understanding of the whole.

Also, the book as a whole can offer insights on concepts that you cannot see without at least one initial read. Therefore, rereading *The Way* at different times in life, and critical sections in times of need, will allow you to gain deeper insights that you could not otherwise.

JOIN US

The Way is part of a grander philosophy and mission. The mission is to be a catalyst that spurs meaningful positive change within people's lives and our society in order to create a world of lasting peace and happiness that everyone can enjoy. We are working to accomplish this mission in many ways. *The Way* is only the beginning. Time is short, and the need is great, so please unite with us.

Our website is the central hub for everything related to **The Way**, "**The 7th Foundation**," "**Our Mission**," and "**The One Movement.**" We are continually working to provide useful resources and ways we can all unite to make a real difference in our world. There is a lot more on the horizon, please join with us and help create something wonderful! **www.7Way.Me** or **www.PeaceAce.com**

> So why "7Way.Me? If you say it like Hey…please 7 way me or 7 way me Now! It's like we are asking for something positive to happen. It references the "7" Steps, the Name of "The Way," and personalizes it with the word "Me." It's also short and hopefully easy to remember :-)

TIPS FOR YOUR JOURNEY

"There is nothing noble in being superior to your fellow man; true nobility is being superior to your former self."
- Ernest Hemingway

As the creator and 1st follower of *The Way*, I would like to offer some tips that helped me as they may help you go farther faster.

YOUR CHOICE – YOUR WAY

Remember, no one is telling or ordering you to follow *The Way*. You are the one who wants to become your best and live a great life, and this is a process that just takes practice. While everyone is bad at most things when we start, you will get better over time. Additionally, some of our greatest barriers are those we place on ourselves. Following *The Way* is your choice, and you can do it in the way you choose. Make it fun. You can jump in with both feet or ease into it.

The Way is not the point or the goal. *The Way* is a circle and a guide to help you on your untraveled path. To be clear, *The Way* helps us live; we do not live for *The Way*. *The Way* is just a book; you are alive! There is not just one way, only your way. *The Way* is a flexible and adaptive system that you customize as life changes.

In the end, there can only be "Your Way" because you are unique and the only one walking your path. Realizing this can help you to make the transition smoother, especially in the beginning.

JOIN WITH PEOPLE & GET HELP

Don't underestimate the power of uniting with other positive people in common cause, for help, and to offer support. This is because it's necessary if you are to have hope, create positive change, and find lasting happiness. You need your people, your tribe, and your loved ones. Without them, you cannot be truly happy. Life can be fun and made easier if we are united. So, as you move through the process, it's important not to discount the benefits of uniting with others in common cause.

STUDENT & TEACHER

We are all ignorant students and enlightened teachers and need each other. Be open to learn and to teach when opportunities arise. This understanding leads to wisdom.

KEEP THE GOAL IN MIND

Remember to focus on the goal and envision it "realized" and how good that would feel for it will create more positive energy. Focusing on the goal is especially helpful when:

- Having a hard time.
- Working on a difficult task.
- Working on long term projects.
- If struggling.

GOOD ON THE HORIZON

Change is happening. You can get somewhere even when there seems little to no hope. As they say, "It's darkest before the dawn." While not literally true, this metaphor demonstrates how positive change can happen very quickly, even when it seems impossible. So, do not give up, instead have hope!

Remember, there are good people in our world, and hope, harmony, synergy, synchronicity, coincidence, and serendipity do exist. Also, never forget that united, we can overcome any seemingly impossible problem. So have hope, all is not lost!

LET THE REST GO

If you are working hard at doing your best, even if what you are doing is not working out well or is not easy and things are a mess, you can still let it go and find peace. Don't be so hard on yourself and forgive yourself; you are a learning human doing what you are supposed to be doing.

. You can feel good because if you are on your "True Path" no matter how difficult or wrong, it's still all good. It's just a challenge to see if you really want this. You are working on it and will make progress, and that's all that matters. You don't know what will happen. You can leave all that you cannot control for now, or for those of faith, in God's hands.

DON'T WAIT FOR TRAGEDY

Don't wait for a major negative event like a health problem or death scare for motivation to act. It's best to be self-motivated rather than have a horrible event be the motivator.

That being said, if going through a major negative life event, the key is to use this extra energy to make positive changes in your life as quickly as possible. Proper use of this energy will help you recover from the event and make your life better. You can turn the negative into positive. See the "Life Manual: Our Practice" for more.

NORMAL DAYS

Normal everyday life may seem boring sometimes to you. However, if you have ever had real trauma and prolonged fear and stress in life, those average days in retrospect seem like something wonderful. In fact, any day that does not have some form of horror and trauma should be seen as a great and wonderful gift!

Your Next Steps

So, don't take these wonderful normal days for granted. Ordinary days are to be seen as a blessing and something to feel great about, laugh, and enjoy. During these average days, be sure to take a moment and be grateful for every moment without a new major problem! Living this way will help you be healthier and ready to deal with the bad days when they arrive.

It's also imperative to use these "normal days" wisely. Sometimes on these days, there is not much to do. You can use this free time to recover and relax or even help others. You can also use it to take great strides toward your life goals. So, don't waste these times. Treat them as a precious, highly valuable finite resource and use them to their fullest.

Your Practice

Ensure that you take the time for "Your Practice" (See the "Life Manual: Our Practice") as for many of us, this is the most easily neglected. Practice includes physical, mental, emotional, and spiritual training with special attention given to the three critical foundational workouts and integration of mini-training opportunities throughout your daily life.

1. Make your three practice sessions every day, even if it's just for a small workout.
2. Stoke "Your Power" and periodically envision your transmutation ability as being on, working well, strong, and shielding you.
3. Use "The Skill" here and there to gain an extra boost.

Meditate

Mediation is covered within the tip above as part of mental training. It's listed here to emphasize its importance, for it will help in all other areas of life. So, be sure to use the "Meditation Mental Focus Sheet" and the 5 different methods. Do this throughout the day to strengthen your mind and improve your attitude.

GAMIFICATION

While life is serious business, you can still make the ordinary fun. Remember to gamify your life. You can listen to positive music and books, dance, sing, play games, laugh, create games out of work, have fun, and smile throughout every day.

COVER ALL THE BASES

Making positive changes in all the diverse areas of life covered within *The Way* will have the most significant overall positive affect. Think of it as "covering all the bases" for those into sports or "keeping all the balls in the air" for those into juggling. If only one key area of life is neglected, it can negatively affect or even bring down everything you are trying to achieve. You are only as strong as your weakest link. Inadequate care of yourself, your government, your close relationships will have devastating effects on your life.

REFINE FUEL SOURCES

Remember to nurture, refine, and look to find better fuel sources of light, air, water, food, and information as you go forward. See the "Life Manual: Fuels" for details.

SEE THE CHANGE

Reaffirming and thinking about what you have accomplished will help you realize that change has taken place, that you are getting somewhere. Reviewing your progress can help create a better and more accurate perspective on life.

BE THE LEADER

You are the "leader" of your life, and it's up to you! We all need you to be the best leader you can. Believe in yourself, and others will.

BELIEVE

To achieve the impossible, you must believe it's possible. It only seems impossible until it's done. We can achieve just about anything if we keep our faith and eye on the goal.

DIAMONDS

Remember, diamonds are made under extreme pressure and look how great they turn out. If you are going through something tough, work to get through it with as much grace as possible. When you do and then come out on the other side, you will be stronger than you would be otherwise. Think of it as your training ground. Do well, and you can rise very high in the ranks of life.

DO IT NOW

"In this moment, there is plenty of time. In this moment, you are precisely as you should be. In this moment, there is infinite possibility." - Victoria Moran

There is no other time to act other than in the "now." You are doing something in the "now" at every moment. Why not choose and follow a positive path to your "True Self?" Now that you have the information, some of you may feel that you need to wait until "the right time" to implement your plan.

You may even feel that you need to wait until something happens to start or to be happy. Some of you may hesitate to start really working on your life until sometime in the future when you are happy or think you will have more time.

For example, you may want to wait until after you get married, have children, get that job, move, make X amount of money, or finish a project.

In truth, starting now with something is better than doing nothing because following the "10 Laws," "Your Daily Way," and integrating other virtues and best practices into your life as you go will create more satisfaction and happiness in your life. Starting right now, no matter how small, will make everything you want easier to achieve and be more fully realized when achieved.

You will be and feel better because as you become more positive and your abilities increase, you are more able to effect positive change within your life and society. Nailing down any essential element of *The Way* as soon as possible ensures that you are more ready and able to overcome the challenges of life and reach your goals.

No Action or Choice is Action & Choice

"Your big opportunity may be right where you are now."
- Napoleon Hill

Understand that doing nothing is still doing something. No choice is a choice. In most cases, not choosing means you are giving your power to someone else, often to those who are not looking out for your best interest. Or it means you are not taking needed positive actions to improve your life or your world.

Non-participation of reasonable people leads to rule by fanatics, extremists, and the destruction of our world. Likewise, silence and non-action when there is great need or evil are seen by many as a lack of caring or even that the silent condones what is happening. Remember, good people only triumph over evil by peacefully overcoming it as we continually work to prevent it from rising in the first place.

In the end, evil, the negative, and disorder win if the positive and good do and say nothing or do the wrong things. Therefore, you must act on your desire to be your best and choose to do whatever you can now. Honestly, this is the only way you will get better and make a real difference in the world.

If you are still hesitating, you can think of it like this. If you start now doing what you can, no matter how small, then when the "right time" does come, you will have somethings in place which will make that "right time" even better and more productive. You can see starting now as preparation, setup, and testing.

In the end, it's all of us united in a common, positive purpose that altogether "We" become the "Superheroes" and create the "Magic" we need. For those of faith, we are all the "Children of God," made in the "Image of God." Therefore, it's all of us, united, one for all and all for one, taking positive action that proves we honor our creator and the gifts we have been given. To say it another way, we can only save our world if the vast majority of us unite and create a wave of positive change that will spread throughout our world.

If not this way, then which? If not now, then when? If not you and all of us, then who? The fact is, you are taking action; the only question left is which side are you are on? Are you part of the problem or the solution?

Parting Wishes

"The biggest adventure you can take is to live the life of your dreams." - Oprah Winfrey

I hope *The Way* has helped you. I wish I was a better writer, that there was more time to refine it, and I was able to create the greatest materials so that *The Way* would make even better sense to everyone. I am not sure why it happened this way, and I was chosen to bring this message forth when I have such a difficult time even forming proper sentences. So please forgive me, and please focus on the message. I had to start somewhere and felt it was better to get something out than to wait until that "someday."

Remember, it does not matter how far down your "True Path" you are, only that you are on it. You are only competing with yourself, and your life's journey is your destination. All that matters is that you are moving forward on your "True Path." You can find satisfaction in the fact that you are working to become your "True Self," live a "True Life," and go to heaven.

You can feel happy knowing you are helping to improve other people's lives and our world. You should feel good about what you have just accomplished and where you are going.

I know you have amazing positive gifts to offer. Today is always the first day of the rest of your life. I am looking forward to seeing what we can all do as individuals and together! The future is ours. We have everything needed, so let's make it wonderful!

God bless you, wishing you peace, happiness, and true success always,

Andrew

MY NOTES

This section is for your notes, insights, thoughts, and to log significant life events.

THE WAY

My Notes

The Way

www.ingramcontent.com/pod-product-compliance
Lightning Source LLC
Chambersburg PA
CBHW071114080526
44587CB00013B/1341